YOUTH EMPLOYMENT AND INDUSTRIAL TRAINING: PROBLEMS AND PROSPECTS

YOUTH EMPLOYMENT AND INDUSTRIAL TRAINING: PROBLEMS AND PROSPECTS

FALENDRA K. SUDAN
Department of Economics, University of Jammu, Jammu
Jammu and Kashmir - 180 006, India

SERIALS PUBLICATIONS
NEW DELHI

First Published - 2008

ISBN : 978-81-8387-173-0

Published by

SERIALS PUBLICATIONS
4830/24, Prahlad Street, Ansari Road
Darya Ganj, New Delhi-110002 (India)
Phone : 23245225. Fax : 91-11-23272135
E-mail: serials@satyam.net.in

CONTENTS

ACKNOWLEDGEMENT

This study was possible due to the support of the senior government officials at the Ministry of Labour & Employment, Government of India, Shram Shakti Bhawan, New Delhi, the Directorate of Technical Education, Government of Jammu and Kashmir and the Principals of the Industrial Training Institutes in the various districts of the state of Jammu and Kashmir. Special thanks are due to Director General, Ministry of Labour & Employment, Government of India, Shram Shakti Bhawan, New Delhi; and Director, Technical Education, Government of Jammu and Kashmir, Jammu/Srinagar. The Director General, Ministry of Labour & Employment, Government of India, Shram Shakti Bhawan, New Delhi has sponsored the study, which is highly acknowledged. I would like to thank Prof. A. N. Sadhu, Prof. O. P. Sharma, and Prof. R. L. Bhat, for their continued and very generous moral support at all times.

Falendra K. Sudan

1

BACKGROUND OF THE STUDY

Globally, more than 1 billion people today are between 15 and 24 years of age. Eighty-five per cent of these young people live in developing countries where many are especially vulnerable to extreme poverty. The ILO estimates that approximately 74 million young women and men are unemployed throughout the world, accounting for 41 per cent of the 180 million unemployed globally, and many more young people are working long hours for low pay, struggling to survive in the informal economy. There are an estimated 59 million young people between 15 and 17 years of age who are engaged in hazardous forms of work. Young people actively seeking to participate in the world of work are two to three times more likely than older generations to find themselves unemployed (ILO, 2003). Decent and productive work is an unfulfilled aspiration of many young people. The United Nations Social Summit in Copenhagen and the United Nations Millennium Summit Declaration of 2001 called for a commitment to develop and implement strategies for decent and productive work for youth, recognizing that it is globally significant problem, with implications for persistent poverty, job instability, and social exclusion (World Bank, 2003). Youth poverty and exclusion are widespread and increasing. Inadequate, insufficient and/or inappropriate education, training and employment, lack of assets, property rights and access to credit and lack of decision-making opportunities exacerbate the social and economic vulnerability of youth, generally. The vulnerability of disadvantaged youth is even greater. Investing in youth is an urgent matter; appropriate policies and programmes must be established and adequate resources allocated in order to address this issue.

The issues of youth unemployment and underemployment have come to the forefront in recent years. Young people are at greater risk in obtaining and retaining employment. The unemployment and underemployment figures for young people are staggering. Education and training are important means of addressing youth employability. Developing young people's employability is central to ensuring their successful transition to the labour market and their access to career-oriented employment. Youth need to acquire the skills, knowledge, competencies and attitudes that will allow them to find work and to cope with an unpredictable labour market. Formal education and training systems often do not reach marginalized youth. Alternative methods of delivering training need to be explored. One of the earliest national training programmes was the Craftsmen Training Scheme (CTS) for semi-skilled and skilled workers. Under this scheme, training is provided in Industrial Training Institutes (ITIs) in 42 engineering and 22 non-engineering trades. The duration of courses varies from one to two years. ITIs are set up both by the respective state governments and by private agencies. As state finances are becoming scarce, more private agencies are setting up private ITIs. Of the total number of 2,720 industrial institutes about 1,700 have been established by private agencies and over 1,000 by the various state governments. They have a total training capacity of 450,000.

YOUTH UNEMPLOYMENT: GLOBAL PERSPECTIVE

Unemployment at the onset of one's working life can lead to serious problems. Lack of employment lowers household income and blocks the crucial development of skills, which come from work experience and on-the-job training. Early workplace skill development is crucial to future earnings growth and unemployment early in working life increases the probability of future joblessness (ILO, 1998). Evidence has shown that early unemployment can permanently affect future employability (ILO, 2004). Policies that lead to youth unemployment result in more difficult challenges for youth that are most vulnerable. Those experiencing unemployment at an early age have years of lower earnings and an increased likelihood of unemployment ahead of them (Mroz, 2001). Global youth unemployment rates are increasing for both women and men. In the ten-year period from 1993 to 2003 there was an increase of approximately 19 million unemployed youth in the world (11.2 million young men and 7.5 million young women) (ILO, 2003). As a result, there has been a rise in the world youth unemployment rate (ILO, 2004).

Unemployment of young people is a serious problem in most of Africa. Although statistics are rare, unemployment in the 15-24 age group is certain to significantly exceed the unemployment rate for the sub-Saharan African labour force as a whole. The problem is more severe in urban areas. According to the 1999 Ethiopia Labour Force Survey, for example, the overall unemployment rate is 8.1 per cent and the youth urban unemployment rate is 37.5 per cent (with women's rate being 43.7 and men's rate 29.4). In Namibia, the total unemployment rate is reported to be 19.5 per cent, while the urban unemployment rate for the 15-19 age group is 56.8 per cent (Kanyenze, et al., 2000). Low demand for labour in a context of a rapidly growing labour force makes it extremely difficult to absorb the new entrants. Labour supply often does not correspond to the needs of the employers, with highly educated young people unable to find jobs to suit their skills or, at the other end of the spectrum, unskilled youth unable to respond to a demand for higher skills. There is an obvious need for both creating an investment climate favourable to employment generation and for improving the human capital of the region.

Youth unemployment is a major challenge in Latin America and the Caribbean. The youth unemployment rate declined between 2000 and 2001 in most of the countries of Latin America, but in 2002 youth unemployment rate increased for most countries for which data are available. On average, the youth unemployment rates are twice as high as the overall rate. Female youth unemployment rates were consistently higher than the male youth unemployment rate. To aggravate the problem, much of new youth employment is being generated in the informal economy (ILO, 2003). Youth unemployment is not, simply, a transitory state to employment, but is a very lengthy process whereby youth move from unemployment, unpaid employment, and low-wage unskilled employment - all of which have low opportunity costs. The youth transition process, including that of youth unemployment, largely reflects larger labour market trends - the large informality of the labour market; the growing skills-wage gap between workers in the formal-informal economy; and declining incomes of informal workers (Fawcett, 2002).

High youth unemployment rates in East Asia illustrate the difficulties new entrants to the labour market have finding jobs. In 2001, 53 per cent of the jobless youth in China were under 35, of which half had been laid off for economic reasons - either restructuring or bankruptcy - and the registered urban youth unemployment rate has been rising since 1998 (ILO, 2002). Youth unemployment is also high in the Republic of Korea, with half of the unemployed under 29 in 2001 compared to less than a fourth in 1999. In Mongolia, the 15-24 age group made up over two-thirds of the unemployed; 44 per cent of the young unemployed were women. Youth unemployment rates are lower for women than for men in East Asia, but the share of youth unemployment in total unemployment is higher for women than for men. A large proportion of the young unemployed are highly qualified, but their specialization does not correspond to the needs of the labour market. In Mongolia, for example, 80 per cent of university students are studying foreign languages, law and international relations. However, in practice, 80 per cent of all job vacancies are related to economic, technical and technological areas, suggesting a need to improve the vocational training system. Furthermore, career guidance and vocational counselling are still underdeveloped in the region.

On average, youth unemployment in India is twice the overall unemployment rate. Indeed, the share of youth among the unemployed is disproportionately high at approximately 59 per cent. Within the youth population, the probability of finding work does not appear to be directly related to the level of educational attainment. In fact, the unemployment rates are higher among the educated youth than among the non-educated. Further, the unemployment rates are higher as one moves up the ladder of general education. More than 56 per cent of the unemployed youth are educated *i.e.* middle school and above. The self-employed constitute 53 per cent of the total employed. This means that people are not necessarily averse to taking up self-employment ventures, though many of them may have done so in the context of non-availability of wage employment opportunities. Youth entrepreneurs constitute 32 per cent of the self-employed (Pant, 2003).

There are signs of a youth bulge in Nepal, where 60 per cent of the population is under the age of 40 years. Twenty per cent of the population is between the ages of 15-30 years. With unemployment rising to astronomical levels, a large percentage of young people are left out of the mainstream. There are 1.5 million youth in the country that are totally unemployed. As the Government fails to develop proper strategies to provide jobs, the problem is gaining urgency day by day. According to the Labour Survey report 1998-99, youths between the ages of 15-29 make up almost 25 per cent of the total population. Of this group, only about 13 per cent live in urban areas. Given this urban-rural distribution and the urban-rural employment situation, there is a mass of youth underemployed in rural areas. As is the case with the urban population in general, urban youth tend to be unemployed rather than underemployed. More than 30 per cent of new job market entrants leave the country in search of jobs (Dhakal, 2002).

Youth unemployment in the Middle East and North Africa is high for both women and men, ranging from 13 per cent in Bahrain to 39 per cent in Algeria. The share of the 15 to 24 population in total unemployment is alarmingly high, over 73 per cent in the Syrian Arab Republic, for example. Youth unemployment rates have increased during the 1990s and, given the very high population growth rates in the region, youth unemployment is a major challenge. Youth unemployment is a continuing problem in the transition economies. In Poland, for example, almost 44 per cent of young people are unemployed and over 38 per cent in Bulgaria. In most transition economies, unemployment rates among the under-25 age group are twice as high as the national average. Young people with less education are more affected than those with an advanced level of education. The main reason is the mismatch between skills offered by young people and skills demanded by the labour market. Youth unemployment in industrialized countries, as a whole, is almost double the total unemployment rate. Although industrialized countries witnessed a drop in the youth unemployment rate between 1997 and 2001, it has increased or remained stagnant since 2001. Germany, for example, has almost doubled its (low) youth unemployment rate between 1990 and 2001. Youth unemployment has also increased slightly in the United Kingdom. Despite some progress, many countries still record very high youth unemployment rates. Italy, for example, has more than a quarter of its labour force below 24 years of age (ILO, 2003).

According to the ILO, more women than men are unemployed in almost all regions of the world. Only in East Asia and sub-Saharan Africa did the regional male unemployment rate exceed that of the female (the rates are equal in the transition economies). The difficulty of finding work is even more drastic for young females (aged 15 to 24 years). In Latin America and the Caribbean as well as the Middle East and North Africa the unemployment rate for young women is over 7 per cent higher than that of young men. Being female and being young can represent a double source of discrimination – young women face greater barriers in entering the labour market and retaining employment in periods of economic downturn. Unemployment figures, on their own, are a limited indicator for the inadequacy of the labour market situation of men and particularly of women, and should not be used in isolation. Many national definitions of unemployment exclude persons who want to work but do not actively "seek" work either because job opportunities are extremely limited, or because such persons have restricted labour mobility, or face discrimination or structural, social or cultural barriers. The majority of persons in this category are women. Although data on discouraged workers are hard to come by, a review of the data available for industrialized economies reveals that females made up approximately two-thirds of total discouraged workers in Australia, Austria, Belgium, Germany, Greece, Netherlands, Norway and Portugal, and the female share of total discouraged workers was near 90 per cent in Italy and Switzerland (ILO, 2004).

Youth unemployment rates are much higher than overall unemployment rates in all regions of the world. In every country for which ILO data is available, youth unemployment rates exceed adult unemployment rates. In the majority of economies, youth unemployment rates are at least double those of adults. Germany is the only economy where the ratio remains around 1, possibly indicating the success of the German apprenticeship system in facilitating the transition from school to work. This also results from statistical definition whereby apprentices with a work contract are counted as employed, in contrast to young people in school-based training in other European countries. Eliminating this statistical effect, youth unemployment rate compared to the overall unemployment rate in Germany would be comparable to other European countries. It is also important to note, that in the past 20 years, Germany has had an extensive policy of early retirement, in order to promote the entrance of younger workers into the labour market (Heidemann, 2000). Many countries in Europe initiated early retirement schemes to "create jobs for unemployed youth". Yet the impact of such measures on youth unemployment was negligible; new entrants to the labour market lacked the experience needed for the jobs that were vacated by older workers (Samorodov, 1999).

Gaining employment is particularly difficult for already poor and socially excluded youth. For those employed, much of that work is in the informal economy under precarious conditions and low pay. The vast majority of the world's youth work in the informal economy (Han, 2004). In Africa, 93 per cent of all new jobs are in this sector; in India and Indonesia, more than 90 per cent of women working outside of agriculture, work in the informal economy; and nearly 75 per cent of manufacturing work in South-East Asia is within the informal economy (Wiego, 2001). In Latin America, almost all newly created jobs for young labour market entrants are in the informal economy. In much of the developing world the decline of the formal economy, accompanied by decreased public or family income support, means that millions of jobless young people are increasingly forced to find work in the informal economy.

It is important to note that almost everywhere, not only in developing countries, but also in transition and industrialized countries, there is a tendency to the informalization of the economy. The informal economy has been able to absorb large numbers of unemployed and underemployed persons and it has been a primary generator of jobs in many parts of the world. As such, it has often contributed to a minimum of social cohesion; social safety nets have been either nonexistent or not functioning properly. In some countries displaced workers and migrants compose the bulk of informal labour; in others, particularly those with a high population growth, we find a large proportion of youth (Capt, 2001). Most youth working in the informal economy lack adequate incomes, social protection, security and representation. In a vicious cycle, poorly productive enterprises, low incomes and inadequate working conditions interact to undermine enterprise competitiveness, which in turn undermines the capability to provide decent employment conditions. If current trends continue, it is likely that most of the jobs available to young people in the future will be low paid and of poor quality.

Recognizing the concentration of women in the informal economy, many non-governmental organizations (NGOs) have focused on income-generation activities. There is more emphasis on credit provision. and group formation than on skill training provision. These interventions are generally based on the assumption that women are supplementing the family income. The interventions in this area are usually aimed at providing them with skills not for profit but for survival (Leach, 2000). This disregards the fact that women are often the sole or major earners, increasingly so with the growing number of female-headed households. Run by small organizations with limited staff and resources, the training courses provided tend to be of poor quality. Additionally, such courses are often in gender-stereotyped skills, such as sewing or cooking, which do not lead into profitable areas of work. Functional adult literacy courses have also been accompanied by small-scale vocational training, usually for women, and often attract similar criticisms.

Underemployment is typically categorized into visible and invisible where the former consists of work of inadequate duration, *i.e.*, both involuntary part-time employment and temporary short-term work, while the latter encompasses work of inadequate productivity (Holger and Strobl, 2001). Attention tends to focus on visible underemployment rather than "inadequate" productivity. For the developed world studies of underemployment have almost exclusively examined involuntary part-time employment in the United States (Stratton, 1996; Bednarzik, 1975; Leppel and Clain, 1988). The studies available have shown that a disproportionately large number of youth in many countries are underemployed, working fewer hours than they would like. Young people may be able to obtain only part-time work, as is often the case in France (particularly among young women) and Indonesia for example, or seasonal work, as happens frequently in the agriculturally based economies of South Asia and sub-Saharan Africa. Underemployment is also high among many young people who work in the household production unit in the rural and urban informal economy. There is a serious lack of data on unemployment and underemployment rates for disadvantaged youth. This partially reflects the range of vulnerabilities some youth face, resulting from discrimination, economic hardship or geographic location, for example. It also reflects societal norms about assessing which youth *can* work. Often people with disabilities, for example, are classified as "unable to work" and are placed in a category of those in need of social protection. Despite this the World Bank demonstrates that in Asia, Latin America and transition countries, the number of "disadvantaged young people with employment problems" greatly exceeds the number of "young unemployed" (Godfrey, 2003). Yet, in most cases, policies are not aimed at those most disadvantaged because they constitute a minority and, therefore, are not cost-effective.

The most socially disadvantaged youth generally experience more problems obtaining employment. They are less likely to obtain good basic education, and are often discriminated against on the basis of social class, ethnic origin, gender, disability, etc. For instance, data from Japan, Sweden, United Kingdom and the United States show above average unemployment rates for ethnic minorities. Poor young people are even more prone to unemployment, and particularly to inactivity. In several advanced economies youth joblessness is more and more concentrated in households in which no member is employed (Bowers; Sonnet; and Bardonne, 2000). Poor youth are also ignored in mainstream development thinking and action. In addition to the problems faced by youth in mainstream development strategies, they have a second burden of poverty, which gives them fewer choices. Poor young women have a triple burden. Over 300 million of the 500 million young people searching for employment are poor (60 per cent).

The United Nations Social Summit in Copenhagen and the United Nations Millennium Summit Declaration of 2001 called for reduction of poverty by 50 per cent by 2015, recognizing the challenge of poverty and the right to decent work, the double and triple burden faced by poor youth, the vicious nexus between poverty and unemployment, the vicious cycle of poverty reproduction through unsustainable use of natural and financial resources and the inability to move to good governance without eradicating the worst forms of poverty and providing work for poor youth, in a given time frame (Wignaraja, 2002). Rural youth constitute approximately 55 per cent of the world's young people. With increasing industrialization, rural areas around the world have experienced a decline in employment opportunities. Young people face difficulties in sustaining jobs in traditional agricultural sectors and in gaining access to education and training. It is evident, despite the lack of comparable data, that many groups of young people are more likely to suffer higher unemployment and underemployment rates due to the nature of their circumstances. These disadvantaged youth must be given more choices, more opportunities for education, skills training, micro credit and more effort must be made to address these issues:

YOUTH LABOUR MARKET AND EMPLOYMENT IN INDIA: AN OVERVIEW

The estimates of the number of "youth" and their proportion in the total population are more difficult than might be expected a priori even for the census years, because of the common errors of age reporting. The 1991 census data have reported the number of youth in India as 153.5 million or 18.3 percent of the total population. However, these data excluded the state of Jammu and Kashmir, where the census was not conducted. If the estimated population of Jammu and Kashmir (7.7 million) had the same age distribution as the rest of India, the number of youth in India would be 154.9 million. These estimates need a modification, if we use the smoothed or adjusted age data, smoothed according to the well-established mathematical techniques to minimize the effects of age misreporting. The smoothed age distribution indicates the number of youth to be 156.4 million in India excluding Jammu and Kashmir and 157.8 million, (18.5 percent of the total population of the country), if an estimate for the population of Jammu and Kashmir is taken into consideration. If an allowance is made for the usual tendency of most censuses to undercount the population, the total population of India and the number of Indian youth on March 1, 1991, would be estimated at 861.2 and 159.3 million, respectively.

According to labour force projection, the number of youth in the labour force (in terms of usual status) is estimated to grow from 85 million in 1991 to 93 million in 1997, 105 million in 2002 and 117 million in 2007. The labour force participation rate for the youth is projected to decline to 50.5 percent by 2007, but the proportion of the youth in the population is expected to rise to 20.8 percent. An adjustment for the net undercount in the 1991 Census will raise these numbers by about 2 percent. The average annual increase in the youth labour force has been of the order of 1.3 million during 1991-97 but it will almost double to 2.4 million during 1997-2007. The number of youth in India already exceeded 165 million in mid-1990 and 175 million by mid-1995. According to the UN estimates, the average annual increase in the number of youth in India was 3.06 million during 1985-90, 2.1 million during 1990-95, and 3.14 million during 1995-2000 and further to a peak of 3.72 million during 2000-2005. Thereafter, the annual increment is expected to decline because of the recent and prospective drop in fertility in India. Further, according to the UN estimates and projections, the proportion of the youth in the total population of India has been fluctuating between 17.7 and 19.4 percent between 1950 and 2005; but it is expected to decline almost steadily to 13 percent by 2050.

The expansion of employment opportunities has been an important objective of development planning in India. There has been a significant growth in employment over the years. However, a relatively higher growth of population and labour force has led to an increase in the volume of unemployment from one plan period to another. In 2002, India's labour force reached 375 million and will continue to expand in the next two decades. Some projections suggest that the labour force increase will mount to more than 8 million per annum. In the recent past, India has achieved the GDP growth of more than 6.5 per cent with just one per cent growth in employment. Most of the large industries have been shedding labour and the labour absorption capacity of the agriculture is low. The unorganized sector is growing at much higher rate than any other sector. However, the workers in unorganized sector seem to be the least educated and trained.

In the recent past, unemployment rate in India has increased significantly from 6 per cent in 1994 to 7.3 percent in 2000. About 27 million people are without jobs. The proportion of unemployed in rural areas is estimated at more than three quarters, out of which three-fifth are educated. The data provided by the National Sample Survey Organization (NSSO) confirm that the rate of unemployment among the youth. The unemployed youth formed 40 to 50 percent of all the rural unemployed and 58 to 60 percent of the urban unemployed in terms of the weekly status. The range of estimates indicated that the absolute number of unemployed youth was between 5.5 and 8.6 million in 1987-88 and between 5.2 and 8.9 million in 1993-94. If the unemployment rate in terms of usual status were to remain unchanged through 2001, the number of unemployed youth would rise to about 6.2 million. On the one hand, this number does not appear alarmingly large for a country with more than one billion persons, but the resulting frustration can indeed pose a serious threat to the stability of the Indian social and political structure. On the other hand, open unemployment is not a true indicator of the gravity of the unemployment problem in an economy such as India, characterized as it is by large-scale underemployment and poor employment quality in the unorganized sector, which accounts for over 90 per cent of the total employment. The organized sector contributes only about 9 per cent to the total employment. On the whole, underemployment in various segments of the labour force is quite high.

High rates of youth unemployment are observed throughout the world. The contributory factors include the high rate of population growth, and of labour force growth, a result of the welcome decline in mortality in excess of the decline in fertility. Fortunately, the rate of population growth in India has begun to decline and now stands at 1.9 percent. In urban India, the rate of natural increase seems to have dropped to 1.5 to 1.6 percent, but the number of urban youth grows partly through rural-urban migration. Contrary to the indications provided by official population projections, no dramatic decline in the rate of growth of the population of India is likely to occur during the current decade. The most optimistic estimate would place it at about 1.6 to 1.7 percent in the next quinquennium. The youth who will join the labour force over the next 15 years are already born. Their participation rates might decline, particularly those of the teenage youth, if they continue in schools and colleges for a longer period than they do now.

The largest share of the new jobs in India would be created in the unorganized sector that employs more than 90 per cent of the workforce and produces more than 60 per cent of the gross domestic product (GDP). The unorganized sector is also more labour intensive. The private sector has a greater role to play in the creation of jobs. Besides, the small and micro enterprises are also labour intensive and must be given due attention in employment generation strategy. The education and training services are supposed to improve access of the poorer sections of the society to employable skills. The major challenge before the country is to ensure the employability of the youth by training them adequately for productive work, by imparting to them marketable skills and the flexibility to learn new things and to innovate, and by inculcating in them a proper work ethic. All these goals are necessary conditions for survival and growth in the changing economic environment in which even a large country is a small part of a global village. If the frequent articulation of these goals is not to remain a mere rhetoric the requisite investments will need to be made by the state to eliminate illiteracy and to ensure high quality education for all.

The majority of workers in the unorganized economy of India have never been to vocational training institutions and many of them have never been to school (Gasskov and Burns, 2001). The formal training system, because of its entry requirements and geographical mapping, is not designed to offer skills to the low-educated people and particularly those who operate in the rural non-farm sector. On the other hand, there are no other providers of the short term, but structured training that would be able to serve the numerous employees of micro enterprises. Workers in this sector continue to learn trades on the job from, also, low-literate and low-skilled craft people. This situation has its impact on the unorganized economy's capability to produce goods and services. The following sectors have high potential employment growth: commercial agriculture, agro-industry and agro-business, forestry and pulp and paper, retail and wholesale trade, tourism, housing and construction, garment industry, the information technology (IT) and IT-enabled services, education, health, financial services, transport and communications, and community services. An important portion of these activities is and will be in the unorganized economy. The enormous opportunities for employment growth associated with these sectors are thought to help considerably in reducing or eliminating unemployment in India by 2020 (Government of India, 2001 and 2002). The current situation, however, is that in India's vast informal economy, skills are acquired over a long period of traditional apprenticeship. The core of the informal economy employs mostly non-skilled and semi-skilled workers in basic trades such as fitters, welders, electricians, tailors, etc. Their skills are rather narrow as trainees are mainly low-literate and have no structured preparation. As a result, many basic goods and services produced are of low quality with the demand for them remaining low as long as there is a significant number of people living below the poverty line who cannot consume better services.

It is likely that a number of businesses of the unorganized economy are involved in production of high quality consumer goods or semi-finished goods for larger enterprises and they therefore grow rapidly and require highly skilled persons. It is exactly such businesses that have a capability to absorb the skilled graduates produced by ITIs. It is estimated that the largest number of new jobs will be created in the services sector of India adding some 120 million jobs by the year 2020. The most promising sectors would involve financing, insurance, education, health, construction and real estate, advertising, printing and packaging, etc. These sectors have witnessed much higher than average rates of growth. The future economy of India is expected to become the knowledge intensive services economy. Development of vocational knowledge and skills should become a significant part of the forthcoming knowledge revolution in India. India will become the fourth largest economy in the world by 2020 as the global markets for textiles, clothing, agricultural products, software and IT-enabling services and other products that are well developed in India, will expand dramatically. However, India's ability to benefit from this trend will depend on its improved capacity to keep pace with rising international standards of price, quality, safety and productivity. India will also have to become far more aggressive in acquiring and applying advanced technologies in agriculture, biotechnology, IT, energy, education, etc. Currently, a significant proportion of workers in India earn below subsistence wages as they apply low productive technologies and working methods. Therefore, the objective of employment generation is not only to ensure availability of jobs but also to ensure that people receive a decent income. This would require masses of people to be educated and trained in applying new technologies. The knowledge and skills of the national workforce will be a major determinant of the future economic growth and the type and number of jobs that can be created. However, only 5 per cent of the country's total workforce in the 20-24 age group is estimated to have undertaken skills training. This figure is far below many other developing countries. To remedy this, it is suggested that annual vocational participation reach the level of 10 million people, an increase of more than five times the current participation.

It must be recognised that the demand for labour cannot always be created to suit the characteristics of labour supply. Shortages and surpluses are found to coexist in the labour market due to the mismatch between skill and other requirements of new employment opportunities and the attributes of available workers. This phenomenon is likely to be more marked in a situation of rapidly changing technologies and work organisation. It would also, therefore, be necessary to intervene on the supply side of the labour market with a view to improving the employability of workers in general, and promoting such institutional structures and arrangements for training and skill upgradation, which could speedily respond to rapidly changing requirements of productive activities, in particular. In order that the training and skill formation systems are closely aligned with the trends in labour demand, it would be essential that the users, that is, the employers, have a major role and involvement in planning and running them.

The above brief review of the structure of unemployment suggests that over the years, the problem of open unemployment is gaining and that of underemployment is declining in importance. These features suggest that the strategy of employment generation would have to lay greater emphasis on augmentation of productivity and income levels of the working poor and the creation of new full time employment opportunities on wage or self employment basis, rather than on schemes for short-term employment generation.

COSTS OF YOUTH UNEMPLOYMENT

Youth unemployment and underemployment impose a heavy cost upon individuals, employers, trade unions, governments and societies. Unemployment in early life may permanently impair employability and, as research has shown, patterns of behaviour and attitudes established at an early stage persist later in life. For employers, youth unemployment means that young people have less to spend on their products and services, and that personal savings are reduced for investment in business, resulting in loss of production. For trade unions, youth unemployment means loss of potential membership and weaker bargaining positions to secure improved rights, protection and working conditions for their members. For governments, youth unemployment means they have a reduced taxation base and higher social welfare costs, that investments in education and training are wasted, and that their support among young people is weak (ILO, 2002). Moreover, rising unemployment levels among youth may be a source of social instability, increased drug abuse and crime. Further, youth unemployment and poor jobs contribute to high levels of poverty. An analysis of youth investments identified with the highest economic returns found that countries under-invest in the healthy development of adolescents and young adults. Some evidence exists that youth-focused interventions are a cost-effective way to improve health, reduce poverty, and benefit society (Knowles; J.R. Behrman, 2003). The costs of neglecting youth can be measured in terms of depletion of human and social capital. There is a loss of economic growth possibilities, which increases as this cohort ages without gaining experience in the work force. More difficult to quantify are the costs of societal instability and endemic conflict.

The social and economic costs of long-term unemployment, joblessness and poverty are not only measured in terms of income support. They include loss of output, erosion of skills, reduced levels of activity, and increased social divisions (Cass, 1989). Unemployment wastes some of the scarce resources used in training workers. Furthermore, workers who are unemployed for long periods become de-skilled as their skills become increasingly out-dated in a rapidly changing job market. This reduces their chances of gaining employment in the future, which, in turn, increases the economic burden on government and society. The lost in productivity magnifies over the course of the life cycle. In the context of the demographics of the current youth cohort, persistent unemployment represents a significant loss of human capital. Young people experience exclusion from the labour market and self-employment opportunities. They rarely possess physical assets such as land or housing which could serve as collateral, and so they have little access to credit. They also experience isolation, vulnerability and powerlessness. Youth from ethnic minorities tend to face even greater barriers to employment. In many European and Central Asian countries, disadvantaged youth find it difficult to secure employment than menial labour (Cava and Lytle, 2003). Their disadvantages derive from lack of access to assets in three interrelated dimensions: (i) economic (assets leading to income generation); (ii) social (access to information, social capital, free-time activities, cultural expression, educational opportunities, care and mentoring in youth friendly venues); and (iii) participation in decision-making (empowerment and governance). On this basis, it appears that youth inclusion policies would be more effective if these different dimensions were combined, rather than having fragmented sectoral interventions (World Bank, 2003).

Considering the pace of economic growth worldwide, the expectation of sufficient formal employment in the short-term is unrealistic. During periods of retrenchment, youth are often the first to be terminated, due to their lack of seniority. However, greater attention to youth income generation opportunities (and the market niches in which they have comparative advantage) can contribute to the economic empowerment of youth as well as being an engine for economic growth. Greater participation of youth in the development of micro-businesses, for example could contribute substantially to growth. The social costs of youth unemployment are far-reaching; it contributes to costly social problems such as poorer health, the breakdown of relationships and families, increased crime and significant additional expenditure requirements. Unemployment erodes the stability of communities and threatens social cohesion as young people become inescapably dependent on welfare programmes and disenfranchised in terms of their participation in mainstream society. The social cost of crime among unemployed young people, for example, is magnified if a society's means of dealing with it encourages further antisocial behaviour and attitudes. The overwhelming evidence is that unemployment, and especially long-term unemployment, exacts a terrible and cumulative toll on individuals. With little to do in any constructive or positive sense, life is boring and empty; it becomes harder to remain motivated. Prolonged unemployment is more likely to be oppressive, resulting in subsistence living, a loss of personal autonomy and control, frustration, anger, low self esteem and social alienation. To be unemployed for a long time, or to be growing up in a family where one or both parents are unemployed, is a difficult start to adult life. Without dramatically improved support systems for reintegrating these young people into mainstream education, training and employment opportunities, it is conceivable that many of them face a future without work and with little or no chance of a decent standard of living. Youth unemployment is also associated with psychological symptoms, such as depression and loss of confidence. Finally, the prevalence of lifestyle risk factors (cannabis use and, less consistently, tobacco and alcohol consumption) is higher in unemployed compared with employed young people.

POLICIES FOR PROMOTING YOUTH EMPLOYMENT IN INDIA

Ever since the initiation of planning in India in 1950, the Government has stressed the goal of increasing employment opportunities and eventually eradicating unemployment from the country. Acceleration of the rate of savings and investment and raising of the level of productivity has been prime goals of the successive five-year plans of the country. Awareness about the difficulties of eliminating unemployment has led the successive governments at the centre and in the states to formulate and implement several schemes for eradicating unemployment and promoting employment. The planners have recognized high rates of unemployment among the youth. It is generally stressed as the problem of unemployment among the "educated" or those who have passed the high school certificate examination (matriculates) or the higher educated. The problem is seen as part of the overall problem of employment creation or development. Yet, some of the special employment schemes have been aimed specifically at the youth to improve their training and skills and to promote self-employment and entrepreneurship. They included: an effort to reorient the Indian educational system in the direction of Vocational Education; an Apprenticeship Training Scheme supported by legislation passed in 1961 and amended in 1973 and 1986; the centrally sponsored scheme of TRYSEM (Training of Rural Youth for Self-Employment); and a Self-Employment Scheme for Educated Unemployed Youth (SEEUY) in urban areas. Some of the schemes have been modified in the light of experience and the findings of evaluations undertaken by various agencies and institutions on behalf of the government. Yet, the overall problem of high rates of unemployment among the youth continues to be virtually intractable. Despite considerable rhetoric on the subject, the actual action has fallen far short of the requirements.

More importantly, under the National Policy on Education (NPE), adopted in 1986 and revised in 1992, high priority has been assigned to "vocationalisation" of secondary education. The goals for 1995 and 2000 envisage the diversion of 10 and 25 percent of the students studying beyond the High School Certificate examination to the vocational stream. The objectives were to enhance the employability of individual students, to reduce the mismatch between the demand for and the supply of skilled manpower and to provide an alternative to those seeking to pursue higher education without a particular interest or purpose. About 150 vocational courses have been introduced in six major areas of agriculture, business and commerce, engineering and technology, health and paramedical services, home science and humanities. Sixty additional vocational courses have been notified under the Apprenticeship Act of 1961.

By March 31, 1994, almost 0.91 million were enrolled in 16,450 vocational sections in 5,701 schools. However, the quality of the vocational courses was a cause for concern. The progress was considered sluggish and the links with industry were weak. A Central Institute for Vocational Education was established at Bhopal in July 1993 to strengthen the activities in the field of vocational education. In the 1950s, the government attempted to link the young work-seekers with the industrial units in the country in the area of formal training. An Apprenticeship Act was enacted in 1961 to make it obligatory for the employers in specified industries to engage apprentices for training between six months to four years. The Act came into force on March 1, 1963. The training was to include both basic skills and on the job or shop floor training according to the standards prescribed by the Government in consultation with the Central Apprenticeship Council. Following amendments in 1973 and 1986, the scheme now covers the training of graduates and diploma holders in engineering and technology, and technician (vocational) apprentices, the latter including those passing out of the vocational higher secondary schools. So far, 132 trades in 218 industries with about 25,000 enterprises have been covered under the scheme. The number of apprentices being trained under the scheme has risen from just 1200 initially to 129,000 in 1991 and 150,000 during 1995-96. However, there is widespread doubt about the extent to which the employers are willing to train the apprentices whom they are required to support through stipends; many of them do not really offer adequate training. A thorough evaluation of the scheme is necessary.

Over the past six decades, there has been a steady expansion in the number of ITIs which train the youth aged 15-25 in 42 engineering and 22 non-engineering trades for a period of one or two years. Depending on the trade, the minimum educational qualification varies between the 8th standard and the 12th standard. Admissions to ITIs are in great demand in many States and they fulfill a useful role in training the craftsmen. However, the outdated equipment and the outmoded training skills of the ITI trainers have often invited adverse comment. An attempt is being made to overcome these limitations with the financial assistance from the World Bank. Overall, however, the quantity and the quality of the output of ITIs do not really meet the needs of the Indian industry. Most firms necessarily rely on on-the-job training and use the earlier training received by their employees as a screening mechanism.

In India, it has been recognized that technical education programmes will not only help to provide an alternative to those pursuing higher education without specific interest, but will also help to promote individual employability (including self-employment) and reduce the mismatch between demand and supply of a skilled work-force. Hence, the policy provides for generic technical courses with international recognition, and salaried and self-employment oriented curricula. To meet this challenge, appropriate bodies and authorities have been created to pursue and monitor policy directives and their implementation, such as the All India Council for Technical Education, National Council of Vocational Education, Central Institute of Vocational Education, State Departments of

Figure 1
Current System of Education in India

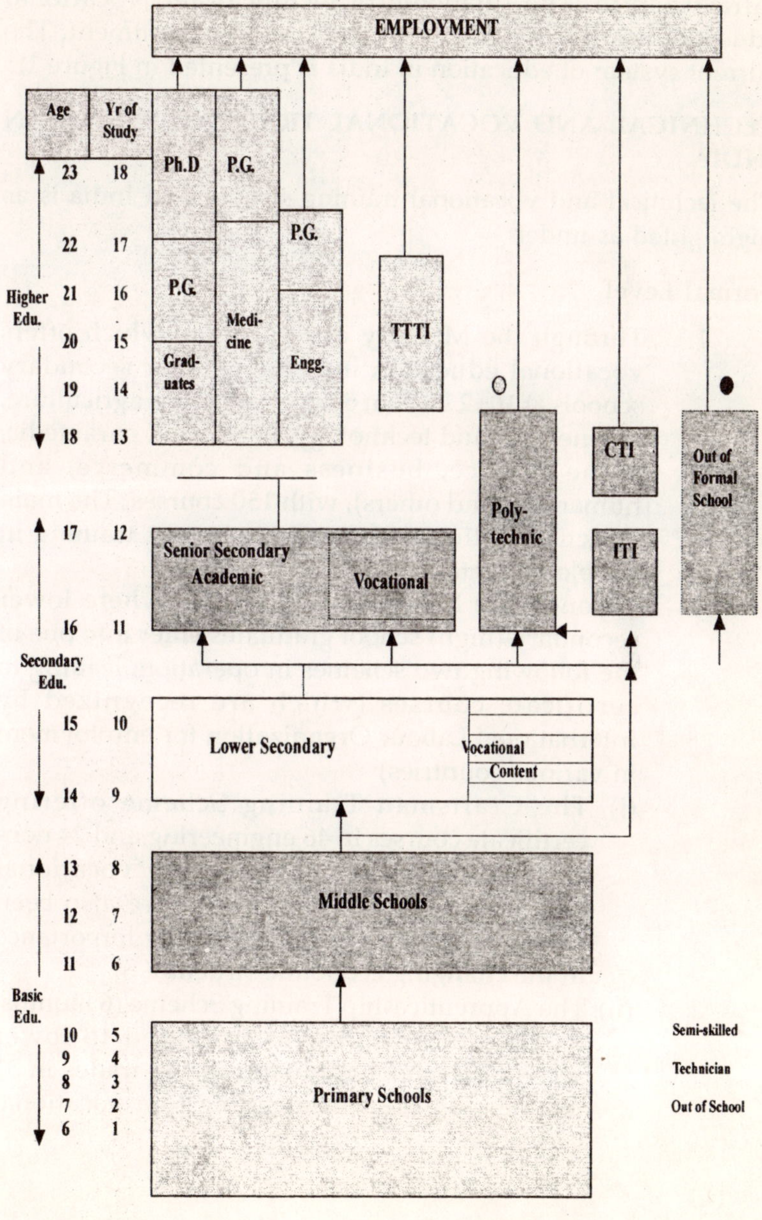

Technical and Vocational Education, National and State Councils for Education, Research and Training and district level infrastructure. The financing of technical and vocational education in India is largely by the central government. The current system of education in India is presented in Figure 1.

TECHNICAL AND VOCATIONAL TRAINING SYSTEM IN INDIA

The technical and vocational training structure in India is as highlighted as under:

Formal Level

1. Through the Ministry of Education, which offers vocational education in certain senior secondary schools at 10+2 level in 6 major areas (*i.e.* agriculture, engineering and technology, health and paramedic, home science, business and commerce, and humanities and others), with 150 courses. The main objective of these courses is to impart training in simple marketable skills to students.
2. Through the Ministry of Labour, - where lower secondary (high) school graduates enter into one of the following two schemes in operation, leading to certificate courses (which are recognized by International Labour Organization for employment in various countries):
   (i) The Craftsman Training Scheme offering certificate courses in 46 engineering and 24 non-engineering trades leading to a 'vocational certificate.' Thirty new trades have also been recently introduced in view of their importance in the changing economic structure.
   (ii) The Apprenticeship Training Scheme (6 months' to 4 years' training) is provided to lower secondary school graduates in 135 trades in 31 engineering branches leading to a vocational certificate.

Non-Formal Level

At the non-formal level, vocational training is provided to school dropouts, neo-literates and disadvantaged groups through *shramik vidya peeths* (skill training schools) and national open schools in certain vocational trades.

(i) **Technician Education:** Graduates from lower secondary schools can also enter into polytechnics to pursue 2/3-year diploma programme at senior secondary level (normally based on an entry test). They are trained to work at supervisory level, and thus act as a vital link between the worker and the engineer in an industry/project. There are over 1,200 polytechnics with an intake capacity of 200,000 students in India. Diploma courses are offered in 149 trades in 18 engineering-based and 11 non-engineering-based areas. Advanced diploma and post-diploma courses are also on offer. Community polytechnics have also been set up in rural areas to meet the training needs of local youth, college dropouts, women and disadvantaged sections of society.

(ii) **Vocational Education in Other Areas:** Vocational education courses are also available in the fields of health and paramedics, business and commerce, hotel management, etc. Certain new trades, such as travel and tourism, fashion design, food technology, beauty culture, etc., have also been introduced recently in view of their employment potential. However, there are few systems of production of a skilled work force for the agricultural sector.

Higher Technical Education

The country has advanced facilities for pursuing higher technical education including prestigious institutes of technology and management, engineering colleges, agriculture and general universities, law and commerce colleges, etc.

Higher education in India is of international standard and globally recognized.

FRAMEWORK FOR THE STUDY

The contribution of technically trained manpower to the economic growth and development is a well-accepted factor. The shortage of personnel with an education in industrial training will have an adverse impact on the state's economy, especially in the industrial sector. A vast body of literature exists to evince that technological change and dynamism in industry is positively related with the nature and extent of technically trained workforce engaged in a country's industrial sector.

In order to attain industrial and technological self-reliance, the planners envisaged the development and building up of indigenous expertise and stock of technically trained manpower as an inalienable part of the state's development strategy. As a sequel to this policy, a tremendous effort was made by the Government to create a massive infrastructure to train and built up locally groomed expertise and skilled manpower. ITIs are one of the major institutions that provide technically trained manpower in state of Jammu and Kashmir. As a result, state has turned into the one of the largest reservoir of technically skilled manpower in the country.

However, the over production of technically trained manpower, with less regard to the absorption capacity of the labour market will result in unemployment among these skilled labour force. "Labour market of ITIs" has become a topic of vital interest in our society today as a result of burning issue of unemployment among the technically trained manpower. In view of rapidly changing social, political and technological climates, the technically trained manpower requirements also change which demands for constant monitoring of manpower requirements. Therefore, an assessment of the impact of training courses in the ITIs and to evaluate the track record of the placement of the trainees is essential for the relevant authorities to identify gaps between the demand and supply of the technically trained personnel as well as to take suitable action in advance.

OBJECTIVES

The main objectives of the present study are:

1. To assess the impact of training courses in the ITIs;
2. To evaluate the track record of the placement of the trainees;
3. To estimate the level of unemployment among technically trained manpower;
4. To analyze the obstacles faced by technically trained manpower in the process of securing jobs in the labour market; and
5. To suggest policy recommendations to overcome the gaps between demand and supply of technically trained manpower pass-out from ITIs and to avoid the surplus or shortage of technically trained manpower in different disciplines accordingly.

METHODOLOGY OF THE PRESENT STUDY

(i) **Targeted Population and Sample Size:** The present study has been conducted in all the areas of the state of Jammu and Kashmir. This study has been confined to technically trained manpower passed out from ITIs in the last five years, viz. 2001, 2002, 2003, 2004, and 2005. The sample size has been restricted to 20% of technically trained manpower passed out from ITIs. The proportional sampling technique has been used to select the male and female trainees. The respondents have been proportionally distributed among all the districts of the state of Jammu and Kashmir. Out of the total 4159 ITI pass outs in the last five years, a proportional sample of 796 ITI pass outs has been selected Table 1. The sample of districts were confined to pass outs of ITI Handwara (Kupwara district), ITI Doda and ITI Ramban (district Doda), ITI Udhampur and ITI Reasi (Udhampur district), ITI Mendhar (Poonch district), ITI Rajouri and ITI Sunderbani (Rajouri district), ITI Jammu and ITI Samba (Jammu district), ITI Kathua and ITI Hiranagar (Kathua district) and for other districts, the sample was to ITI pass outs at district headquarters.

For the assessment of the demand of the industries of the courses run by the ITIs, a sample of 193 industrial units have been selected and their distribution across the districts of the state of Jammu and Kashmir. An attempt has also been made to assess the demand of the prospective trainees of the courses run by the ITIs, for which a random sample of 350 prospective trainees has been selected covering 25 prospective trainees from all the districts of the state.

(ii) **Method of Data Collection:** The field survey method has been used to collect primary data and information. Three types of questionnaires – (a) Assessment of Impact of Training Courses in ITIs and Track Record of Placement of Trainees; (b) Demand Assessment of Industries of the Courses Run by ITIs; and (c) Demand Assessment of Prospective Trainees of the Courses Run by ITIs. The questionnaires have been prepared in English to collect the data and information related to the present study, for which the services of trained research investigators have been utilized. A separate questionnaire has been used to collect secondary data and information from the respective ITIs.

Table 1
Sample Size of the Present Study

District	*Total ITI pass outs*	*Sample ITI pass outs*	*Sample of industrial units*	*Sample of prospective trainees*
Anantnag	587	80	25	24
Baramulla	172	37	25	15
Doda	204	42	25	8
Jammu	542	107	25	31
Kathua	528	103	25	16
Leh	270	54	25	7
Poonch	76	22	25	11
Rajouri	301	62	25	12
Srinagar	581	105	25	19
Udhampur	284	56	25	11
Pulwama	193	39	25	11
Kupwara	54	14	25	6
Kargil	195	39	25	6
Budgam	172	36	25	16
Total	4159	796	350	193

(iii) **Sources of the Data:** The secondary data and information regarding enrolment in training courses, pass-outs of technically trained manpower and staff utilization during the period of five years viz. 2001, 2002, 2003, 2004, and 2005 has been collected from the respective ITIs. In this study, employment status of technically trained manpower pass-outs from ITIs has been classified using five main categories. The technically trained manpower who are permanently or temporarily engaged in full time work in formal employment sectors such as government, non-government organisations (NGOs) and private sectors has been considered as the employed technically trained manpower. The technically trained manpower engaged in own or family business has been considered as self-employed. Unemployed technically trained manpower has been considered as those who are without work and seeking for employment. The technically trained manpower without work and not seeking employment has not been considered for further analysis, as they could not be categorized with respect to work or employment.

(iv) **Method of Processing and Analysing:** The collected data has been classified as employment status of technically trained manpower pass-outs from ITIs (according to gender, management/cadre level of employed ITI pass-outs, sector of employment by type of course, sector of employment by income group, income level of employed ITI pass-outs, income level of employed ITI pass-outs by gender, income level by type of course, waiting time of ITI pass-outs according to type of course, major reasons for the failure to obtain a permanent employment, unemployed ITI pass-outs according to type of course, employment rates/unemployment rates by type of course, views regarding their failure in obtaining permanent employment, and obstacles faced by ITI pass-outs in finding suitable employment. The data analysis has been done using simple descriptive statistics.

LIMITATIONS OF THE STUDY

In India, in general and Jammu and Kashmir, in particular, there is considerable lack of data and information on the issues of demand and supply of technically trained manpower coming out of the ITIs, which results in poorly designed technically trained manpower policies and plans. The studies related to assessment of the impact of training courses in the ITIs including the analysis of the track record of the placement of the trainees in the context of pass-outs of ITIs and demand assessment of the ITI courses by industries and prospective trainees is virtually non-existent and the present study has been a median attempt in this direction. It is emphasized that to get a clear picture on the actual absorption pattern of ITI pass-outs into the labour market and for policy initiatives to be considered for relevant in the tertiary education curricular, a series of such studies should be conducted.

DESIGN OF THE STUDY

The present study has been designed in six chapters. The first chapter is introductory one and presents the objectives and methodology of the study. The chapter two is based on the secondary data and information and highlights the status of technical education especially enrolment, retention and pass outs in the ITIs of the state of Jammu and Kashmir. The third chapter examines the impact of training courses in the ITIs including the analysis of the track record of the placement of the trainees in the context of pass-outs of ITIs. The chapters four and five examine the demand assessment of the ITI courses by the industries and prospective trainees. The last chapter provides the conclusions and recommendations of the study.

2

INDUSTRIAL TRAINING FACILITIES IN J&K

In the state of Jammu and Kashmir, the Directorate of Technical Education (DTE) was established in 1981 by the creation of a unified institute for administration and control of the ITIs and vocational training institute. This was done to coordinate the various training programmes and efficient utilization of the available resources and integrated development of the technical and vocational training in the state. At the time of the establishment of DTE, there were 21 ITIs and 2 polytechnics. Over the period, the DTE diversified its activities and the number of ITIs and polytechnics has increased to 37 and 12 respectively. By the year 1994, all the major towns of the state has one ITI meant for providing fundamental type of industrial training.

ITIs are providing Craftsman Training leading to the award of Diploma/Certificate in Craftsmanship, and Apprenticeship training in the field, leading to the award of Diploma/Certificate in Apprenticeship. Craftsman Training courses are job-oriented, with the purpose of providing skilled workers and are conducted under the technical leadership of the National Council for Vocational Training (NCVT) through a network of the ITIs in the state. Apprenticeship training is for actual industrial workers, who are trained on the job as fully skilled workers. The scheme is conducted through National Apprenticeship Council (NAC) at the national level. Both NCVT and NAC are under the Ministry of Labour, Government of India.

In 1956, the Craftsman Training Scheme (CTS) was introduced in India. Under the scheme, training is being imparted through ITIs for meeting the requirements of skilled labour for the industrial/engineering sector. It also provides opportunities for large-scale self-employment of the youth. In the state of Jammu and Kashmir, the scheme was introduced in 1958 and two ITIs were established in the capital cities of Srinagar and Jammu. Since than, more and more ITIs were added to provide the vocational training facilities in remote areas with a view to provide industrial and technical skills to youth to be better qualified for employment/self-employment within and outside the state.

Table 1
Place and Year of Establishment of ITIs

Kashmir Division		*Jammu Division*	
Place	*Year Established*	*Place*	*Year Established*
Srinagar*	1958	Jammu*	1958
Anantnag*	1962	Kistwar*	1962
Baramulla*	1962	Rajouri	1962
Bandipora	1979	Hiranagar	1962
Shopian	1979	Udhampur	1975
Badgam	1980	Poonch	1975
Kupwara	1980	Gool	1975
Pulwama	1981	Ramban	1979
Uri	1981	Doda	1980
Pattan	1985	Kathua	1980
Tral	1985	Bhadarwah	1981
Ganderbal	1985	Mendhar	1985
Leh	1985	Reasi	1985
Kargil	1985	Sunderbani	1985
Chrarisharief	1988	Bhaddu/Billawar	1985
Sopore	1988	R.S. Pura	1988
Kulgam	1988	Basholi	1988
Handwara	1994	Samba	1994
Women's ITI Srinagar	1994		

Note: *indicates major ITIs with a capacity of more than 200 seats.

TRAINING INSTITUTES

The place and year of establishment of ITIs in the state of Jammu and Kashmir are given in Table 1. A perusal of the table clearly reveals that first ITI was established in the year 1958 in both the Kashmir and Jammu division of the state. In Kashmir division, three ITIs are having a total capacity of more than 200 seats, whereas in Jammu division, the ITIs with a capacity of 200 seats stood at two. The district-wise distribution of ITIs are given in Table 2, which makes it clear that district Baramulla has comparatively more ITIs and its number stood at 5, whereas districts of Leh and Kargil have one ITI each.

Table 2
District-wise Distribution of ITIs

Kashmir Division		*Jammu Division*	
District	Number of ITIs	District	Number of ITIs
Srinagar	3	Jammu	3
Anantnag	2	Doda	4
Baramulla	5	Rajouri	2
Budgam	2	Poonch	2
Kupwara	2	Udhampur	3
Pulwama	3	Kathua	4
Leh	1		
Kargil	1		

TRAINING FACILITIES

Out of 67 trades designated by the NCVT under the CTS, training facilities are available in 21 trades in ITIs in the state of Jammu and Kashmir, which are further divided as: engineering trades (18) and non-engineering trades (3). The engineering trades are: welder, mechanic (diesel, plumber), mason (building constructor), mechanic (tractor), carpenter, computer operator and programme assistant, information technology and electronics systems maintenance, painter (general), mechanic (motor vehicle), fitter, turner, machinist, electrician, instrument mechanic, mechanic radio and television, mechanic AC/ refrigeration, and electronic mechanic. The non-engineering trades are cutting and tailoring, stenography (English), and calico printing.

AFFILIATION STATUS

A total of 267 trade units (a unit is generally of 19 trainees including the supernumeraries) are available in all the ITIs of the state. Of these, 221 trade units are affiliated with the NCVT, while the remaining 46 units have not been affiliated due to lack of infrastructure such as space, machinery/equipment or staff.

DEFICIENCIES OF INFRASTRUCTURE

There are significant deficiencies in the availability of infrastructure in both the affiliated and un-affiliated trades, which is affecting the quality of training being imparted in these ITIs. Some of the buildings in both the Kashmir and Jammu division are without their own buildings (See Table 3).

Table 3
ITIs without Own Building

Kashmir Division	*Jammu Division*
Tral*	Basholi*
Shopian*	Billawar*
Kulgam	Gool*
Pattan	Doda

Note: * These ITIs do not have the land as well as funds for constructing their own buildings

Besides above, the equipment maintenance workshops at Jammu and Budgam established under the World Bank Programme in 1999 do not have the required staff. The second instructor with Diploma level qualification should be provided to the trades as per the revised norms of the NCVT in each of the trades in the ITIs.

MODERNIZATION OF THE VOCATIONAL TRAINING STRUCTURE

A centrally sponsored scheme, amounting Rs. 30.60 crores in the first phase has been submitted to the Ministry of Labour,

Government of India to modernize the training facilities, which will boost self-employment and curb unemployment in the State. Some of the important features of the proposed scheme are: (a) 31 obsolete and unpopular trades will be deleted from the ITIs of the state, which are to be replaced by 69 modern trades; (b) the modern concept of multi-skill training will be introduced in the state; (c) obsolete equipments in 102 existing trade units will be replaced by modern and more versatile equipments; (d) short time courses to cater to the need of different target groups will be introduced in 9 ITIs in the state; (e) ITIs at Kulgam, Tral, Doda and Basholi will be provided with their own buildings; (f) ITI Srinagar will be reconstructed on modern lines at a more appropriate site in order to meet the need for ISO 9002 standardisation of the institute; (g) a women's ITI will be established at Jammu and hostel facilities will be provided to the women's ITI at Srinagar; (h) facilities for the vocational training of women will be significantly improved by the establishment of women's wing in 5 ITIs, in different areas of the state; (i) vocational instructors of unpopular trades being closed up, will be retrained in modern/popular trades; (j) the staffing pattern in the state directorate will be brought in line with the DGE&T pattern by removing the deficiencies; and (k) the seat capacity for vocational training will go up from the present 4946 seats to 6065 seats to ensure one seat for every 1670 persons so that it will be closer to the national average of 1575 persons.

In sum, there is need to give vocational trainings the status of the priority sector so that the youth of the state can take up the self-employment in a big way and can be able to find suitable employment as skilled workers. Thus, there is need for heavy investment in this sector so as to raise the standards and quality of training to be provided to the youth of the state, which in turn would have greater acceptability in the employment markets. However, if there is a failure on this front, the youth of the state will have no option but to pursue aimless education, which will deteriorate the already alarming unemployment among the youth with unforeseen repercussions.

VI. ENROLMENT, RETENTION AND PASS OUTS

Out of 36 ITIs, the data regarding the enrolment, retention and pass outs has been available for 29 ITIs for the period of five years viz. 2001, 2002, 2003, 2004 and 2005. The total enrolment of the trainees in various courses/trades offered during the reference period was 10985 in the 29 ITIs of the state of Jammu and Kashmir, out of which 7351 (66.91 percent) were males and 3634 (33.09 percent) were females. Out of 7351 males enrolled, 4873 (66.29 percent) were appeared in the final test and out of 3634 females enrolled, 2753 (75.75 percent) were appeared in the final test and of those who appeared in the final test, 62.57 percent and 71.70 percent of the males and females respectively were declared pass (See Table 4). Thus, about two-third of males and three-fourth of the females ITI enrolled trainees were retained and appeared in final trade test and the drop out/ wastage was significant (33.0 percent and 25.0 percent respectively for males and females).

The course-wise data regarding enrolment, retention and pass outs is also given in Table 4, which reveals that all male ITI trainees appeared in the final test of the course of instrument mechanic followed by more than 80 percent in the courses of Urdu calligraphy and diesel mechanic were declared pass. Similarly, more than 70 percent of the male ITI trainees appeared in the courses of computer operator, A.C & refrigerator, electrician, motor and mechanic and more than 60 percent in the courses of electronic mechanic, plumber, fitter, and machinist were declared pass. In case of female trainees, the proportion of the pass outs was comparatively higher in courses of Urdu calligraphy followed by computer operator, cutting and tailoring, and electronic mechanic. On the whole, the pass outs in the courses like radio & T.V mechanic, turner, and tractor mechanic were less than 50.0 percent, which needs attention of the authorities so that the proportion of the ITI pass outs in these specific courses could be increased further.

The data regarding the enrolment, retention and pass outs for the 29 ITI, are given in the Tables 5 to 33. A perusal of the data given in these tables makes it evident that in some of the courses/trades, the enrolment of the trainees was comparatively lower than the number of sanctioned trainees per course and the female trainees were confined to one-third of the courses offered by the ITIs. In most of the courses catering to the supply of technically trained manpower for the industrial sector, the enrolment of the female trainees was virtually non-existent, which needs serious attention by the relevant authorities. The women trainees were mostly enrolled in courses like cutting and tailoring, stenography and computer operator. Thus, there is gender bias in enrolment in the ITI courses and therefore, there is urgent need to remove such biases by motivating more and more young women to enroll in courses catering to the industrial employment.

Table 4
Enrolment, Retention and Pass Outs in 29 ITIs by Type of Course/Trade (No./%)

Training course/trade	*No. enrolled at its beginning*		*No. of trainees appeared for trade test*		*No. of trainees passed in final trade test*		*% of trainees passed in final trade test*	
	Male	*Female*	*Male*	*Female*	*Male*	*Female*	*Male*	*Female*
Electrician	1627	-	967	-	682	-	70.52	-
Motor Mechanic	583	-	340	-	244	-	71.76	-
Radio and T.V. Mechanic	616	155	315	57	145	28	46.03	49.12
Turner	144	-	69	-	31	-	44.93	-
Machinist	55	-	20	-	12	-	60.00	-
Fitter	260	-	142	-	95	-	65.52	-
Mason	140	-	120	-	70	-	58.33	-
Carpenter	224	-	137	-	80	-	58.39	-
Welder	576	-	401	-	214	-	53.37	-
Tractor Mechanic	266	-	188	-	86	-	45.74	-
A.C & Refrigerator	33	-	16	-	12	-	75.00	-
Computer Operator	504	299	416	202	324	158	77.88	78.21
Information Technology	63	-	27	-	16	-	59.26	-
Stenography	1367	858	1029	626	576	345	55.97	59.89
Cutting and Tailoring	30	2109	46	1767	20	1368	43.47	77.42
Painter General	162	66	70	39	37	11	52.86	28.20
Instrument Mechanic	55	-	21	-	21	-	100	-
Plumber	271	-	253	-	168	-	66.40	-
Electronic Mechanic	265	132	196	71	135	54	68.87	76.05
Urdu Calligraphy	13	15	11	11	9	10	81.81	90.91
Diesel Mechanic	97	-	89	-	72	-	80.89	-
Total	7351	3634	4873	2753	3049	1974	62.57	71.70

A perusal of the data in Table 5 makes it clear that out of 1133 trainees enrolled in ITI Jammu, 76.62 percent and 23.38 percent respectively were males and females and a total of 573 trainees were retained and appeared in the final trade test (46.28 percent of males and 64.41 percent of females) and of them 58.31 percent (male) and 71.76 percent (female) trainees were declared pass during the period under reference. Thus, there is wide gap between enrolment and retention. It is significant to note that all the trainees appeared in final test of the courses of machinist and instrument mechanic were declared pass, whereas in the courses of tractor mechanic, stenography and turner, the proportion of the pass outs was very low. In ITI Samba, 493 trainees were enrolled in various courses, of which majority of them were males and all the females enrolled were retained and appeared in final test and most of them (97.10 percent) were declared pass. In the courses of electrician, turner and fitter, the proportion of the pass outs was cent percent, whereas the performance in the courses of tractor mechanic, radio & T.V mechanic and welder was comparatively very low.

In ITI Reasi, two-third of the enrolled trainees were males and rest were females and of them two-third of males and a significantly higher proportion of the females (93.14 percent) were retained and appeared in the final test, however, the proportion of ITI pass outs was lower, the half in case of both the sexes. The proportion of the pass outs in trade of welder was very low (15.0 percent). More female trainees than males were enrolled and retained in ITI Udhampur and of them about one-third of males and 95.86 percent of the females were declared pass Table 8. In ITI Gool, 59.7 percent and 40.83 percent of the enrolled trainees were respectively males and females, of them 64.19 percent and 72.45 percent were retained and appeared in the final test and 65.26 percent and 70.42 percent respectively were declared pass during the period under reference.

Out of 414 enrolled trainees in ITI Kathua, 70.05 percent of them were males and rest was females. More than 70.0 percent males and cent percent females were retained and appeared in final test, of them about half of males and more than 80.0 percent

Table 5

Enrolment, Retention and Pass Outs in ITI Jammu by Type of Course/Trade (No./%)

Training course/trade	*No. of sanctioned trainees per course*	*No. enrolled at its beginning*		*No. of trainees appeared for trade test*		*No. of trainees passed in final trade test*		*% of trainees passed in final trade test*	
		Male	*Female*	*Male*	*Female*	*Male*	*Female*	*Male*	*Female*
Electrician	48	111	-	52	-	40	-	76.92	-
Motor Mechanic	16	95	-	37	-	27	-	72.79	-
Radio & T.V. Mechanic	19	35	-	17	-	13	-	76.47	-
Turner	12	34	-	17	-	7	-	41.17	-
Machinist	12	31	-	6	-	6	-	100	-
Fitter	16	43	-	17	-	11	-	64.70	-
Mason	16	48	-	30	-	16	-	53.33	-
Carpenter	16	43	-	29	-	13	-	44.82	-
Welder	12	34	-	19	-	6	-	31.57	-
Tractor Mechanic	16	60	-	29	-	8	-	27.58	-
A.C & Refrigerator	19	33	-	16	-	12	-	76.00	-
Computer Operator	24	84	29	39	16	34	14	87.18	87.50
Information Technology	19	35	3	17	-	6	-	35.29	-
Stenography	32	107	63	54	46	18	18	33.33	39.13
Cutting and Tailoring	32	-	159	-	104	-	88	-	84.62
Painter General	16	39	11	15	4	9	2	60.00	50.00
Instrument Mechanic	19	36	-	9	-	9	-	100	-
Total	344	868	265	403	170	235	122	58.31	71.76

Table 6

Enrolment, Retention and Pass Outs in ITI Samba by Type of Course/Trade (No./%)

Training course/trade	*No. of sanctioned trainees per course*	*No. enrolled at its beginning*		*No. of trainees appeared for trade test*		*No. of trainees passed in final trade test*		*% of trainees passed in final trade test*	
		Male	*Female*	*Male*	*Female*	*Male*	*Female*	*Male*	*Female*
Electrician	16	62	-	13	-	13	-	100	-
Electronic Mechanic	16	5	-	-	-	-	-	-	-
Fitter	16	37	-	4	-	4	-	100	-
Motor Mechanic	16	69	-	25	-	20	-	80.00	-
Tractor Mechanic	16	54	-	41	-	14	-	34.15	-
Welder	12	48	-	27	-	13	-	48.15	-
Plumber	16	85	-	85	-	44	-	51.76	-
Cutting and Tailoring	16	-	69	-	69	-	67	-	97.10
Radio & T.V Mechanic	16	47	-	29	-	13	-	44.83	-
Turner	32	17	-	2	-	2	-	100	-
Total	172	424	69	226	69	123	67	54.42	97.10

Table 7

Enrolment, Retention and Pass Outs in ITI Reasi by Type of Course/Trade (No./%)

Training course/trade	*No. of sanctioned trainees per course*	*No. enrolled at its beginning*		*No. of trainees appeared for trade test*		*No. of trainees passed in final trade test*		*% of trainees passed in final trade test*	
		Male	*Female*	*Male*	*Female*	*Male*	*Female*	*Male*	*Female*
Electrician	16	90	-	53	-	32	-	60.38	-
Fitter	16	42	-	15	-	12	-	80.00	-
Welder	16	25	-	20	-	3	-	15.00	-
Stenography	16	50	26	50	26	20	10	40.00	38.46
Cutting and Tailoring	16	-	76	-	69	-	36	-	52.17
Total	80	207	102	138	95	67	46	48.55	48.42

Table 8

Enrolment, Retention and Pass Outs in ITI Udhampur by Type of Course/Trade (No./%)

Training course/trade	*No. of sanctioned trainees per course*	*No. enrolled at its beginning*		*No. of trainees appeared for trade test*		*No. of trainees passed in final trade test*		*% of trainees passed in final trade test*	
		Male	*Female*	*Male*	*Female*	*Male*	*Female*	*Male*	*Female*
Electrician	16	33	-	13	-	6	-	46.15	-
Welder	12	47	-	16	-	11	-	68.76	-
Stenography	16	68	18	39	12	27	10	69.23	83.33
Cutting and Tailoring	32	-	157	-	109	-	106	-	97.24
Total	76	148	175	68	121	44	116	64.70	95.86

Table 9

Enrolment, Retention and Pass Outs in ITI Gool by Type of Course/Trade (No./%)

Training course/trade	*No. of sanctioned trainees per course*	*No. enrolled at its beginning*		*No. of trainees appeared for trade test*		*No. of trainees passed in final trade test*		*% of trainees passed in final trade test*	
		Male	*Female*	*Male*	*Female*	*Male*	*Female*	*Male*	*Female*
Electrician	19	53	-	33	-	16	-	48.48	-
Painter General	12	19	14	7	5	6	4	85.71	80.00
Stenography	19	48	41	34	39	26	24	76.47	61.53
Cutting and Tailoring	16	22	43	21	27	14	22	66.67	81.48
Total	66	142	98	95	71	62	50	65.26	70.42

of the females trainees were declared pass Table 10. In the courses of turner, welder, painter, and stenography, the proportion of the pass outs in final test was reportedly very low as compared to the courses of electrician and motor mechanic. In ITI Hiranagar, about two-third and one-third of the enrolled trainees were males and females respectively, and of them a significantly high proportion were retained (88.58 percent of males and 75.56 percent of the females) and declared pass in final test (more than two third of males and 84.32 percent of the females). In the courses of stenography and computer operator, all the male trainees appeared in the final test were declared pass, whereas 57.14 percent of the females were declared pass in stenography course, whereas the proportion of the pass outs in ITI Bhaddu/Billawar was comparatively very low and needs improvement, except for the course of stenography.

In ITI Mendhar, a very high proportion of the enrolled trainees in the courses offered were males and the retention rate in case of female trainees was cent percent, however, only one-third of the females appeared in the final test were declared pass. In case of male trainees, the proportion of the pass outs in final test was cent percent in the course of radio & T.V mechanic, followed by about two-third in trade of electrician. About three-fourth of the enrolled trainees in ITI Doda were males and a significantly very high proportion of them were retained and appeared in final test, however, the proportion of the trainees declared pass in the courses of welder, plumber and stenography was low and significantly very low in stenography in case of female trainees (12.5 percent). The poor performance in these trades has its repercussions on their sustainability, which needs attention. In ITI Ramban, less than two-third of the enrolled trainees were male, however, more than two-third and three-fourth of the male and female trainees respectively were retained and appeared in the final test and of them 48.42 percent and 64.41 percent males and females respectively were declared pass. The proportion declared pass was significant in all the courses offered except the course of stenography (37.14 percent males and about one-third of females).

Table 10

Enrolment, Retention and Pass Outs in ITI Kathua by Type of Course/Trade (No./%)

Training course/trade	*No. of sanctioned trainees per course*	*No. enrolled at its beginning*		*No. of trainees appeared for trade test*		*No. of trainees passed in final trade test*		*% of trainees passed in final trade test*	
		Male	*Female*	*Male*	*Female*	*Male*	*Female*	*Male*	*Female*
Electrician	16	75	-	48	-	34	-	70.83	-
Turner	16	30	-	20	-	6	-	30.00	-
Motor Mechanic	16	35	-	23	-	18	-	78.26	-
Welder	12	61	-	56	-	26	-	46.43	-
Painter General	16	28	7	13	7	6	2	46.15	33.33
Stenography	16	61	26	44	26	16	20	36.36	76.92
Cutting and Tailoring	16	-	91	-	91	-	81	-	89.01
Total	108	290	124	204	124	106	103	51.96	82.40

Table 11

Enrolment, Retention and Pass Outs in ITI Hiranagar by Type of Course/Trade (No./%)

Training course/trade	*No. of sanctioned trainees per course*	*No. enrolled at its beginning*		*No. of trainees appeared for trade test*		*No. of trainees passed in final trade test*		*% of trainees passed in final trade test*	
		Male	*Female*	*Male*	*Female*	*Male*	*Female*	*Male*	*Female*
Electrician	16	37	-	37	-	18	-	48.65	-
Fitter	19	17		17	-	5	-	29.41	-
Turner	16	22	-	14	-	5	-	35.71	-
Welder	12	45	-	45	-	28	-	62.22	-
Carpenter	16	46		31	-	19	-	61.29	-
Painter General	16	11	7	11	-	5	-	45.45	-
Stenography	16	52	14	46	14	46	8	100	57.14
Cutting and Tailoring	32	-	101	-	86	-	76	-	-
Computer Operator	16	24	13	24	2	24	2	100	100
Total	159	254	135	225	102	150	86	66.67	84.31

Table 12
Enrolment, Retention and Pass Outs in ITI Bhaddu/Billawar by Type of Course/Trade (No./%)

Training course/trade	*No. of sanctioned trainees per course*	*No. enrolled at its beginning*		*No. of trainees appeared for trade test*		*No. of trainees passed in final trade test*		*% of trainees passed in final trade test*	
		Male	*Female*	*Male*	*Female*	*Male*	*Female*	*Male*	*Female*
Electrician	19	40	-	28	-	12	-	42.86	-
Stenography	18	36	18	25	18	25	7	100	38.88
Radio & T.V Mechanic	19	24	-	13	-	1	-	7.69	-
Total	56	100	18	66	18	38	7	57.57	38.88

Table 13
Enrolment, Retention and Pass Outs in ITI Mendhar by Type of Course/Trade (No./%)

Training course/trade	*No. of sanctioned trainees per course*	*No. enrolled at its beginning*		*No. of trainees appeared for trade test*		*No. of trainees passed in final trade test*		*% of trainees passed in final trade test*	
		Male	*Female*	*Male*	*Female*	*Male*	*Female*	*Male*	*Female*
Electrician	16	38	-	26	-	17	-	65.38	-
Plumber	16	79	-	58	-	22	-	37.93	-
Stenography	16	55	15	35	15	21	5	60.00	33.33
Radio & T.V Mechanic	16	37	-	13	-	13	-	100	-
Total	64	209	15	132	15	73	5	55.30	33.33

Table 14
Enrolment, Retention and Pass Outs in ITI Doda by Type of Course/Trade (No./%)

Training course/trade	*No. of sanctioned trainees per course*	*No. enrolled at its beginning*		*No. of trainees appeared for trade test*		*No. of trainees passed in final trade test*		*% of trainees passed in final trade test*	
		Male	*Female*	*Male*	*Female*	*Male*	*Female*	*Male*	*Female*
Electrician	16	52	-	48	-	42	-	87.50	-
Welder	8	15	-	15	-	7	-	46.67	-
Plumber	16	62	-	61	-	25	-	40.98	-
Stenography	16	43	18	38	16	16	2	42.10	12.50
Cutting and Tailoring	16	-	38	-	38	-	33	-	86.84
Total	72	172	56	162	54	90	35	55.55	64.81

Table 15
Enrolment, Retention and Pass Outs in ITI Ramban by Type of Course/Trade (No./%)

Training course/trade	*No. of sanctioned trainees per course*	*No. enrolled at its beginning*		*No. of trainees appeared for trade test*		*No. of trainees passed in final trade test*		*% of trainees passed in final trade test*	
		Male	*Female*	*Male*	*Female*	*Male*	*Female*	*Male*	*Female*
Electrician	16	38	-	34	-	16	-	47.06	-
Welder	12	43	-	26	-	17	-	65.38	-
Carpenter	16	7	-	-	-	-	-	-	-
Stenography	16	54	23	35	15	13	5	37.14	33.33
Cutting and Tailoring	16	-	54	-	44	-	33	-	75.00
Total	76	142	77	95	59	46	38	48.42	64.41

About two-third of the enrolled trainees in ITI Rajouri were males and rest of them were females and of them 47.56 percent and 63.63 percent of male and female trainees were retained and about two-third of them declared pass. In all the courses, the proportion of the pass outs was above two-third except stenography (37.93 percent of the males). In ITI Sunderbani, 73.31 percent and 26.69 percent of the male and female trainees respectively were enrolled and 72.82 percent and 78.87 percent of them were retained and appeared in the final test and of them 54.22 percent of the male trainees and 66.07 percent of the female trainees were declared pass, however, in case of all the trades, the performance was good except the course of stenography.

In ITI Leh, a high proportion of the female trainees were enrolled, however, the proportion of the trainees retained and appeared in the final test was below one-half, which is a matter of concern and as such the drop out rate and wastage is quite significant. Out of the 198 trainees appeared in the final test, 65.0 percent of the males and 48.07 percent of the females were declared pass. In course of stenography, the performance of the female trainees was poor, whereas in the trade of radio & T.V mechanic the performance of the female trainees was cent percent. In ITI Kargil, out of the enrolled trainees, a significantly high proportion of them were retained and appeared in final test and declared pass in almost all the courses offered.

Out of 866 trainees enrolled in ITI Srinagar, more than three-fourth of them were males and a very high proportion of them were retained and appeared in final test and declared pass. In three courses viz. turner, plumber, and cutting and tailoring the pass percentage was very high (cent percent), followed by courses like electrician, computer operator, motor mechanic, stenography, fitter, electronic mechanic (more than three-fourth). In ITI Ganderbal, 71.71 percent of the trainees enrolled were males and of them 67.0 were retained. About 80.17 percent of the female trainees appeared in the final test and of them 55.91 percent were declared pass and such proportion for the male trainees stood at more than two-third. In the trades such as motor mechanic and fitter, the proportion of the pass outs were low and recorded as 42.42 percent and 47.60 percent respectively. In the course of carpenter, the pass percentage was cent percent, whereas in other trades the pass percentage was more than two-third (computer operator) and more than three-fourth (electrician and welder).

The enrolment ratio was 53.91 percent and 46.09 percent respectively for male and female trainees in ITI Bandipore, of them 51.91 percent of the males and 92.68 percent of the females were retained and appeared in the final test and 55.86 percent and 48.24 percent respectively were declared pass. In ITI Baramulla, out of 455 trainees enrolled, 78.16 percent and 21.84 percent respectively were males and females, and of them 51.89 percent and 87.86 percent were retained and appeared in the final test and 54.61 percent and 82.92 percent respectively were declared pass. However, the pass percentage in the courses of radio & T.V mechanic and electrician was very low as compared to other ITIs and stood at 26.0 percent and 37.14 percent respectively. The pass percentage in other trades was also significantly low except the trade of stenography (81.48 percent). For the female trainees, the proportion of pass outs was significantly high (more than 80.0 percent) except computer operator (41.67 percent).

In ITI Badgam, more than two-third of the enrolled trainees were retained and 52.36 percent of the males and 72.89 percent of the females were declared pass. In the trades of motor mechanic and radio & T.V mechanic the proportion of the pass outs were cent percent. All the female trainees appeared in the final test of electronic mechanic were declared pass, whereas in the trade of stenography, such proportion stood at 37.50 percent. At the same time, one-fourth of the trainees appeared in final test of welder and about one-third of the trainees appeared in final test of stenography were declared pass. Similarly, 58.82 percent and 42.67 percent of the trainees appeared in final test were declared pass in ITI Tral.

In ITI Handwara, 72.73 percent of the enrolled trainees were males, however, comparatively small proportion of them were retained and appeared in the final test. The pass percentage was also comparatively lower than other ITIs and stood at 43.90

Table 16

Enrolment, Retention and Pass Outs in ITI Rajouri by Type of Course/Trade (No./%)

Training course/trade	*No. of sanctioned trainees per course*	*No. enrolled at its beginning*		*No. of trainees appeared for trade test*		*No. of trainees passed in final trade test*		*% of trainees passed in final trade test*	
		Male	*Female*	*Male*	*Female*	*Male*	*Female*	*Male*	*Female*
Electrician	16	53	-	19	-	19	-	100	-
Electronic Mechanic	16	37	-	23	-	16	-	69.56	-
Carpenter	16	27	-	10	-	7	-	70.00	-
Painter General	16	7	2	-	-	-	-	-	-
Stenography	16	59	33	29	15	11	9	37.93	60.00
Cutting and Tailoring	16	-	81	-	57	-	38	-	66.67
Computer Operator	16	63	16	36	12	24	9	66.67	75.00
Total	112	246	132	117	84	77	56	65.81	66.67

Table 17

Enrolment, Retention and Pass Outs in ITI Sunderbani by Type of Course/Trade (No./%)

Training course/trade	*No. of sanctioned trainees per course*	*No. enrolled at its beginning*		*No. of trainees appeared for trade test*		*No. of trainees passed in final trade test*		*% of trainees passed in final trade test*	
		Male	*Female*	*Male*	*Female*	*Male*	*Female*	*Male*	*Female*
Electrician	16	56	-	38	-	29	-	76.31	-
Motor Mechanic	16	51	-	35	-	23	-	65.71	-
Carpenter	16	21	-	15	-	10	-	66.67	-
Stenography	16	67	20	54	20	15	4	27.77	20.00
Cutting and Tailoring	16	-	51	-	36	-	33	-	91.67
Total	80	195	71	142	56	77	37	54.22	66.07

Table 18

Enrolment, Retention and Pass Outs in ITI Leh by Type of Course/Trade (No./%)

Training course/trade	*No. of sanctioned trainees per course*	*No. enrolled at its beginning*		*No. of trainees appeared for trade test*		*No. of trainees passed in final trade test*		*% of trainees passed in final trade test*	
		Male	*Female*	*Male*	*Female*	*Male*	*Female*	*Male*	*Female*
Electrician	16	18	-	4	-	2	-	50.00	-
Stenography	16	4	57	4	28	4	7	100	25.00
Cutting and Tailoring	16	2	27	-	18	-	12	-	66.67
Radio & T.V Mechanic	16	23	21	12	6	7	6	58.33	100
Total	64	47	105	20	52	13	25	65.00	48.07

Table 19

Enrolment, Retention and Pass Outs in ITI Kargil by Type of Course/Trade (No./%)

Training course/trade	*No. of sanctioned trainees per course*	*No. enrolled at its beginning*		*No. of trainees appeared for trade test*		*No. of trainees passed in final trade test*		*% of trainees passed in final trade test*	
		Male	*Female*	*Male*	*Female*	*Male*	*Female*	*Male*	*Female*
Electrician	16	64	-	59	-	46	-	77.96	-
Stenography	16	52	9	48	9	43	7	89.58	77.77
Cutting and Tailoring	16	-	70	-	70	-	64	-	91.43
Radio & T.V Mechanic	16	32	-	28	-	24	-	85.71	-
Total	64	148	79	135	79	113	71	83.70	89.87

Table 20

Enrolment, Retention and Pass Outs in ITI Srinagar by Type of Course/Trade (No./%)

Training course/trade	*No. of sanctioned trainees per course*	*No. enrolled at its beginning*		*No. of trainees appeared for trade test*		*No. of trainees passed in final trade test*		*% of trainees passed in final trade test*	
		Male	*Female*	*Male*	*Female*	*Male*	*Female*	*Male*	*Female*
Electrician	38	72	-	70	-	66	-	94.28	-
Electronic Mechanic	38	72	-	68	-	51	-	75.00	-
Motor Mechanic	38	114	-	103	-	87	-	84.46	-
Turner	14	14	-	11	-	11	-	100	-
Machinist	28	24	-	14	-	6	-	42.85	-
Fitter	19	17	–	17	-	13	-	76.47	-
Mason	19	14	-	14	-	9	-	62.28	-
Plumber	19	38	-	38	-	38	-	100	-
Carpenter	19	13	-	13	-	2	-	15.38	-
Radio & T.V Mechanic	19	16	-	14	-	3	-	21.43	-
Welder	14	42	-	38	-	30	-	78.95	-
Computer Operator	48	142	48	132	42	117	30	88.63	71.43
Stenography	54	62	37	58	32	45	28	77.58	87.50
Cutting and Tailoring	36	5	117	5	113	5	110	100	97.34
Instrument Mechanic	19	19	-	17	-	12	-	70.58	-
Total	422	664	202	612	187	465	168	75.98	89.84

Table 21

Enrolment, Retention and Pass Outs in ITI Ganderbal by Type of Course/Trade (No./%)

Training course/trade	*No. of sanctioned trainees per course*	*No. enrolled at its beginning*		*No. of trainees appeared for trade test*		*No. of trainees passed in final trade test*		*% of trainees passed in final trade test*	
		Male	*Female*	*Male*	*Female*	*Male*	*Female*	*Male*	*Female*
Electrician	20	40	-	35	-	27	-	77.14	-
Fitter	16	20	-	21	-	10	-	47.60	-
Motor Mechanic	16	72	-	33	-	14	-	42.42	-
Welder	12	61	-	31	-	24	-	77.42	-
Carpenter	10	38	-	14	-	14	-	100	-
Cutting and Tailoring	16	-	96	-	73	-	44	-	60.27
Computer Operator	20	63	20	63	20	43	8	68.25	40.00
Total	110	294	116	197	93	132	52	67.00	55.91

Table 22

Enrolment, Retention and Pass Outs in ITI Ganderbal by Type of Course/Trade (No./%)

Training course/trade	*No. of sanctioned trainees per course*	*No. enrolled at its beginning*		*No. of trainees appeared for trade test*		*No. of trainees passed in final trade test*		*% of trainees passed in final trade test*	
		Male	*Female*	*Male*	*Female*	*Male*	*Female*	*Male*	*Female*
Electrician	20	40	-	35	-	27	-	77.14	-
Fitter	16	20	-	21	-	10	-	47.60	-
Motor Mechanic	16	72	-	33	-	14	-	42.42	-
Welder	12	61	-	31	-	24	-	77.42	-
Carpenter	10	38	-	14	-	14	-	100	-
Cutting and Tailoring	16	-	96	-	73	-	44	-	60.27
Computer Operator	20	63	20	63	20	43	8	68.25	40.00
Total	110	294	116	197	93	132	52	67.00	55.91

Table 23

Enrolment, Retention and Pass Outs in ITI Baramulla by Type of Course/Trade (No./%)

Training course/trade	*No. of sanctioned trainees per course*	*No. enrolled at its beginning*		*No. of trainees appeared for trade test*		*No. of trainees passed in final trade test*		*% of trainees passed in final trade test*	
		Male	*Female*	*Male*	*Female*	*Male*	*Female*	*Male*	*Female*
Electrician	20	97	-	35	-	13	-	37.14	-
Turner	16	27	-	5	-	-	-	-	-
Motor Mechanic	16	35	-	35	-	20	-	57.14	-
Tractor Mechanic	16	58	-	28	-	14	-	50.00	-
Welder	12	58	-	28	-	13	-	46.43	-
Stenography	32	73	42	54	35	44	30	81.48	85.71
Cutting and Tailoring	16	-	78	-	68	-	67	-	98.53
Radio & T.V Mechanic	16	50	8	50	8	13	-	26.00	-
Fitter	16	24	-	-	-	-	-	-	-
Carpenter	16	25	-	6	-	2	-	33.33	-
Computer Operator	24	54	12	54	12	23	5	42.59	41.67
Total	200	501	140	260	123	142	102	54.61	82.92

Table 24

Enrolment, Retention and Pass Outs in ITI Budgam by Type of Course/Trade (No./%)

Training course/trade	*No. of sanctioned trainees per course*	*No. enrolled at its beginning*		*No. of trainees appeared for trade test*		*No. of trainees passed in final trade test*		*% of trainees passed in final trade test*	
		Male	*Female*	*Male*	*Female*	*Male*	*Female*	*Male*	*Female*
Electrician	20	40	-	21	-	13	-	61.90	-
Electronic Mechanic	20	32	6	19	2	15	2	78.94	100
Motor Mechanic	20	33	5	19	-	19	-	100	-
Radio & T.V Mechanic	20	38	-	19	-	19	-	100	-
Welder	15	67	-	50	-	12	-	24.00	-
Stenography	19	51	46	36	32	16	12	33.33	37.50
Cutting and Tailoring	19	-	82	19	73	-	64	-	87.67
Computer Operator	19	-	19	-	-	-	-	-	-
Total	152	261	158	183	107	94	78	52.36	72.89

Table 25

Enrolment, Retention and Pass Outs in ITI Tral by Type of Course/Trade (No./%)

Training course/trade	*No. of sanctioned trainees per course*	*No. enrolled at its beginning*		*No. of trainees appeared for trade test*		*No. of trainees passed in final trade test*		*% of trainees passed in final trade test*	
		Male	*Female*	*Male*	*Female*	*Male*	*Female*	*Male*	*Female*
Electrician	16	39	-	17	-	10	-	58.82	-
Cutting and Tailoring	16	-	75	-	75	-	32	-	42.67
Total	32	39	75	17	75	10	32	58.82	42.67

Table 26

Enrolment, Retention and Pass Outs in ITI Handwara by Type of Course/Trade (No./%)

Training course/trade	*No. of sanctioned trainees per course*	*No. enrolled at its beginning*		*No. of trainees appeared for trade test*		*No. of trainees passed in final trade test*		*% of trainees passed in final trade test*	
		Male	*Female*	*Male*	*Female*	*Male*	*Female*	*Male*	*Female*
Electrician	20	72	-	56	-	24	-	42.85	-
Electronic Mechanic	20	58	14	42	11	16	2	38.09	18.18
Radio & T.V Mechanic	20	52	4	10	4	5	1	50.00	25.00
Stenography	16	26	7	15	2	9	2	60.00	100
Cutting and Tailoring	16	-	34	-	13	-	4	-	30.77
Computer Operator	16	-	19	-	-	-	-	-	-
Total	108	208	78	123	30	54	9	43.90	30.00

Table 27

Enrolment, Retention and Pass Outs in ITI Anantnag by Type of Course/Trade (No./%)

Training course/trade	*No. of sanctioned trainees per course*	*No. enrolled at its beginning*		*No. of trainees appeared for trade test*		*No. of trainees passed in final trade test*		*% of trainees passed in final trade test*	
		Male	*Female*	*Male*	*Female*	*Male*	*Female*	*Male*	*Female*
Electrician	20	77	-	54	-	46	-	85.18	-
Electronic Mechanic	20	60	12	44	6	37	6	84.09	100
Fitter	20	60	-	51	-	40	-	78.43	-
Diesel Mechanic	20	97	-	89	-	72	-	80.89	-
Tractor Mechanic	20	94	-	90	-	50	-	55.55	-
Urdu Calligraphy	16	13	15	11	11	9	10	81.81	90.90
Mason	16	78	-	76	-	45	-	59.21	-
Painter General	20	58	32	24	23	11	3	45.83	13.04
Stenography	40	106	70	91	62	61	30	67.03	48.38
Cutting and Tailoring	40	1	175	1	162	1	120	100	74.07
Computer Operator	24	29	12	47	11	38	11	80.85	100
Information Technology	24	28	-	10	-	10	-	100	-
Welder	12	30	-	30	-	24	-	80.00	-
Total	292	731	316	618	275	444	180	71.84	65.45

percent and 30.0 percent respectively for males and females. The performance of ITI Anantnag is reportedly better and out of 893 retained trainees, 71.84 percent of the males and 65.45 percent of the females were declared pass. The cent percent male pass outs were recorded in trades of information technology and cutting and tailoring and in other course also the percentage pass outs in different trades such as electrician, electronic mechanic, diesel mechanic, Urdu calligraphy, computer and welder stood at more than 80.0 percent. In ITI Kulgam, the performance of the trainees was comparatively poor and the proportion pass outs stood at 44.77 percent and 62.50 percent respectively for males and females.

In ITI Pulwama, the performance was comparatively better. Similar is the situation of Women's ITI Srinagar. In ITI Chrarisharief, the retention rate was comparatively very low in case of male trainees and just one-half of them appeared in the final test and of them 91.14 percent of the male trainees were declared pass. In ITI Shopian, 62.16 percent of the male trainees and 69.86 percent of the female trainees were declared pass, whereas in ITI Pattan, such proportion was comparatively very low in case of male trainees and significantly high in case female trainees (93.75 percent).

On the whole, the proportion of the male trainees enrolled in ITIs was comparatively more than the female trainees except the ITIs of Udhampur, Leh, and Tral. The retention rate for male trainees was comparatively low (less than 60 percent) in ITIs of Jammu, Samba, Udhampur, Rajouri, Leh, Bandipore, Baramulla, Tral, Handwara, Kulgam, and Chararisharief, whereas the retention rate for female trainees was comparatively low (less than 50 percent) in ITIs of Leh, Handwara, and Pattan. The lower retention rate implies high drop out and wastage, which needs immediate attention of the relevant authorities so that the rate of retention should be enhanced from the present lower levels. Similarly, the cent percent retention of enrolled female trainees in ITIs of Kathua, Bhaddu/Billawar, Mendhar, Kargil, and Tral; above 80.0 percent in ITIs of Reasi, Doda, Srinagar, Ganwderbal, Bandipore, Baramulla, Anantnag, and Shopian deserve

Table 28
Enrolment, Retention and Pass Outs in ITI Kulgam by Type of Course/Trade (No./%)

Training course/trade	*No. of sanctioned trainees per course*	*No. enrolled at its beginning*		*No. of trainees appeared for trade test*		*No. of trainees passed in final trade test*		*% of trainees passed in final trade test*	
		Male	*Female*	*Male*	*Female*	*Male*	*Female*	*Male*	*Female*
Electrician	19	19	-	-	-	-	-	-	-
Stenography	19	54	36	34	25	24	13	70.58	52.00
Radio & T.V Mechanic	19	46	8	33	7	6	7	18.18	100
Total	57	119	44	67	32	30	20	44.77	62.50

Table 29
Enrolment, Retention and Pass Outs in ITI Pulwama by Type of Course/Trade (No./%)

Training course/trade	*No. of sanctioned trainees per course*	*No. enrolled at its beginning*		*No. of trainees appeared for trade test*		*No. of trainees passed in final trade test*		*% of trainees passed in final trade test*	
		Male	*Female*	*Male*	*Female*	*Male*	*Female*	*Male*	*Female*
Electrician	16	57	-	39	-	39	-	100	-
Plumber	16	69	-	69	-	39	-	56.52	-
Stenography	16	67	22	47	14	23	14	48.93	100
Cutting and Tailoring	16	-	90	-	77	-	54	-	70.13
Computer Operator	20	45	3	21	-	21	-	100	100
Radio & T.V Mechanic	16	19	-	-	-	-	-	-	-
Total	100	257	115	176	91	122	68	69.31	74.72

Table 30

Enrolment, Retention and Pass Outs in Women's ITI Srinagar by Type of Course/Trade (No./%)

Training course/trade	*No. of sanctioned trainees per course*	*No. enrolled at its beginning*		*No. of trainees appeared for trade test*		*No. of trainees passed in final trade test*		*% of trainees passed in final trade test*	
		Male	*Female*	*Male*	*Female*	*Male*	*Female*	*Male*	*Female*
Electronic Mechanic	20	-	100	-	52	-	44	-	84.61
Stenography	20	-	100	-	73	-	44	-	60.27
Cutting and Tailoring	20	-	100	-	78	-	76	-	97.43
Computer Operator	20	-	108	-	87	-	79	-	90.80
Radio & T.V Mechanic	20	-	100	-	20	-	8	-	40.00
Total	100	-	508	-	310	-	251	-	80.96

Table 31

Enrolment, Retention and Pass Outs in ITI Chrarisharief by Type of Course/Trade (No./%)

Training course/trade	*No. of sanctioned trainees per course*	*No. enrolled at its beginning*		*No. of trainees appeared for trade test*		*No. of trainees passed in final trade test*		*% of trainees passed in final trade test*	
		Male	*Female*	*Male*	*Female*	*Male*	*Female*	*Male*	*Female*
Electrician	20	61	-	42	-	39	-	92.85	-
Stenography	20	40	41	16	34	12	14	75.00	41.17
Cutting and Tailoring	20	-	73	-	51	-	39	-	76.47
Radio & T.V Mechanic	20	55	13	21	12	21	6	100	50.00
Total	80	156	127	79	97	72	59	91.14	60.82

Table 32

Enrolment, Retention and Pass Outs in ITI Shopian by Type of Course/Trade (No./%)

Training course/trade	*No. of sanctioned trainees per course*	*No. enrolled at its beginning*		*No. of trainees appeared for trade test*		*No. of trainees passed in final trade test*		*% of trainees passed in final trade test*	
		Male	*Female*	*Male*	*Female*	*Male*	*Female*	*Male*	*Female*
Electrician	16	39	-	36	-	20	-	55.55	-
Stenography	16	58	26	38	21	26	11	68.42	52.38
Cutting and Tailoring	16	-	52	-	52	-	40	-	76.92
Total	48	97	78	74	73	46	51	62.16	69.86

Table 33

Enrolment, Retention and Pass Outs in ITI Pattan by Type of Course/Trade (No./%)

Training course/trade	*No. of sanctioned trainees per course*	*No. enrolled at its beginning*		*No. of trainees appeared for trade test*		*No. of trainees passed in final trade test*		*% of trainees passed in final trade test*	
		Male	*Female*	*Male*	*Female*	*Male*	*Female*	*Male*	*Female*
Stenography	16	28	-	23	-	10	-	43.47	-
Cutting and Tailoring	16	-	32	-	16	-	15	-	93.75
Radio & T.V Mechanic	16	72	1	39	-	13	-	33.33	-
Total	48	100	33	62	16	23	15	37.09	93.75

appreciation and incentives. In ITIs of Reasi, Ramban, Handwara, Kulgam, and Pattan, the proportion of the male ITI pass outs stood at less than one-half and in the ITIs of Reasi, Bhaddu/Billawar, Mendhar, Leh, Bandipore, Tral, and Handwara, the proportion of the female ITI pass outs were recorded at less than one-half, which implies the need for improvement in teaching methodology, library and laboratory infrastructure, etc. In some of the ITIs, the availability of the teaching and non-teaching staff is also reportedly inadequate to cater to the need of effective training, which also need attention of the relevant authorities.

3

IMPACT OF TRAINING COURSES AND TRACK RECORD OF PLACEMENT OF TRAINEES

PROFILE OF RESPONDENTS

In the following paragraphs, an account of the profile of the sample ITI pass outs has been presented, which includes the age, sex, and marital status of the respondents and the educational and occupational status of their parents, which would be helpful in understanding their educational, employment and income attainments.

(a) **Age of the Respondents:** In the present study, a sample of 796 ITI pass outs during the period of five years viz. 2001, 2002, 2003, 2004 and 2005 have been selected across the districts of the state of Jammu and Kashmir. Out of sample respondents, 15 percent, 53.1 percent, 25.4 percent and 6.4 percent were found respectively in the age group of below 20 years, between 20-25 years, between 25-30 years and above 30 years. Thus, the majority of the sample ITI pass outs were found in the youthful age groups. In district Kupwara, all the sample respondents were concentrated in the age groups of 20-25 years (85.7 percent) and 25-30 years (14.3 percent). In other districts, the sample respondents were distributed across the age groups shown in Table 1, except the districts of Pulwama, Leh, Kargil, Doda and Poonch where none of the sample ITI pass outs were found in the relatively older age group of above 30 years, which clearly reflects that a higher proportion of them are very young and energetic, and highly productive if they could be provided with suitable job opportunities.

(b) **Sex of the Respondents:** The data presented in Table 2 shows that 60.3 percent and 39.7 percent of the ITI pass outs were males and females respectively, which clearly reflects the gender imbalance in their enrolments in industrial training courses. However, the districts of Leh, Kargil and Udhampur are exceptions in this regard, where the proportion of female ITI pass outs was significantly high (70.4 percent in Leh, 64.1 percent in Kargil and 62.5 percent in Udhampur). In the districts of Badgam and Anantnag, the proportion of female ITI pass outs was 44.5 and 45.0 respectively.

(c) **Marital Status of the Respondents:** Two-third of the sample respondents were unmarried, which means that one-third of them were married. It is significant to note that more than half of the sample ITI pass outs were married in district of Leh, whereas the proportion of married sample respondents was much lower in districts of Doda (4.7 percent), Kupwara (14.3 percent), Badgam (22,2 percent), Poonch (27.3 percent) and Kathua (29.13 percent). This clearly reveals that the social understanding of the ITI pass outs is comparatively high in most of the districts due to which they enter the nuptial ties at later ages. However, this may also be due to higher prevalence of unemployment among the ITI pass outs in these districts, which may be delaying their entry into the marriage. Keeping such apprehensions aside, as we will examine the

Table 1

District-wise Distribution of Sample ITI Trainees by Age

Age (Years)	*I*	*II*	*III*	*IV*	*V*	*VI*	*VII*	*VIII*	*IX*	*X*	*XI*	*XII*	*XIII*	*XIV*	*Total*
< 20	-	6	14	6	2	9	7	5	11	7	4	9	23	17	120
		(16.2)	(13.3)	(16.7)	(5.1)	(11.2)	(12.9)	(12.8)	(26.2)	(12.5)	(18.2)	(14.5)	(21.5)	(16.5)	(15.0)
20-25	12	18	59	22	26	39	32	19	29	23	15	26	47	56	423
	(85.7)	(48.6)	(56.2)	(61.1)	(66.7)	(48.8)	(59.3)	(48.7)	(69.0)	(41.1)	(68.2)	(41.9)	(43.9)	(54.4)	(53.1)
25-30	2	10	24	6	11	27	15	15	2	18	3	19	27	23	202
	(14.3)	(27.02)	(22.8)	(16.7)	(28.2)	(33.7)	(27.8)	(38.5)	(4.8)	(32.1)	(13.6)	(30.6)	(25.2)	(22.3)	(25.4)
> 30	-	3	8	2	-	5	-	-	-	8	-	8	10	7	51
		(8.2)	(7.7)	(5.5)		(6.3)				(14.3)		(12.9)	(9.4)	(6.8)	(6.4)
Total	14	37	105	36	39	80	54	39	42	56	22	62	107	103	796
	(100)	(100)	(100)	(100)	(100)	(100)	(100)	(100)	(100)	(100)	(100)	(100)	(100)	(100)	(100)

Note: I: Kupwara; II: Baramulla; III: Srinagar; IV: Badgam; V: Pulwama; VI: Anantnag; VII: Leh; VIII: Kargil; IX: Doda; X: Udhampur; XI: Poonch; XII: Rajouri; XIII: Jammu; and XIV: Kathua

Table 2
District-wise Distribution of Sample ITI Trainees by Sex

Sex	*I*	*II*	*III*	*IV*	*V*	*VI*	*VII*	*VIII*	*IX*	*X*	*XI*	*XII*	*XIII*	*XIV*	*Total*
Male	11	24	73	20	26	44	16	14	29	21	17	40	83	62	480
	(78.6)	(64.8)	(69.5)	(55.5)	(66.7)	(55.0)	(29.6)	(35.9)	(69.1)	(37.5)	(77.3)	(64.5)	(77.6)	(60.2)	(60.3)
Female	3	13	32	16	13	36	38	25	13	35	5	22	24	41	316
	(21.4)	(35.2)	(30.5)	(44.5)	(33.3)	(45.0)	(70.4)	(64.1)	(30.9)	(62.5)	(22.7)	(35.5)	(22.4)	(39.8)	(39.7)
Total	14	37	105	36	39	80	54	39	42	56	22	62	107	103	796
	(100)	(100)	(100)	(100)	(100)	(100)	(100)	(100)	(100)	(100)	(100)	(100)	(100)	(100)	(100)

Note: Same as Table 1

Table 3
District-wise Distribution of Sample ITI Trainees by Marital Status

Marital Status	*I*	*II*	*III*	*IV*	*V*	*VI*	*VII*	*VIII*	*IX*	*X*	*XI*	*XII*	*XIII*	*XIV*	*Total*
Married	2	13	32	8	12	29	23	21	2	26	6	27	37	30	268
	(14.3)	(35.1)	(30.5)	(22.2)	(30.7)	(36.3)	(42.6)	(53.9)	(4.7)	(46.4)	(27.3)	(43.5)	(34.6)	(29.13)	(33.7)
Unmarried	12	24	73	28	27	51	31	18	40	30	16	35	70	73	528
	(85.7)	(64.9)	(69.5)	(77.8)	(69.3)	(63.7)	(57.4)	(46.1)	(95.3)	(53.6)	(72.7)	(56.5)	(65.4)	(70.9)	(66.3)
Total	14	37	105	36	39	80	54	39	42	56	22	62	107	103	796
	(100)	(100)	(100)	(100)	(100)	(100)	(100)	(100)	(100)	(100)	(100)	(100)	(100)	(100)	(100)

Note: Same as Table 1

employment situation later in this section, the marital status of the ITI pass outs reveals better social status of their households.

(d) **Parental Educational Level:** Information on the parents' level of education is presented in Table 4 and Table 5 respectively for fathers and mothers of ITI pass outs. A major area of concern on ITI pass outs' parental education is their literacy level. It is significant to note that very low proportion of the parents of ITI pass outs were without any formal education, but at the same time 38.8 percent of fathers and 55.2 percent of mothers had education up to middle standard. From the data in the Tables 4 and 5, it is clear that only 8.4 percent of the parents of ITI pass outs were educated up to graduation and above. About 26 percent and 21 percent of fathers and mothers of ITI pass outs respectively were educated up to high school level and 18.5 percent and 7.4 percent of the fathers and mothers of ITI pass outs respectively were educated up to higher secondary level. Thus, mothers of ITI pass outs had lower educational level compared to their fathers. Gender disparity in education is a source of concern in all levels of education irrespective of age of respondents.

The district-wise analysis of the parents' educational level reveals that the fathers of the ITI pass outs in districts of Srinagar, Badgam, Pulwama, Kargil and Jammu have better educational status and none of them are without any formal education. Similarly, none of the mothers of the ITI pass outs in districts of Srinagar, Poonch and Jammu were without any formal education. A very lower proportion of parents of the ITI pass outs had educational level up to master's degree and they were concentrated in major cities like Srinagar and Jammu. The findings of this study on the parental education are an indication that most of the ITI pass outs come from families with low social economic status.

Table 4
Highest Educational Level of Fathers of ITI Pass Outs

Educational Level	*I*	*II*	*III*	*IV*	*V*	*VI*	*VII*	*VIII*	*IX*	*X*	*XI*	*XII*	*XIII*	*XIV*	*Total*
No forma	1	7	-	-	-	6	5	-	7	11	3	7	-	17	63
education	-	(18.9)				(7.5)	(9.3)		(16.7)	(19.6)	(13.6)	(11.3)		(16.5)	(7.9)
Primary	4	5	8	6	12	18	13	9	8	7	5	17	14	26	152
	(28.6)	(13.5)	(7.6)	(16.7)	(30.7)	(22.5)	(24.1)	(23.1)	(19.1)	(12.5)	(22.7)	(27.4)	(13.1)	(25.2)	(19.1)
Middle	4	4	18	4	9	15	14	16	4	7	7	14	16	25	157
	(28.6)	(10.8)	(17.1)	(11.1)	(23.1)	(18.7)	(25.9)	(41.0)	(9.5)	(12.5)	(31.8)	(6.4)	(14.9)	(24.3)	(19.7)
High School	6	15	29	13	10	20	12	9	6	16	7	172	25	26	211
	(42.8)	(40.6)	(27.6)	(36.1)	(25.6)	(25.00)	(22.2)	(23.1)	(14.3)	(28.6)	(31.8)	(27.4)	(23.4)	(25.2)	(26.5)
Higher	-	6	35	6	8	14	5	5	10	15	-	7	27	9	147
Secondary		(16.2)	(3.3)	(16.7)	(20.5)	(17.5)	(2.1)	(12.8)	(23.8)	(26.8)		(11.3)	(25.2)	(8.7)	(18.5)
Bachelor's degree	-	-	12	4	-	7	5	-	7	-	-	-	13	-	48
			(11.4)	(11.1)		(8.7)	(2.1)		(16.7)				(12.1)		(6.1)
Master's degree	-	-	3	3	-	-	-	-	-	-	-	-	12	-	18
			(2.9)	(8.3)									(11.2)		(2.3)
Total	14	37	105	36	39	80	54	39	42	56	22	62	107	103	796
	(100)	(100)	(100)	(100)	(100)	(100)	(100)	(100)	(100)	(100)	(100)	(100)	(100)	(100)	(100)

Note: Same as Table 1

Table 5
Highest Educational Level of Mothers of ITI Pass Outs

Education of Level	*I*	*II*	*III*	*IV*	*V*	*VI*	*VII*	*VIII*	*IX*	*X*	*XI*	*XII*	*XIII*	*XIV*	*Total*
No formal	1	11	-	4	4	14	8	4	7	9	-	14	-	16	91
	-	(29.7)		(11.1)	(10.3)	(17.5)	(14.8)	(10.2)	(16.7)	(25.0)		(22.6)		(15.5)	(11.4)
Primary	7	16	18	6	16	23	10	13	16	14	9	15	36	28	227
	(50.0)	(43.3)	(17.1)	(16.7)	(41.0)	(28.7)	(18.5)	(33.3)	(38.1)	(6.2)	(40.9)	(24.2)	(34.6)	(27.2)	(28.5)
Middle	7	5	27	6	11	28	16	11	14	16	8	14	25	25	213
	(50.0)	(13.5)	(25.7)	(16.7)	(28.2)	(35.00)	(29.6)	(28.2)	(33.3)	(28.6)	(36.4)	(22.6)	(23.4)	(24.3)	(26.7)
High School	-	5	24	15	8	12	18	9	5	14	5	10	23	26	174
		(13.5)	(22.9)	(41.6)	(20.5)	(15.0)	(33.3)	(23.1)	(11.9)	(25.0)	(22.7)	(16.1)	(21.5)	(25.2)	(21.8)
Higher Secondary	-	-	16	5	-	3	2	2	-	3	-	9	14	5	59
			(15.2)	(13.9)		(3.7)	(3.7)	(5.1)		(5.4)		(14.5)	(13.1)	(4.8)	(7.4)
Bachelor's degree	-	-	13	-	-	-	-	-	-	-	-	-	7	3	23
			(12.4)										(6.5)	(2.9)	(2.9)
Master's degree	-	-	7	-	-	-	-	-	-	-	-	-	2	-	9
			(6.7)										(1.8)		(1.1)
Total	14	37	105	36	39	80	54	39	42	56	22	62	107	103	796
	(100)	(100)	(100)	(100)	(100)	(100)	(100)	(100)	(100)	(100)	(100)	(100)	(100)	(100)	(100)

Note: Same as Table 1

(e) **Parental Occupational Level:** The occupational level of the parents of ITI pass outs are given in tables 6 and 7. A perusal of the data in table 6 makes it evident that 30.6 percent, 48.2 percent and 21.1 percent of the fathers of ITI pass outs were engaged in farming, non-farming and self-employed activities respectively. Due to successful implementation of land reforms and rapid increase in population and consequent sub-division and fragmentation of landholdings, higher proportion of the parents were engaged in non-farming and self-employed economic pursuits to eke out their livelihoods, which may also be one of the potent reasons of enrolment of their children in industrial training courses. The parents of ITI pass outs were aware of the growing unemployment among the non-technically educated personnel and therefore sent their children to get industrial trainings. However, in case of mothers of ITI pass outs, very high proportion of them are still engaged in farming and household related activities, which is a clear indication of their low economic status. The district level analysis of the employment level of the parents reveals more or less the same picture.

RATING OF FACTORS INFLUENCING TRAINING DECISIONS

In the following paragraphs, an attempt has been made to analyze the factors influencing the training decisions viz. academic rating during training, types of courses/trades opted and their rating by the trainees, reasons and factors influencing enrolment decisions in ITIs.

(a) **Academic Rating during Studentship:** The data related to academic rating during ITI training by the pass outs are presented in table 8. A perusal of the data makes it evident that 17.1 percent, 31.4 percent and 28.5 percent of the ITI pass outs have rated their own academic respectively as excellent, very good and good, and 14.6 percent, 6.3 percent and 2.1 percent respectively have rated their own academic respectively as not so bad, bad and very bad. Thus, majority of the ITI pass outs have rated the academic during their training as good and a small proportion of them has rated their academic rating as bad. The district-wise academic rating by the trainees also reveals more or less the same picture with exceptions of the districts of Kupwara, Baramulla, Badgam, Pulwama, Doda, Udhampur and Poonch, where none of the ITI pass outs has rated their academic as bad and very bad during training.

(b) **Types of Courses/Trades Opted during Training:** Table 9 provides data on types of courses/trades opted by ITI Pass outs during training, which makes it clear that 61.0 percent of the ITI pass outs had opted for courses/trades like electrician (20.8 percent), cutting and tailoring (24.7 percent), and stenography (15.5 percent). All the ITI pass outs opted for trade of cutting and tailoring were reportedly females. The courses of computer operator, electronic mechanic and plumber were opted by 8.1 percent, 6.0 percent and 5.0 percent of the ITI pass outs. Two of the courses/trades viz. electrician, and cutting and tailoring were opted by the ITI pass outs in all the districts and were more common among males (electrician) and females (cutting and tailoring), followed by courses/trades of stenography, computer operator, electronic mechanic and plumber. About 3.0 percent, 1.2 percent, 1.5 percent, 3.3 percent, 3.8 percent, 2.5 percent, and 3.5 percent of the ITI pass outs have opted the courses/trades of fitter, turner, machinist, motor mechanic, welder, carpenter, and Radio and T.V mechanic respectively. The courses/trades of tractor mechanic and information technology were opted by a meager proportion of the ITI pass outs (tractor mechanic: 0.63 percent and information

Table 6
Occupational Level of Fathers of ITI Pass Outs

Occupation	*I*	*II*	*III*	*IV*	*V*	*VI*	*VII*	*VIII*	*IX*	*X*	*XI*	*XII*	*XIII*	*XIV*	*Total*
Farming	6	18	22	9	23	24	14	14	18	16	7	13	36	24	244
	(42.8)	(48.7)	(20.9)	(25.0)	(58.97)	(30.0)	(25.9)	(35.9)	(42.8)	(28.6)	(31.8)	(20.0)	(33.6)	(23.3)	(30.6)
Non-farming	4	11	54	17	9	43	33	19	16	31	11	36	57	43	384
	(28.6)	(29.7)	(51.4)	(47.2)	(23.07)	(53.8)	(61.1)	(48.7)	(38.1)	(55.4)	(50.0)	(58.1)	(53.3)	(41.7)	(48.2)
Self-employed	4	8	29	10	7	13	7	6	8	9	4	13	14	36	168
	(28.6)	(21.6)	(27.7)	(27.8)	(17.95)	(16.2)	(12.9)	(15.4)	(19.0)	(16.1)	(18.2)	(20.9)	(13.1)	(34.9)	(21.1)
Total	14	37	105	36	39	80	54	39	42	56	22	62	107	103	796
	(100)	(100)	(100)	(100)	(100)	(100)	(100)	(100)	(100)	(100)	(100)	(100)	(100)	(100)	(100)

Note: Same as Table 1

Table 7
Occupational Level of Fathers of ITI Pass Outs

Occupation	*I*	*II*	*III*	*IV*	*V*	*VI*	*VII*	*VIII*	*IX*	*X*	*XI*	*XII*	*XIII*	*XIV*	*Total*
Farming	6	28	42	19	13	34	32	18	22	26	11	33	43	36	363
	(42.8)	(75.6)	(40.0)	(52.8)	(33.3)	(42.5)	(59.2)	(46.1)	(52.4)	(46.4)	(50.0)	(53.2)	(40.2)	(34.9)	(45.6)
Non-farming	2	4	9	4	4	7	5	4	6	5	2	6	9	7	74
	(14.4)	(10.8)	(8.6)	(11.1)	(10.3)	(8.7)	(9.3)	(10.3)	(14.3)	(8.9)	(9.1)	(9.7)	(8.4)	(6.8)	(9.3)
House-wife	6	5	54	13	22	39	17	17	14	25	9	23	55	60	359
	(42.8)	(13.5)	(51.4)	(36.1)	(56.4)	(48.8)	(31.5)	(43.6)	(33.3)	(44.6)	(40.9)	(37.1)	(51.4)	(58.3)	(45.1)
Total	14	37	105	36	39	80	54	39	42	56	22	62	107	103	796
	(100)	(100)	(100)	(100)	(100)	(100)	(100)	(100)	(100)	(100)	(100)	(100)	(100)	(100)	(100)

Note: Same as Table 1

Table 8

Occupational Level of Fathers of ITI Pass Outs

Occupation	I	II	III	IV	V	VI	VII	VIII	IX	X	XI	XII	XIII	XIV	*Total*
Excellent	2	6	27	6	4	13	7	4	8	13	4	9	24	9	136
	(14.3)	(16.2)	(25.7)	(16.7)	(10.3)	(16.2)	(12.9)	(10.3)	(19.0)	(23.2)	(18.2)	(14.5)	(22.4)	(8.7)	(17.1)
Very Good	5	13	24	9	23	11	23	9	13	21	7	13	36	43	250
	(35.7)	(35.1)	(22.9)	(25.0)	(58.9)	(13.7)	(42.6)	(23.1)	(30.9)	(37.5)	(31.8)	(20.9)	(33.6)	(41.7)	(31.4)
Good	7	10	27	11	5	23	16	16	17	17	5	25	21	27	227
	(50.0)	(27.0)	(25.7)	(30.5)	(12.8)	(28.7)	(29.6)	(41.0)	(40.5)	(30.4)	(22.7)	(40.3)	(19.6)	(26.2)	(28.5)
Not so Bad	-	8	13	10	7	20	4	7	4	5	6	7	14	11	116
		(21.6)	(12.4)	(27.8)	(17.9)	(25.0)	(7.4)	(17.9)	(9.5)	(8.9)	(27.3)	(11.3)	(13.1)	(10.7)	(14.6)
Bad	-	-	9	-	-	10	4	3	-	-	-	8	7	9	50
			(8.6)			(12.5)	(7.4)	(7.7)				(12.9)	(6.5)	(8.7)	(6.3)
Very Bad	-	-	5	-	-	3	-	-	-	-	-	-	5	4	17
			(4.8)			(3.6)							(4.7)	(3.9)	(2.1)
Total	14	37	105	36	39	80	54	39	42	56	22	62	107	103	796
	(100)	(100)	(100)	(100)	(100)	(100)	(100)	(100)	(100)	(100)	(100)	(100)	(100)	(100)	(100)

Note: Same as Table 1

Table 9

Types of the Courses/Trades Opted during Training

Type of Trade	*I*	*II*	*III*	*IV*	*V*	*VI*	*VII*	*VIII*	*IX*	*X*	*XI*	*XII*	*XIII*	*XIV*	*Total*
Electrician	8	8	17	4	6	14	12	9	11	17	6	18	19	17	166
	(57.2)	(21.6)	(16.2)	(11.1)	(15.4)	(17.5)	(22.2)	(23.1)	(26.2)	(30.4)	(27.3)	(29.0)	(17.7)	(16.5)	(20.8)
Cutting and	3	6	16	9	11	21	16	13	9	16	7	15	26	29	197
Tailoring	(21.4)	(16.2)	(15.3)	(25.0)	(28.2)	(26.3)	(29.6)	(33.3)	(21.4)	(28.6)	(31.8)	(24.2)	(24.3)	(28.1)	(24.7)
Electronic	3	-	9	6	-	11	-	-	11	3	-	5	-	-	48
Mechanic	(21.4)		(8.6)	(16.7)		(13.7)			(26.2)	(5.3)		(8.1)			(6.0)
Fitter	-	-	6	-	-	5	-	-	5	2	-	-	4	2	24
			(5.7)			(6.2)			(11.9)	(3.6)			(3.7)	(1.9)	(3.0)
Turner	-	-	5	-	-	-	-	-	-	-	-	-	-	5	10
			(4.8)											(4.8)	(1.2)
Machinist	-	-	3	-	-	-	-	-	-	-	-	6	3	-	12
			(2.8)									(9.7)	(2.8)		(1.5)
Motor Mechanic	-	6	7	-	-	-	-	-	-	-	-	-	7	6	26
		(16.2)	(6.7)										(6.5)	(5.8)	(3.3)
Tractor Mechanic	-	2	-	-	-	-	-	-	-	-	-	-	3	-	5
		(5.5)											(2.8)		(0.63)
Welder	-	-	8	3	-	-	-	-	-	4	-	-	3	12	30
			(7.6)	(8.3)						(7.1)			(2.8)	(11.6)	(3.8)

Contd.....

Type of Trade	*I*	*II*	*III*	*IV*	*V*	*VI*	*VII*	*VIII*	*IX*	*X*	*XI*	*XII*	*XIII*	*XIV*	*Total*
Carpenter	-	2	-	-	-	-	-	-	-	-	-	6	4	8	20
		(5.4)										(9.7)	(3.7)	(7.7)	(2.5)
Plumber	-	-	7	-	8	-	-	-	6	14	5	-	-	-	40
			(6.7)		(20.5)				(14.3)	(25.0)	(22.7)				(5.0)
Stenography	-	8	13	8	7	16	17	12	-	-	-	12	16	14	123
		(21.6)	(12.4)	(22.2)	(17.9)	(20.0)	(31.5)	(30.7)				(19.3)	(14.9)	(13.6)	(15.5)
Computer	-	5	14	-	7	13	-	-	-	-	-	-	15	10	64
Operator		()	(13.3)		(17.9)	(16.3)							(14.0)	(9.7)	(8.1)
Radio and TV	-	-	-	6	-	-	9	5	-	-	4	-	4	-	28
Mechanic				(16.7)			(16.7)	(12.8)			(18.2)		(3.7)		(3.5)
Information	-	-	-	-	-	-	-	-	-	-	-	-	3	-	3
Technology													(2.8)		(0.4)
Total	14	37	105	36	39	80	54	39	42	56	22	62	107	103	796
	(100)	(100)	(100)	(100)	(100)	(100)	(100)	(100)	(100)	(100)	(100)	(100)	(100)	(100)	(100)

Note: Same as Table 1

technology: 0.4 percent), which is due to the fact that only two ITIs viz. ITI Baramulla and ITI Jammu are providing training in trade of tractor mechanic and ITI Jammu is providing training in the field of information technology. This needs immediate attention of the authorities so that emerging and highly employment oriented courses like information technology may be introduced in all the ITIs.

The district-wise analysis of the types of the courses/trades opted by ITI pass outs during training reveals that 57.2 percent and 21.4 percent respondents had opted courses/trades of electrician, and cutting and tailoring and electronic mechanic in district Kupwara. The courses/trades like electrician and stenography were opted by 21.6 percent followed by courses/trades of cutting and tailoring, and motor mechanic by 16.2 percent of the ITI pass outs in district Baramulla. The courses/trades of electrician, cutting and tailoring, computer operator and stenography were opted by 16.2 percent, 15.3 percent, 13.3 percent and 12.4 percent of the ITI pass outs respectively in district Srinagar. The courses/trades of electrician and stenography was opted by one-third of ITI pass outs in districts of Udhampur and Rajouri, and Leh and Kargil respectively. It is significant to note that all the courses/trades were not provided by ITIs and opted by the sample respondents. For example, the sample ITI pass outs of ITI Handwara had opted three courses/trades (electrician, cutting and tailoring, and electronic mechanic), four courses/trades (electrician, cutting and tailoring, stenography and Radio and T.V mechanic) in ITI Leh and ITI Kargil, and in ITI Mendhar (electrician, cutting and tailoring, plumber, and Radio and T.V mechanic). Thus, there is urgent need to add more vocational courses in those of the ITIs, where fewer courses/trades is currently being operationalized, which would provide more options to the prospective trainees.

(c) **Rating of Types of Courses/Trades Offered by ITIs:** The majority of the ITI pass outs have rated the courses/trades offered by ITIs as middle high to very high 10. For example, 14.45 percent, 25.90 percent and 19.87 percent of the ITI pass outs have rated the course/trade of electrician as very high, high and middle high respectively. A more or less similar rating of the courses/trades of cutting and tailoring, plumber, stenography and computer operator has been made by them. The courses/trades such as fitter, turner, machinist, motor mechanic, tractor mechanic, welder and carpenter have also been rated as high and very high. This is due to the fact that most of the ITI pass outs in these courses/trades are currently employed or self-employed and earning sustainable livelihoods. It is interesting to note that 21.08 percent and 17.77 percent of the ITI pass outs in courses/trades of electrician, and cutting and tailoring have rated these courses as low. Similarly, 5.0 percent and 6.25 percent of the ITI pass outs in the courses/trades of plumber, stenography and computer operator have rated these courses as low. The low rating of these courses in the range of 5.0 percent to 21.08 percent is mainly attributed to their failure to obtain a job or being unable to be self-employed after the training in respective courses/trades. Keeping in view the high level of incidence of unemployment and underemployment in the state of Jammu and Kashmir, the prospective trainees should also be trained in management aspects to enable them to venture in self-employment after completing their courses/trades at ITIs. The prospective trainees should also be educated about various self-employment programmes being run by government agencies, for which regular visits of the functionaries of the line departments, banking and industries be arranged to expose the trainees to the need and importance of self-employment and means and ways to be engaged as self-employed.

Table 10
Rating of the Type of Courses/Trade Offered by ITIs

Type of Trade	*Rating of the Type of Courses/Trade Offered*					
	Very high	*High*	*Middle high*	*Middle*	*Low*	*Total*
Electrician	24 (14.45)	43 (25.90)	33 (19.87)	31 (18.67)	35 (21.08)	166 (100)
Cutting and Tailoring	36 (18.27)	51 (25.88)	36 (18.27)	39 (19.79)	35 (17.77)	197 (100)
Electronic Mechanic	9 (18.75)	11 (22.92)	16 (33.33)	12 (25.00)	-	48 (100)
Fitter	6 (25.00)	9 (37.5)	7 (29.17)	2 (8.33)	-	24 (100)
Turner	3 (30.00)	5 (50.00)	2 (20.00)	-	-	10 (100)
Machinist	4 (33.33)	6 (50.00)	2 (16.67)	-	-	12 (100)
Motor Mechanic	9 (34.62)	8 (30.77)	6 (23.08)	3 (11.54)	-	26 (100)
Tractor Mechanic	2 (20.00)	3 (60.00)	-	-	-	5 (100)
Welder	7 (23.33)	9 (30.00)	11 (36.67)	3 (10.00)	-	30 (100)
Carpenter	5 (25.00)	6 (30.00)	7 (35.00)	2 (10.00)	-	20 (100)
Plumber	4 (10.00)	12 (30.00)	10 (25.00)	12 (30.00)	2 (5.00)	40 (100)
Stenography	32 (26.02)	41 (33.33)	27 (21.95)	17 (13.82)	6 (4.88)	123 (100)
Computer Operator	24 (37.60)	13 (20.13)	10 (15.63)	13 (20.31)	4 (6.25)	64 (100)
Radio and TV Mechanic	6 (21.42)	4 (14.29)	14 (50.00)	4 (14.29)	-	28 (100)
Information Technology	- (66.67)	2	1 (33.33)	-	-	3 (100)

(d) **Reasons and Factors for Decisions to Enroll in ITIs:** The sample respondents were asked to give the reasons for their decisions to enroll in ITIs. A perusal of the data given in table 11 makes it evident that more than half of the ITI pass outs reported that they wanted to focus on a field that they were interested in ITI as very important and important reason. Similarly, 45 percent of them reported that they could get more practical training in ITI and it was too expensive to study at a polytechnic as very important and important reasons to enroll in ITI and a similar proportion of them reported that they wanted to go to an ITI rather than stay at school and they could not get a job as least important and not important reasons to enroll in ITIs. More than half of them reported that they enrolled in ITI because there was an ITI near their homes, and their parents wanted them to study at ITI as very important and important reasons. It is surprising to note that 43.28 percent of them also reported that they do not know what they really wanted to do as very important and important reason, which clearly reveals the lack of awareness and motivation and non-seriousness on the part of the ITI trainees in pursuing a course/trade. Thus, there is urgent need to provide proper counseling and awareness to the prospective trainees before getting them admitted in various courses/trades, which would help them in taking up only those of the courses/trades in which they are really interested.

Table 11
Reasons for Decisions to Enroll in ITIs

Reasons to Enroll	*Very Important*	*Important*	*Somewhat Important*	*Least Important*	*Not Important*	*Total*
I wanted to focus on a field that I was interested in ITI	36 (27.27)	33 (25.00)	28 (21.21)	24 (18.18)	11 (8.34)	132 (100)
I could get more practical training in ITI	32 (23.36)	30 (21.90)	33 (24.08)	20 (14.60)	22 (16.06)	137 (100)
It was too expensive to study at a polytechnic	26 (21.14)	29 (23.58)	23 (18.70)	27 (21.95)	18 (14.63)	123 (100)

Contd....

Reasons to Enroll	*Very Impor-tant*	*Impor-tant*	*Some-what Impor-tant*	*Least Impor-tant*	*Not Impor-tant*	*Total*
I could not get into a polytechnic	19 (19.59)	20 (20.62)	17 (17.52)	14 (14.43)	27 (27.84)	97 (100)
I wanted to go to an ITI rather than stay at school	16 (21.05)	14 (18.42)	12 (15.79)	11 (14.47)	23 (30.26)	76 (100)
I could not get a job	18 (23.38)	12 (15.58)	16 (20.78)	18 (23.38)	13 (16.88)	77 (100)
There was an ITI near my home	13 (30.23)	11 (25.58)	7 (16.28)	8 (18.60)	4 (9.30)	43 (100)
My parents wanted me to study in an ITI	10 (22.73)	13 (29.54)	8 (18.18)	9 (20.45)	4 (9.10)	44 (100)
I did not know what I really wanted to do	15 (22.39)	14 (20.89)	14 (20.89)	13 (19.40)	11 (16.42)	67 (100)

Table 12
Factors Influencing Decisions to Enroll in ITI

Factors Influencing Decisions	*Very Impor-tant*	*Impor-tant*	*Some-what Impor-tant*	*Least Impor-tant*	*Not Impor-tant*	*Total*
I was interested in it	36 (27.27)	33 (25.00)	28 (21.21)	24 (18.18)	11 (8.33)	132 (100)
To get a job	114 (43.35)	54 (20.54)	43 (16.35)	33 (12.55)	19 (7.22)	263 (100)
It was the easiest programme/course	67 (45.89)	23 (15.75)	33 (12.55)	13 (8.90)	10 (6.85)	146 (100)
My family wanted me to study in this field	10 (22.73)	13 (29.54)	8 (18.18)	9 (20.45)	4 (9.09)	44 (100)
The course I wanted to study at the ITI was full	103 (48.82)	42 (19.90)	35 (16.59)	17 (8.06)	14 (6.63)	211 (100)

The respondents were also asked to reveal the factors influencing their decisions to enroll in ITI Table 12. A perusal of the data in table 3.12 makes it evident that a majority of them enrolled in the courses/trades in ITIs because they were interested in them and to get a job as very important and important factors influencing their decisions. However, it is surprising to note that the more than two-third of them enrolled in courses/trades at ITIs because of the easy programme structure. A similar proportion of them reported that the courses they wanted to study at ITI were full, so they were compelled to enoll in other courses/trades of least interest, which is really cause of concern and calls for immediate attention of the appropriate authorities so that a proportional balance is maintained in demand and supply of the courses/trades being offered at ITIs.

LEVEL OF ACADEMIC SATISFACTION OF ITI PASS OUTS

The level of academic satisfaction of ITI pass outs has been examined in terms of rating of quality of training provisions, study provisions and conditions and knowledge and skill gained at ITIs.

(a) **Rating of Quality of Training Provisions at ITI:** The data on rating of quality of training provisions at ITI as perceived by the ITI pass outs has been given in table 13, which reveals that the 28.01 percent and 35.05 percent of the respondents respectively were very satisfied and satisfied with quality of teaching, 40.70 percent and 29.27 percent respectively were very satisfied and satisfied with study methods, 23.49 percent and 48.87 percent respectively were very satisfied and satisfied with language of instruction and 26.88 percent and 37.06 percent respectively were very satisfied and satisfied with provisioning of library materials. In terms of computer laboratories and practical workshops, 36.00 percent and 38.33 percent, and 21.11 percent and 39.32 percent of ITI pass outs respectively were very satisfied and satisfied. It is significant to note that 34.42 percent and 22.11 percent of them were unsatisfied and very unsatisfied respectively in terms of availability of the staff to help them when needed. Similarly, 27.39 percent and 24.87 percent of them were unsatisfied and very unsatisfied respectively with the conditions of buildings. The level of satisfaction was also reportedly very low in case of provisioning of lecture handouts to the trainees. Thus, there is need to improve the conditions of the existing buildings and availability of staff to help the trainees in need and the staff may be motivated to provide the lecture handouts to the trainees so that they could use them and supplement with other reading materials.

Table 13
Rating of Quality of Training Provisions at ITI

Rating of Quality of Training Provisions	*Very Satisfied*	*Satis-fied*	*Some-what Satis-fied*	*Unsatis fied*	*Very unsatis fied*	*Total*
Quality of teaching	223	279	164	75	55	796
	(28.01)	(35.05)	(20.60)	(9.42)	(6.91)	(100)
Staff available to help me when needed	65	89	192	274	176	796
	(8.16)	(11.18)	(24.12)	(34.42)	(22.11)	(100)
Condition of buildings	97	194	89	218	198	796
	(12.18)	(24.37)	(11.18)	(27.39)	(24.87)	(100)
Lecture handouts	24	17	156	399	200	796
	(3.02)	(2.13)	(19.60)	(50.12)	(25.12)	(100)
Help with study methods	324	233	187	52	-	796
	(40.70)	(29.27)	(23.50)	(6.53)		(100)
Help with language problems	187	389	122	78	20	796
	(23.49)	(48.87)	(15.33)	(9.79)	(2.51)	(100)
Computer laboratories	21	23	16	-	-	60
	(36.00)	(38.33)	(26.67)			(100)
Practical workshops	168	313	197	88	30	796
	(21.11)	(39.32)	(24.75)	(11.06)	(3.77)	(100)
Library material	214	295	178	71	38	796
	(26.88)	(37.06)	(22.36)	(8.92)	(4.77)	(100)

(b) **Rating of Study Provisions and Conditions at ITI:** About two-third of the ITI pass outs were satisfied with the assistance/advice offered by the instructors, opportunity of out for examinations, academic advice offered, teaching quality of lectures, structure of the programmes, provision of practical works, contacts with fellow trainees, availability of teaching equipments, quality of laboratories, and equipment and stocking of libraries. More than one-third of them were satisfied with supply of teaching materials, catering facilities and quality of buildings (see Table 14). Thus, as discussed in last paragraph, there is urgent to improve the provisioning of supply of teaching materials and conditions of catering facilities and buildings so that the overall quality of study provisions and conditions at ITI could be improved, which would go a long way in improving the performance and quality of ITI pass outs.

Table 14
Rating of Quality of Training Provisions at ITI

Rating of Study Provisions and Conditions	*Very Satisfied*	*Satis-fied*	*Some-what Satis-fied*	*Unsatis fied*	*Very unsatis fied*	*Total*
Assistance/advice for examinations	314 (39.45)	246 (30.90)	142 (17.84)	71 (8.92)	23 (2.89)	796 (100)
Opportunity of out of examinations	156 (19.60)	372 (46.73)	173 (21.73)	79 (9.92)	16 (2.01)	796 (100)
Academic advice offered	243 (30.52)	247 (31.03)	176 (22.11)	100 (12.56)	30 (3.77)	796 (100)
Teaching quality of lectures	223 (28.01)	279 (35.05)	164 (20.60)	75 (9.42)	55 (6.9)	796 (100)
Structure of programme	189 (23.74)	293 (36.81)	184 (23.11)	104 (13.06)	26 (3.27)	796 (100)
Provision of practical work	192 (24.12)	331 (41.58)	147 (18.47)	83 (10.43)	43 (5.40)	796 (100)
Contacts with fellow trainees	379 (47.61)	227 (28.52)	124 (15.58)	55 (6.91)	11 (1.38)	796 (100)
Availability of teaching equipment	232 (29.14)	319 (40.07)	162 (20.35)	44 (5.53)	10 (1.26)	796 (100)
Quality of laboratories	168 (21.10)	313 (39.32)	197 (24.75)	88 (11.05)	30 (3.77)	796 (100)
Supply of teaching materials	132 (16.58)	186 (23.37)	232 (29.14)	148 (18.60)	98 (12.31)	796 (100)

Contd....

Rating of Study Provisions and Conditions	*Very Satisfied*	*Satis-fied*	*Some-what Satis-fied*	*Unsatis fied*	*Very unsatis fied*	*Total*
Equipment and stocking of libraries	214 (26.88)	295 (37.06)	178 (22.36)	71 (8.92)	38 (4.77)	796 (100)
Catering facilities	177 (22.24)	129 (16.21)	124 (15.58)	175 (21.98)	191 (23.99)	796 (100)
Quality of the buildings	97 (12.18)	194 (24.37)	89 (11.18)	218 (27.38)	198 (24.87)	796 (100)

(c) **Rating of Knowledge and Skill Gained at ITI:** The data given in Table 15 makes it evident that the more than one-third of the sample respondents were satisfied with interpersonal skills, written communication skills, oral communication skills and problem-solving skills, self-confidence development and team work and leadership skills acquired during

Table 15
Rating of Knowledge and Skill Gained at ITI

Rating of Knowledge and Skill Gained	*Very Satisfied*	*Satis-fied*	*Some-what Satis-fied*	*Unsatis fied*	*Very unsatis fied*	*Total*
Interpersonal Skills	143 (17.96)	165 (20.73)	192 (24.12)	173 (21.73)	123 (15.45)	796 (100)
Written Communication Skills	131 (16.45)	157 (19.72)	286 (35.93)	162 (20.35)	60 (7.54)	796 (100)
Oral Communication Skills	178 (22.36)	169 (21.23)	274 (34.42)	120 (15.07)	55 (6.91)	796 (100)
Problem-solving Skills	98 (12.31)	211 (26.51)	289 (36.31)	114 (14.32)	84 (10.55)	796 (100)
Creative thinking	43 (5.40)	133 (16.71)	87 (10.92)	310 (38.94)	223 (28.01)	796 (100)
Independent learning	87 (10.93)	156 (19.60)	173 (21.73)	285 (35.80)	95 (11.93)	796 (100)
Self-confidence Development	93 (11.68)	177 (22.24)	218 (27.38)	274 (34.42)	34 (4.27)	796 (100)
Teamwork and Leadership	88 (11.05)	173 (21.73)	203 (25.50)	210 (26.38)	122 (15.33)	796 (100)

training in their respective courses/trades at ITIs. The skill gained in creative thinking and independent learning was rated low and more than two-third of the respondents were unsatisfied or very unsatisfied in creative thinking aspect and 47.78 percent of ITI pass outs were unsatisfied or very unsatisfied in aspect of independent learning. Thus, the aspects of creative thinking and independent learning needs to improved, which could improve their employability, productivity and levels of earnings and help facilitate innovations and modifications in work processes.

EMPLOYMENT PROFILE OF ITI PASS OUTS

In the following paragraphs, the employment profile of the ITI pass outs is presented, which includes the present employment status, employment status by gender, sector of current employer, nature of business done by current employer, employment status of employed by management/cadre, sector of employment by type of course, duration of job search by unemployed, main reasons for not finding a job, duration of job search by currently employed, term of current employer, duration of stay with current employer, sector of current employer, nature of business done by current employer, present tenure, major reasons for failure to obtain a permanent employment, present job related to field of training, reasons behind taking a job not related to field of training, intention to change job in future and reasons behind intended change in job.

(a) **Present Employment Status of ITI Pass Outs:** The data presented in Table 16 makes it clear that out of sampled 796 ITI pass outs, 389 (48.8 percent) were reportedly unemployed and 407 (51.2 percent) were employed. Out of 389 unemployed ITI pass outs, 89.2 percent were never employed before and 10.8 percent have resigned/laid off/ separated from the previous employment. Those of the respondents who were gainfully employed, 48.3 percent, 22.4

percent and 22.4 percent respectively were employed locally, within the respective districts, and outside their respective districts and 22.6 percent were self-employed. The district-wise analysis of the data presented in table 16 reveals that 62.5 percent and 37.5 percent were locally employed and self-employed respectively in district Kupwara. About half of the ITI pass outs were gainfully employed in all the districts of the state of Jammu and Kashmir except the districts of Pulwama and Leh, where the proportion of gainfully employed ITI pass outs stood at 43.6 percent and 42.6 percent respectively. About one-fourth of the employed ITI pass outs were self-employed in districts of Srinagar, Badgam, Leh, Kargil, Doda, Poonch and Rajouri, whereas in other districts the proportion of self-employed were about one-fifth except Kupwara, where self-employed were reportedly 37.5 percent. Thus, self-employment is one of the lucrative options for ITI pass outs to eke out a livelihood and there is need to promote awareness regarding self-employment programmes and schemes among the prospective trainees during the tenure of their stay at ITIs.

(b) **Employment Status of ITI Pass Outs by Gender:** Out of 407 employed ITI pass outs, 78.4 percent and 21.6 percent were males and females respectively. In district Kupwara, all the employed ITI pass outs were males. In all other districts, the proportion of male employed ITI pass outs was higher than females except the district Kargil, where they were reportedly in equal proportion. In districts of Leh and Udhampur, the gender imbalance in employment was not so sharp as in other districts and 43.5 percent and 41.1 percent of the employed ITI pass outs were females Table 16. The main reason for lower proportion of the employed female ITI pass outs is their enrollment pattern, as a higher proportion of them were enrolled in the course/

Table 16

Present Employment Status of ITI Pass Outs

Employment Status	*I*	*II*	*III*	*IV*	*V*	*VI*	*VII*	*VIII*	*IX*	*X*	*XI*	*XII*	*XIII*	*XIV*	*Total*
1. Unemployed	6	17	54	16	22	42	31	19	19	27	11	26	47	52	389
	(42.8)	(45.9)	(51.4)	(44.4)	(56.4)	(52.5)	(57.4)	(48.7)	(45.2)	(48.2)	(50.0)	(41.9)	(43.9)	(50.5)	(48.8)
1.a. Never been	6	17	46	16	19	37	28	19	17	23	11	24	39	45	347
employed before	(100)	(100)	(85.2)	(100.0)	(86.4)	(88.1)	(90.3)	(100.0)	(89.5)	(85.2)	(100.0)	(92.3)	(82.9)	(86.5)	(89.2)
1.b. Resigned/	-	-	8	-	3	5	3	-	2	4	-	2	8	7	42
Laid off/Separated from previous employment			(14.8)	(13.6)	(11.9)		(9.7)		(10.5)	(14.8)		(7.7)	(17.1)	(13.5)	(10.8)
2. Gainfully	8	20	51	20	17	38	23	20	23	29	11	36	60	51	407
employed	(57.1)	(54.1)	(48.6)	(55.5)	(43.6)	(47.5)	(42.6)	(51.3)	(54.8)	(51.8)	(50.0)	(58.1)	(56.1)	(49.5)	(51.2)
2.a. Employed	5	10	22	8	9	17	11	11	14	17	8	16	27	21	196
locally	(62.5)	(50.0)	(43.1)	(40.0)	(52.9)	(44.7)	(47.8)	(55.0)	(60.9)	(58.6)	(72.7)	(44.4)	(45.0)	(41.2)	(48.2)
2.b. Employed	-	6	9	4	4	10	6	4	3	4	-	7	20	14	91
within district		(30.0)	(17.6)	(20.0)	(23.5)	(26.3)	(26.1)	(20.0)	(13.1)	(13.8)		(19.4)	(33.3)	(27.4)	(22.4)
2.c. Employed	-	-	7	3	-	3	-	-	-	2	-	4	-	9	28
outside district			(13.7)	(15.0)		(7.9)				(6.9)		(11.1)		(17.6)	(6.9)
2.d. Self-	3	4	13	5	4	8	6	5	6	6	3	9	13	7	92
employed	(37.5)	(20.0)	(25.5)	(25.0)	(23.5)	(21.1)	(26.1)	(25.0)	(26.1)	(20.7)	(27.3)	(25.0)	(21.7)	(13.8)	(22.6)
Total	14	37	105	36	39	80	54	39	42	56	22	62	107	103	796
	(100)	(100)	(100)	(100)	(100)	(100)	(100)	(100)	(100)	(100)	(100)	(100)	(100)	(100)	(100)

Note: Same as Table 1

trade of cutting and tailoring, which provides them meager job opportunities in organized as well unorganized sectors. However, they could be motivated to take up self-employment as the market for their services is very large and returns are also very lucrative, for which there is need to make them aware regarding various schemes being run by governmental and non-governmental agencies for assisting them to start their own small enterprises on individual as well as group basis.

(c) **Sector of Current Employer of Employed ITI Pass Outs:** The data regarding sector employer of employed ITI pass outs id given in Table 17. A cursory glance at Table 17 makes it evident that private sector is the dominant employment-providing sector to the ITI pass outs, where about half of them were employed and 22.6 percent each were employed in government and self-employed sector. Non-governmental organizations (NGOs) are providing employment opportunities to a very small proportion (5.4 percent) of the ITI pass outs. The district-wise analysis of the data reveals that NGO sector jobs for ITI pass outs are virtually non-existing in most of the districts. Thus, as discussed earlier the programmes and schemes of self-employment needs to propagated among the ITI pass outs so that they could productively engaged in building and advancing the economy of the state of Jammu and Kashmir.

(d) **Nature of Business done by Current Employer of Employed ITI Pass Outs:** The current employer of the ITI pass outs are reportedly engaged in various businesses and economic activities. The electricity/ gas and water supply is the dominant economic activity where 24.1 percent of ITI pass outs were employed, followed by manufacturing (17.5 percent), wholesale/retail/repairs/hotels (16.8 percent), construction (11.1 percent), transport and

Table 16

Employment Status of ITI Pass Outs by Gender

Employment Status	*I*	*II*	*III*	*IV*	*V*	*VI*	*VII*	*VIII*	*IX*	*X*	*XI*	*XII*	*XIII*	*XIV*	*Total*
Male	8	16	43	16	14	31	13	10	19	17	9	29	51	43	319
	(100)	(80.0)	(84.3)	(80.0)	(82.3)	(81.6)	(56.5)	(50.0)	(82.6)	(58.6)	(81.8)	(80.5)	(85.0)	(84.3)	(78.4)
Female	-	4	8	4	3	7	10	10	5	12	2	6	9	8	88
		(20.0)	(15.7)	(20.0)	(17.7)	(18.4)	(43.5)	(50.0)	(17.4)	(41.4)	(18.2)	(19.5)	(15.0)	(15.7)	(21.6)
Total	8	20	51	20	17	38	23	20	23	29	11	36	60	51	407
	(100)	(100)	(100)	(100)	(100)	(100)	(100)	(100)	(100)	(100)	(100)	(100)	(100)	(100)	(100)

Note: Same as Table 1

Table 17

Sector of Current Employer of Employed ITI Pass Outs

Sector	*I*	*II*	*III*	*IV*	*V*	*VI*	*VII*	*VIII*	*IX*	*X*	*XI*	*XII*	*XIII*	*XIV*	*Total*
Government	2	6	14	4	5	7	4	5	6	5	3	7	13	11	92
	([illegible])	(30.0)	(27.4)	(20.0)	(29.4)	(18.4)	(17.4)	(25.0)	(26.1)	(17.24)	(27.3)	(19.4)	(21.7)	(21.6)	(22.6)
Private	3	10	20	11	8	17	13	10	11	18	5	16	30	29	201
	(37.5)	(50.0)	(39.2)	(55.0)	(47.1)	(44.7)	(56.5)	(50.0)	(47.8)	(62.1)	(45.4)	(44.4)	(50.0)	(56.9)	(49.4)
NGO	-	-	4	-	-	6	-	-	-	-	-	4	4	4	22
			(7.8)			(15.8)						(11.1)	(6.7)	(7.8)	(5.4)
Self-employed	3	4	13	5	4	8	6	5	6	6	3	9	13	7	92
	(37.5)	(20.0)	(25.5)	(25.0)	(23.5)	(21.1)	(26.1)	(25.0)	(26.1)	(20.7)	(27.3)	(25.0)	(21.7)	(13.8)	(22.6)
Total	8	20	51	20	17	38	23	20	23	29	11	36	60	51	407
	(100)	(100)	(100)	(100)	(100)	(100)	(100)	(100)	(100)	(100)	(100)	(100)	(100)	(100)	(100)

Note: Same as Table 1

storage (8.2 percent), real estate and business services (5.4 percent), and agriculture and forestry (4.4 percent). The district-wise analysis of the data presented in Table 18 reveals that manufacturing, and electricity/gas/water supply are the main economic activities of employment of ITI pass outs in districts of Kupwara and Baramulla. It is significant to note that in districts of Jammu, Kathua and Srinagar, the ITI pass outs were engaged almost all types of economic activities given in table 18 with minor modifications of agriculture and forestry in Srinagar.

(e) **Employment Status of Employed ITI Pass Outs by Management/Cadre:** The data on employment status of employed ITI pass outs by management/cadre is given in Table 19. A perusal of the Table 19 makes it clear that one-fourth of them were engaged as technician followed by supervisory position (15.5 percent), sales and service personnel, and operator (11.1 percent), and skilled workers (10.2 percent). About 6.7 percent of the ITI pass outs were engaged in managerial position and 8.3 percent of them were working as clerks. A smaller proportion of them were also engaged as craft workers (6.3 percent) and elementary workers (5.1 percent). The district-wise analysis of the data makes it evident that all of the employed ITI pass outs in district Kupwara were engaged as technician (60 percent) and operators (40 percent). Similarly, technician is dominant cadre in district Baramulla also. The districts of Anantnag, Jammu and Kathua represents all the positions occupied by ITI pass outs. Similar is the situation in district Srinagar except the elementary occupation. The districts of Leh and Udhampur are dominant in terms of managerial position occupied by employed ITI pass outs. This is mainly due to the fact that these respondents have also educated up to graduation and post-graduation level, which have paved their

Table 18
Nature of Business done by Current Employer of Employed ITI Pass Outs

Nature of Business	*I*	*II*	*III*	*IV*	*V*	*VI*	*VII*	*VIII*	*IX*	*X*	*XI*	*XII*	*XIII*	*XIV*	*Total*
Academic	-	-	4	-	-	-	-	-	-	-	-	-	5	2	11
			(10.5)										(10.6)	(4.5)	(3.5)
Manufacturing	3	3	7	2	2	9	3	-	-	6	-	3	8	9	55
	(60.0)	(18.7)	(18.4)	(13.3)	(15.4)	(30.0)	(17.6)			(26.1)		(11.1)	(17.0)	(20.4)	(17.5)
Wholesale/retail	-	3	3	6	5	7	5	4	3	-	-	6	7	4	53
/repairs/hotels		(18.7)	(7.9)	(40.0)	(38.5)	(23.3)	(29.4)	(26.7)	(17.6)			(22.2)	(14.9)	(9.1)	(16.8)
Electricity/gas/	2	6	9	5	6	4	4	3	6	4	4	9	7	7	76
water supply	(40.0)	(37.5)	(23.9)	(33.3)	(46.1)	(13.3)	(23.5)	(20.0)	(35.3)	(17.4)	(50.0)	(33.3)	(14.9)	(15.9)	(24.1)
Community/	-	4	4	2	-	6	-	-	-	-	-	4	4	4	28
social services		(25.0)	(10.5)	(13.3)		(20.0)						(14.8)	(8.5)	(9.1)	(8.9)
Construction	-	-	3	-	-	-	2	3	3	6	2	5	6	5	35
			(7.9)				(11.7)	(20.0)	(17.6)	(26.1)	(25.0)	(18.5)	(12.7)	(11.4)	(11.1)
Transport/storage	-	-	5	-	-	-		5	-	3	-	-	6	7	26
			(13.1)					(33.3)		(13.1)			(12.7)	(15.9)	(8.2)
Real estate/	-	-	3	-	-	-	3	-	-	4	2	-	2	3	17
business services			(7.9)				(17.6)			(17.4)	(25.0)		(4.2)	(6.8)	(5.4)
Agriculture/	-	-	-	-	-	4		-	5	-	-	-	2	3	14
forestry						()			(29.4)				(4.2)	(6.8)	(4.4)
Total	5	16	38	15	13	30	17	15	17	23	8	27	47	44	315
	(100)	(100)	(100)	(100)	(100)	(100)	(100)	(100)	(100)	(100)	(100)	(100)	(100)	(100)	(100)

Note: Same as Table 1

Table 19
Employment Status of Employed ITI Pass Outs by Management/Cadre

Position	*I*	*II*	*III*	*IV*	*V*	*VI*	*VII*	*VIII*	*IX*	*X*	*XI*	*XII*	*XIII*	*XIV*	*Total*
Technician	3	9	13	6	4	6	5	4	3	7	3	5	8	5	81
	(60.0)	(56.25)	(34.2)	(40.0)	(30.7)	(20.0)	(29.4)	(26.7)	(17.6)	(30.4)	(37.5)	(18.5)	(17.0)	(11.4)	(25,7)
Supervisory	-	3	4	3	2	5	6	5	3	5	-	3	6	4	49
		(18.75)	(10.5)	(20.0)	(15.4)	(16.7)	(35.3)	(33.3)	(17.6)	(21.7)		(11.1)	(12.7)	(12.7)	(15.5)
Managerial	-	-	2	-	-	2	3	-	2	4	-	-	5	3	21
			(5.3)			(6.7)	(17.6)		(11.7)	(17.4)			(10.6)	(6.8)	(6.7)
Clerk	-	-	2	-	2	3	-	-	3	3	-	3	6	4	26
			(5.3)		(15.4)	(10.0)			(17.6)	(13.0)		(11.1)	(12.7)	(9.1)	(8.3)
Sales & service	-	2	3	-	-	3	-	3	4	4	2	5	4	5	35
		(12.5)	(7.9)			(10.0)		(20.0)	(23.5)	(17.4)	(25.0)	(18.5)	(8.5)	(11.4)	(11.1)
Craft worker	-	-	4	-	2	4	-	-	-	-	-	4	3	3	20
			(10.5)		(15.4)	(13.3)						(14.8)	(6.4)	(6.8)	(6.3)
Operator	2	-	6	-	3	3	-	3	2	-	-	4	7	5	35
	(40.0)		(15.8)		(23.1)	(10.0)		(20.0)	(11.7)			(14.8)	(14.9)	(11.4)	(11.1)
Skilled worker	-	2	4	3	-	2	3	-	-	-	3	3	5	7	32
		(12.5)	(10.5)	(20.0)		(6.7)	(17.6)				(37.5)	(11.1)	(10.6)	(15.9)	(10.2)
Elementary	-	-	-	3	-	2	-	-	-	-	-	-	3	8	16
				(20.0)		(6.7)							(6.4)	(18.2)	(5.1)
Total	5	16	38	15	13	30	17	15	17	23	8	27	47	44	315
	(100)	(100)	(100)	(100)	(100)	(100)	(100)	(100)	(100)	(100)	(100)	(100)	(100)	(100)	(100)

Note: Same as Table 1

ways up to managerial position. Thus, it is not wrong to infer that technical training supplemented by higher education has helped the employed ITI pass outs to attain better employment.

(f) **Sector of Employment of Employed ITI Pass Outs by Type of Course:** The data given in Table 20 revels that out of 103 employed ITI pass outs in electrician

Table 20

Sector of Employment of Employed ITI Pass Outs by Type of Course

Type of Trade	*Sector of Employment*				
	Government	*Private*	*NGO*	*Self Employed*	*Total*
Electrician	29 (28.1)	44 (42.7)	8 (7.8)	22 (21.4)	103 (100)
Cutting and Tailoring	-	13 (36.11)	-	23 (63.9)	36 (100)
Electronic Mechanic	4 (15.4)	16 (61.5)	-	6 (23.1)	26 (100)
Fitter	3 (16.7)	15 (83.3)	-	-	18 (100)
Turner	3 (30.0)	7 (70.0)	-	-	10 (100)
Machinist	-	9 (100)	-	-	9 (100)
Motor Mechanic	-	16 (76.2)	-	5 (23.8)	21 (100)
Tractor Mechanic	-	-	-	5 (100)	5 (100)
Welder	-	13 (54.2)	-	11 (45.8)	24 (100)
Carpenter	-	8 (50.0)	4 (25.0)	4 (25.0)	16 (100)
Plumber	3 (9.1)	23 (69.7)	-	7 (21.2)	33 (100)
Stenography	20 (42.5)	17 (36.2)	10 (21.3)	-	47 (100)
Computer Operator	27 (69.2)	7 (17.9)	-	5 (12.8)	39 (100)
Radio and TV Mechanic	-	13 (76.5)	-	4 (23.5)	17 (100)
Information Technology	3 (100)	-	-	-	3 (100)
Total	92 (22.6)	201 (49.4)	22 (5.4)	92 (22.6)	407 (100)

course/trade, majority of them were reportedly engaged in private sector (42.7 percent) followed by government sector (28.1 percent) and self-employment sector (21.4 percent). Those of the ITI pass outs that have opted for trade of cutting and tailoring, majority of them were working as self-employed (63.9 percent) followed by private sector (36.11 percent). It is important to note that almost all the ITI pass outs who have pursued the course of cutting and tailoring were reportedly females and in order to provide them with better income, it is required to motivate them to avail the benefits of the on-going programmes and schemes of self-employment run by the government and NGOs. None of the ITI pass outs in trades of fitter, turner, machinist, stenography and information technology was engaged as self-employed. On the whole, the private sector is the dominant sector for absorbing a higher proportion of the ITI pass outs in almost all courses/trades except tractor mechanic and information technology. However, in case of the trade like information technology, this appears false in real practice, because the private sector is the highest absorber of the informational technology professionals elsewhere. The current situation is due to the fact that only three ITI pass outs have been included in the sample and all of them were engaged in government sector.

(g) **Duration of Job Search and Main Reasons for Not Finding a Job by Unemployed ITI Pass Outs:** Out of 389 unemployed ITI pass outs, 319 (82.0 percent) are currently looking for a job. The duration of job search by the unemployed ITI pass outs varies from less than 6 months in case of 12.6 percent to less than 2 years in case of 22.9 percent (see table 20). The main reasons reported by unemployed ITI pass outs for not finding a job were economic recession/no jobs available (46.27 percent), very few job opening and

Table 20
Duration of Job Search by Unemployed ITI Pass Outs

Currently Looking for job	*I*	*II*	*III*	*IV*	*V*	*VI*	*VII*	*VIII*	*IX*	*X*	*XI*	*XII*	*XIII*	*XIV*	*Total*
a. Yes	6	13	47	11	18	33	27	17	16	22	8	21	38	42	319
	(100.0)	(76.5)	(87.0)	(68.7)	(81.2)	(78.6)	(87.1)	(89.5)	(84.2)	(81.5)	(72.7)	(80.7)	(80.8)	(80.7)	(82.0)
b. No	-	4	7	5	4	9	4	2	3	5	3	5	9	10	70
		(23.5)	(13.0)	(31.3)	(18.2)	(21.4)	(12.9)	(10.5)	(15.8)	(18.5)	(27.3)	(19.3)	(19.2)	(19.3)	(18.0)
Total	6	17	54	16	22	42	31	19	19	27	11	26	47	52	389
	(100)	(100)	(100)	(100)	(100)	(100)	(100)	(100)	(100)	(100)	(100)	(100)	(100)	(100)	(100)
Duration of job search															
< 6 months	-	3	8	-	-	6	3	-	-	-	-	6	7	7	40
		(23.1)	(17.0)			(18.2)	(11.1)					(28.6)	(18.4)	(16.7)	(12.6)
6 months–1 year	3	6	12	6	8	9	11	7	6	9	4	9	9	13	112
	(50.0)	(46.2)	(25.5)	(54.5)	(44.4)	(27.3)	(40.7)	(41.2)	(37.5)	(40.9)	(50.0)	(42.8)	(23.7)	(30.9)	(35.1)
1- 2 years	3	4	17	5	4	7	7	5	7	6	4	6	7	12	94
	(50.0)	(30.7)	(36.2)	(45.5)	(22.2)	(21.2)	(25.9)	(29.4)	(43.7)	(27.3)	(0.0)	(28.6)	(18.42)	(28.6)	(29.5)
> 2 years	-	-	10	-	6	11	6	5	3	7	-	-	15	10	73
			(21.3)		(33.3)	(33.3)	(22.3)	(29.4)	(18.8)	(31.8)			(39.5)	(23.8)	(22.9)
Total	6	13	47	11	18	33	27	17	16	22	8	21	38	42	319
	(100)	(100)	(100)	(100)	(100)	(100)	(100)	(100)	(100)	(100)	(100)	(100)	(100)	(100)	(100)

Note: Same as Table 1

there is strong competition (58.3 percent), lack of work experience (more than thee-fourth), poor preparation/training (about one-half), lack of professional requirements (more than one-half), and no personal connections/no strong referrals (more than two-third) Table 21.

Table 21
Main Reasons for Not Finding a Job

Reasons	*Very Important*	*Important*	*Somewhat Important*	*Least Important*	*Not Important*	*Total*
Economic recession/ No jobs available	87 (27.27)	67 (21.00)	79 (24.76)	66 (20.69)	20 (6.27)	319 (100)
Very few job openings and there is strong competition	113 (35.42)	73 (22.88)	43 (13.48)	51 (15.99)	39 (12.23)	319 (100)
Lack of work experience	162 (50.79)	88 (27.59)	34 (10.66)	20 (6.27)	15 (4.70)	319 (100)
Poor preparation/ training in my field	64 (20.06)	93 (29.15)	76 (23.82)	56 (17.55)	30 (9.40)	319 (100)

(h) **Duration of Job Search and Term of Current Employer of Employed ITI Pass Outs:** The data related to duration of job search and term of current employer of employed ITI pass outs is given in Tables 22 and 23 respectively. A cursory glance at Table 22 reveals that about one-third of them spent between 6 months and 1 year in finding the current employment, and about one-fifth each of them have spent less than 6 months and less than 2 years in finding current employment. 27 percent of the currently employed ITI pass outs have spent between 1-2 years in finding the current employment. On the whole, the job search interval is reportedly not very long in majority of the currently employed ITI pass outs, which also includes those who are currently engaged in self-

Table 22
Duration of Job Search by Currently Employed ITI Pass Outs

Duration of job search	*I*	*II*	*III*	*IV*	*V*	*VI*	*VII*	*VIII*	*IX*	*X*	*XI*	*XII*	*XIII*	*XIV*	*Total*
< 6 months	2	6	12	3	4	7	2	4	5	7	-	6	9	13	80
	(25.0)	(30.0)	(23.53)	(15.0)	(23.5)	(18.4)	(8.7)	(20.0)	(21.7)	(24.2)		(16.7)	(15.0)	(25.5)	(19.6)
6 months-1 year	3	9	16	11	7	9	8	6	8	6	7	8	16	24	138
	(37.5)	(45.0)	(31.37)	(55.0)	(41.1)	(23.6)	(34.8)	(30.0)	(34.8)	(20.7)	(63.6)	(22.2)	(26.7)	(47.1)	(33.9)
1- 2 years	3	3	13	3	4	13	7	3	6	9	4	11	21	10	110
	(37.5)	(15.0)	(25.49)	(15.0)	(23.5)	(34.2)	(30.4)	(15.0)	(26.1)	(31.-)	(36.7)	(30.5)	(35.0)	(19.6)	(27.0)
> 2 years	-	2	10	3	2	9	6	7	4	7	-	11	14	4	79
		(10.0)	(19.62)	(15.0)	(11.7)	(23.9)	(26.1)	(35.0)	(17.4)	(24.2)		(30.5)	(23.3)	(7.8)	(19.4)
Total	8	20	51	20	17	38	23	20	23	29	11	36	60	51	407
	(100)	(100)	(100)	(100)	(100)	(100)	(100)	(100)	(100)	(100)	(100)	(100)	(100)	(100)	(100)

Note: Same as Table 1

Table 23

Term of Current Employer of Employed ITI Pass Outs

Current Employer	*I*	*II*	*III*	*IV*	*V*	*VI*	*VII*	*VIII*	*IX*	*X*	*XI*	*XII*	*XIII*	*XIV*	*Total*
1st	3	6	14	6	7	15	8	6	7	9	5	11	21	22	140
	(60.0)	(37.5)	(36.8)	(40.0)	(53.8)	(50.0)	(47.1)	(40.0)	(41.2)	(39.1)	(62.5)	(40.7)	(14.9)	(50.0)	(44.4)
2nd	2	7	9	9	6	9	6	5	6	6	3	7	9	10	94
	(40.0)	(43.7)	(23.7)	(60.0)	(46.2)	(30.0)	(35.3)	(13.3)	(35.3)	(26.1)	(37.5)	(25.9)	(19.1)	(22.7)	(29.8)
3rd	-	3	15	-	-	6	3	4	4	8	-	9	17	12	81
		(18.7)	(39.5)			(20.0)	(17.6)	(26.7)	(23.5)	(34.8)		(33.3)	(36.2)	(27.3)	(25.7)
Total	5	16	38	15	13	30	17	15	17	23	8	27	47	44	315
	(100)	(100)	(100)	(100)	(100)	(100)	(100)	(100)	(100)	(100)	(100)	(100)	(100)	(100)	(100)

Note: Same as Table 1

Table 24

Duration of Stay with Current Employer of Employed ITI Pass Outs

Duration of Stay	*I*	*II*	*III*	*IV*	*V*	*VI*	*VII*	*VIII*	*IX*	*X*	*XI*	*XII*	*XIII*	*XIV*	*Total*
< 1 year	2	6	11	3	4	7	6	4	6	10	3	11	16	13	102
	(40.0)	(37.5)	(28.9)	(20.0)	(30.7)	(23.3)	(35.3)	(26.7)	(35.3)	(43.5)	(37.5)	(40.7)	(34.0)	(29.5)	(32.4)
1 - 2 years	3	6	9	6	3	9	8	5	7	7	5	7	12	11	98
	(60.0)	(37.5)	(23.7)	(40.0)	(23.1)	(30.0)	(4.1)	(33.3)	(41.2)	(30.4)	(62.5)	(25.9)	(25.5)	(25.0)	(31.1)
3 - 4 years	-	4	15	6	6	9	3	6	4	6	-	6	13	15	93
		(25.0)	(39.5)	(40.0)	(46.1)	(30.0)	(17.6)	(40.0)	(23.6)	(26.1)		(22.2)	(27.6)	(34.1)	(29.5)
> 4 years	-	-	3	-	-	5	-	-	-	-	-	3	6	5	22
			(7.9)			(16.7)						(11.1)	(12.8)	(11.4)	(6.9)
Total	5	16	38	15	13	30	17	15	17	23	8	27	47	44	315
	(100)	(100)	(100)	(100)	(100)	(100)	(100)	(100)	(100)	(100)	(100)	(100)	(100)	(100)	(100)

Note: Same as Table 1

employment. It is significant to note that the lack of initial capital to start own business, lack of confidence to venture into self-employment, and generally parents expectation to be supported after they have done their part in educating their children may be compelling reasons for the ITI pass outs to seek employment as opposed to self employment, which may have increased the duration of job search. Over the period, more than half of the employed ITI pass outs have changed their jobs and 29.8 percent and 25.7 percent of them have reported that their current employer is second and third employer respectively, which reveals the low level of job satisfaction among the currently employed (see table 23). However, more than one-third of the currently employed ITI pass outs were working with their current employer for more than three years (see table 24).

(i) **Present Tenure of Employed ITI Pass Outs and Reasons for failure to obtain a Permanent Employment:** Out of 315 currently employed ITI pass outs, 37.8 percent, 30.5 percent, 16.5 percent and 15.2 percent respectively were engaged on contractual, temporary, probationary and permanent basis (see table 25). Due to liberalization measures, the employers in government sector as well as private sector prefer to employ the labour on non-permanent basis, so that they could be retrenched as and when required, which is causing a lot of hardships to the ITI pass outs. This needs careful examination by the manpower planners and decision-makers. Out of 267 non-permanent employed ITI pass outs, one-third of them cited low standard of English as the main reason for the failure to get a permanent employment. The poor performance at tests and interviews conducted by recruiting agencies were cited by more than one-fifth as a reason followed by discrimination by race, caste, religion and politics, and poor performance at ITI

Table 25
Present Tenure of Employed ITI Pass Outs

Tenure	*I*	*II*	*III*	*IV*	*V*	*VI*	*VII*	*VIII*	*IX*	*X*	*XI*	*XII*	*XIII*	*XIV*	*Total*
Contractual	3	6	19	7	5	9	7	6	5	9	4	11	13	15	119
	(60.0)	(37.5)	(50.0)	(46.7)	(38.5)	(30.0)	(41.2)	(40.0)	(29.4)	(39.1)	(50.0)	(40.7)	(25.6)	(34.1)	(37.8)
Permanent	-	4	4	-	-	5	4	3	-	4	-	6	11	7	48
		(25.0)	(10.5)			(16.7)	(23.5)	(20.0)		(17.4)		(22.2)	(23.4)	(15.9)	(15.2)
Probationary	-	2	4	-	-	7	6	-	6	7	2	4	9	5	52
		(12.5)	(10.5)			(23.3)	(35.3)		(35.3)	(30.4)	(25.0)	(14.8)	(19.2)	(11.4)	(16.5)
Temporary	2	4	11	8	8	9	-	6	6	3	2	6	14	17	96
	(40.0)	(25.0)	(28.9)	(53.3)	(61.5)	(30.0)		(40.0)	(35.3)	(13.1)	(25.0)	(22.2)	(29.8)	(38.6)	(30.5)
Total	5	16	38	15	13	30	17	15	17	23	8	27	47	44	315
	(100)	(100)	(100)	(100)	(100)	(100)	(100)	(100)	(100)	(100)	(100)	(100)	(100)	(100)	(100)

Note: Same as Table 1

(more than one-tenth) of the ITI pass outs for their failure to obtain a permanent job (see table 26).

Table 26
Major Reasons for Failure to Obtain a Permanent Employment

Main Reasons	*No.*	*Percentage*
Discrimination by race, caste, religion & politics	33	12.36
Poor performance at the ITI	59	12.09
Low standard of English	89	33.33
Poor performance at tests and interviews	64	23.97
Sex discrimination	7	2.62
Status of school attended during secondary education	6	2.25
Other	9	3.37
Total	267	100

(j) **Relation Between Employment and Field of Training:** A cursory glance at the data presented in Table 27 makes it evident that 79.0 percent of the employed ITI pass outs were engaged in jobs related to the field of training and 21.0 percent have landed in jobs, which are not related to the field of training at ITI. More or less the same is applicable for district level analysis with minor variations. Out of 66 employed ITI pass outs, who were landed in jobs not related to the field of training, more than half of them reported that they could not get a satisfactory job in their field of training because either the pay was low or they do not like the job available. A similar proportion of them have reported that their training was inadequate and they could not compete with other pass outs in the same field, and there was an opening in currently employed field, for which they immediately applied. Besides above, some other reasons such as "they have not (yet) been able to/ could not find a job that is/was better linked to their level of education, in doing present job they have/ had better career opportunities, they do/did not mind having a job that is/was not linked to their

Table 27

Present Job related to Field of Training

Tenure	*I*	*II*	*III*	*IV*	*V*	*VI*	*VII*	*VIII*	*IX*	*X*	*XI*	*XII*	*XIII*	*XIV*	*Total*
a. Yes	5	12	29	11	10	23	13	13	13	17	6	23	38	36	249
	(100)	(75.0)	(76.3)	(73.3)	(76.9)	(76.7)	(76.5)	(86.7)	(76.5)	(73.9)	(75.0)	(85.2)	(80.8)	(81.8)	(79.0)
b. No	-	4	9	4	3	7	4	2	4	6	2	4	9	8	66
		(25.0)	(23.7)	(26.7)	(23.1)	(23.3)	(23.5)	(13.3)	(23.5)	(26.1)	(25.0)	(14.8)	(19.2)	(18.2)	(21.0)
Total	5	16	38	15	13	30	17	15	17	23	8	27	47	44	315
	(100)	(100)	(100)	(100)	(100)	(100)	(100)	(100)	(100)	(100)	(100)	(100)	(100)	(100)	(100)

Note: Same as Table 1

studies, they have/had to accept work that is/was not closely linked to their studies at the beginning of their career, their current/past job allows/allowed them to look after their family's needs, they can/could earn more money in their current/past job, their current/past job is/was more interesting, their current/past job allows/allowed them to work part-time or when they want/wanted to, their current/past job is/was more secure, they have been/was promoted to a position less closely linked to their studies (than was their previous position), and their current/past job allows/allowed them to work where they want/wanted to 28.

Table 28
Reasons Behind Taking a Job Not Related to Field of Training in ITI

Reasons	*Very Important*	*Important*	*Somewhat Important*	*Least Important*	*Not Important*	*Total*
a. I could not get a satisfactory job in my field of training; either the pay is low or I do not like the job available	23 (34.8)	14 (21.2)	16 (24.2)	8 (12.1)	5 (7.6)	66 (100)
b. My training is inadequate; I could not compete with other pass outs in the same field	26 (39.4)	12 (18.2)	10 (15.2)	7 (10.6)	11 (16.7)	66 (100)
c. There was an opening in this field, which I immediately applied for	19 (28.8)	17 (25.7)	11 (16.7)	9 (13.6)	10 (15.2)	66 (100)
d. Others						
d.1. I have not (yet) been able to/could not find a job that is/was better linked to my level of education	22 (33.3)	18 (27.3)	14 (21.2)	8 (12.1)	4 (6.1)	66 (100)
d.2. In doing this job I	24 (36.4)	17 (25.7)	16 (24.3)	5 (7.6)	4 (6.1)	66 (100)

have/had better career opportunities						
d.3. I do/did not mind having a job that is/was not linked to my studies	21 (31.8)	11 (16.7)	14 (21.2)	8 (12.1)	12 (18.2)	66 (100)
d.4. I have/had to accept work that is/was not closely linked to my studies at the beginning of my career	20 (30.3)	14 (21.2)	17 (25.7)	9 (13.6)	6 (9.1)	66 (100)
d.5. My current/past job allows/allowed me to look after my family's needs	17 (25.7)	11 (16.7)	18 (27.3)	13 (19.7)	7 (10.6)	66 (100)
d.6. I can/could earn more money in my current/past job	11 (16.7)	19 (28.8)	16 (24.2)	14 (21.2)	6 (9.1)	66 (100)
d.7. My current/past job is/was more interesting	15 (22.7)	17 (25.7)	13 (19.7)	16 (24.2)	5 (7.6)	66 (100)
d.8. My current/past job allows/allowed me to work part-time or when I want/wanted to	14 (21.2)	13 (19.7)	19 (28.8)	14 (21.2)	6 (9.1)	66 (100)
d.9. My current/past job is/was more secure	14 (21.2)	12 (18.2)	14 (21.2)	16 (24.2)	10 (15.1)	66 (100)
d.10. I have been/was promoted to a position less closely linked to my studies (than was my previous position)	16 (24.2)	19 (28.8)	15 (22.7)	9 (13.6)	7 (10.6)	66 (100)
d.11. My current/past job allows/allowed me to work where I want/wanted to	19 (28.8)	17 (25.7)	12 (18.2)	15 (22.7)	3 (4.5)	66 (100)

(k) **Intention to Change Job in Future and Reasons Behind Intended Change:** Out of 66 employed ITI pass outs, who were landed in jobs not related to the field of training, 44 (66.7 percent) intends to change their jobs in future and they are distributed across the districts of the state of Jammu and Kashmir, which clearly reflects strong level of

Table 29
Intention to Change Job in Future

Tenure	*I*	*II*	*III*	*IV*	*V*	*VI*	*VII*	*VIII*	*IX*	*X*	*XI*	*XII*	*XIII*	*XIV*	*Total*
a. Yes	-	3	6	2	3	4	2	2	3	4	2	2	6	5	44
		(75.0)	(66.7)	(50.0)	(100)	(57.1)	(50.0)	(100)	(75.0)	(66.7)	(100)	(50.0)	(66.7)	(62.5)	(66.7)
b. No	-	1	3	2	-	3	2	-	1	2	-	2	3	3	22
		(25.0)	(33.3)	(50.0)		(42.9)	(50.0)		(25.0)	(33.3)		(50.0)	(33.3)	(37.5)	(33.3)
Total	-	4	9	4	3	7	4	2	4	6	2	4	9	8	66
	(100)	(100)	(100)	(100)	(100)	(100)	(100)	(100)	(100)	(100)	(100)	(100)	(100)	(100)	(100)

Note: Same as Table 1

Table 31
Gross Monthly Income of Employed ITI Pass Outs (Rs.)

Monthly Salary	*I*	*II*	*III*	*IV*	*V*	*VI*	*VII*	*VIII*	*IX*	*X*	*XI*	*XII*	*XIII*	*XIV*	*Total*
< 5000	3	9	26	15	13	25	13	12	15	14	8	17	23	27	220
	(60.0)	(56.3)	(68.4)	(100)	(100)	(83.3)	(76.5)	(80.0)	(88.2)	(60.8)	(100)	(62.9)	(48.9)	(54.5)	(69.8)
5000-7500	2	4	8	-	-	2	4	3	2	5	-	4	12	10	56
	(40.0)	(25.0)	(21.1)			(6.7)	(23.5)	(20.0)	(11.8)	(21.7)		(14.8)	(25,3)	(22.7)	(17.8)
7500-10000	-	3	-	-	-	-	-	-	-	2	-	2	6	4	17
		(18.7)								(8.7)		(7.4)	(12.7)	(9.1)	(5.4)
> 10000	-	-	4	-	-	3	-	-	-	2	-	4	6	3	22
			(10.5)			(10.0)				(8.7)		(14.8)	(12.7)	(6.8)	(6.9)
Total	5	16	38	15	13	30	17	15	17	23	8	27	47	44	315
	(100)	(100)	(100)	(100)	(100)	(100)	(100)	(100)	(100)	(100)	(100)	(100)	(100)	(100)	(100)

Note: Same as Table 1

dissatisfaction with the current jobs (see table 29). Out of 44 ITI pass outs who have shown their intention to change the job in future, half of them have reported that their present job is outside their field of training and their salary is also low and the same proportion of them have shown their desire to concentrate on graduate studies to enhance their job prospects Table 30.

Table 30
Reasons Behind Intended Change in Job

Reasons	*Very Important*	*Important*	*Somewhat Important*	*Least Important*	*Not Important*	*Total*
Present job is outside my field of training	14 (31.8)	12 (27.3)	9 (20.4)	7 (15.9)	2 (4.5)	44 (100)
Present job pay is low	13 (29.5)	9 (20.4)	7 (15.9)	11 (25.0)	4 (9.1)	44 (100)
To concentrate in my graduate studies	7 (15.9)	15 (34.1)	6 (13.6)	8 (18.2)	8 (18.2)	44 (100)

INCOME PROFILE OF ITI PASS OUTS

After discussing the occupational profile of the ITI pass outs in previous section, the income profile is discussed in the following paragraphs, which includes gross monthly salary of employed and self-employed, and income level by gender, type of course and sector of employment.

(a) **Gross Monthly Income of Employed and Self-employed ITI Pass Outs:** The gross monthly income of the employed and self-employed ITI pass outs is given in Table 31 and 32 respectively. A perusal of the data in Table 31 reveals that majority of the employed ITI pass outs (69.8 percent) were getting gross monthly income of less than Rs. 5000, 17.8 percent, 5.4 percent and 6.9 percent of them were getting gross monthly income between Rs. 5000-7500, Rs. 7500-10000 and above Rs. 10000 respectively. In districts of Badgam, Pulwama, and

Table 32

Gross Monthly Income of Self- Employed ITI Pass Outs (Rs.)

Monthly Income	*I*	*II*	*III*	*IV*	*V*	*VI*	*VII*	*VIII*	*IX*	*X*	*XI*	*XII*	*XIII*	*XIV*	*Total*
< 5000	2	2	-	-	2	-	-	-	3	-	3	4	5	6	27
	(66.7)	(50.0)			(50.0)				(50.0)		(100)	(44.4)	(38.4)	(85.7)	(29.3)
5000- 7500	1	2	4	3	2	3	4	5	3	3	-	5	3	-	38
	(33.3)	(50.0)	(30.7)	(60.0)	(50.0)	(37.5)	(66.7)	(100)	(50.0)	(50.0)		(55.6)	(23.1)		(41.3)
7500-10000	-	-	3	2	-	5	2	-	-	3	-	-	1	1	18
			(18.7)	(40.0)		(62.5)	(33.3)			(50.0)			(7.7)	(14.3)	(19.6)
> 10000	-	-	5	-	-	-	-	-	-	-	-	-	4	-	9
			(38.6)										(30.7)		(9.8)
Total	3	4	13	5	4	8	6	5	6	6	3	9	13	7	92
	(100)	(100)	(100)	(100)	(100)	(100)	(100)	(100)	(100)	(100)	(100)	(100)	(100)	(100)	(100)

Note: Same as Table 1

Poonch, all of the employed ITI pass outs were getting lower gross monthly income, whereas in the districts of Kupwara, Kargil, Leh, and Doda, all of them belong to the income group of below Rs. 7500 per month. In the districts of Rajouri, Jammu and Srinagar, 14.8 percent, 12.7 percent and 10.5 percent of them were found in monthly income group of above Rs. 10000.

A cursory glance at data in Table 32 makes it clear that out of 92 self-employed ITI pass outs, majority of them (41.3 percent) were earning between Rs. 5000-7500 monthly and less than one-third and one-fifth were earning below Rs. 5000 and between Rs. 7500-10000 on monthly basis. About a tenth of them were found in higher income group and they were concentrated in districts of Srinagar and Jammu. From the above, it is not wrong to infer that the gross monthly income of the self-employed ITI pass outs is comparatively more than those of employed ITI pass outs. Thus, self-employment is comparatively more lucrative avenues for the prospective trainees and needs to be strongly propagated during the training periods at respective ITIs so that a greater proportion of them should venture into self-employment as their career.

(b) **Income Level of Employed ITI Pass Outs by Gender, Type of Course and Sector of Employment:** The Tables 33, 34 and 35 are devoted to income level of employed ITI pass outs by gender, type of course and sector of employment. Out of 319 male and female-employed ITI pass outs, 60.5 percent and 60.7 percent respectively were earning less than Rs. 5000 per month and 18.8 percent males and 38.9 percent females were earning between Rs. 5000-7500. 11.0 percent and 9.7 percent of the males were earning between Rs. 7500-10000 and above Rs. 10000 respectively. It is significant to note that none of the female ITI pass out was reportedly earning above Rs. 7500, which clearly reflects gender disparity in levels of earnings, as can be noticed elsewhere.

Table 33
Income Level of Employed ITI Pass Outs by Gender (Rs.)

Gender	*Income Level*				
	< 5000	*5000-7500*	*7500-10000*	*> 10000*	*Total*
Male	193	60	35	31	319
	(60.5)	(18.8)	(11.0)	(9.7)	(100)
Female	54	34	-	-	88
	(61.4)	(38.6)			(100)
Total	247	94	35	31	407
	(60.7)	(23.1)	(8.6)	(7.6)	(100)

The income level of the employed ITI pass outs by the type of course/trade pursued by them is given in Table 34. The data presented in table 34 reveals that 82.5 percent, 77.8 percent and 66.7 percent of the ITI pass outs in courses/trades like electrician, cutting and tailoring and computer operator respectively were earning monthly income to the tune of less than Rs. 5000. Half of the ITI pass outs in courses/trades such as electronic mechanic, motor mechanic, machinist, plumber and radio and T.V mechanic were earning less than Rs. 5000 per month. At the same time, electrician (8.7 percent), electronic mechanic (14.5 percent), filler (16.7 percent), stenography (19.1 percent) and computer operator (15.4 percent) were earning more than Rs. 10000. Thus, it is not wrong to infer that even in the same trade the level of earning differ largely on account of longer duration of employment, better employment opportunities, higher educational attainments, etc.

Similarly, a significantly high proportion (81.6 percent) of the ITI pass outs working in private sector were earning less than Rs. 5000 and 47.8 percent, 54.5 percent and 29.3 percent of ITI pass outs respectively working in government, NGO and self-employed sector were earning less than Rs. 5000. At the same time, 23.9 percent and 9.8 percent of the ITI pass out respectively working government sector and self-employed sector were earning above Rs. 10000 (see table 35). Thus, high variations are noticed in income levels of the workers in government, private and self-employed sector and the private sector are comparatively low-paid sector to the ITI pass outs as compared to government and self-employed sector. Keeping in view the limitations of the government sector to expand, the opportunities lies in expanding more and more the rapidly growing self-employed sector.

Table 34
Income Level of Employed ITI Pass Outs by Type of Course (Rs.)

Type of Trade	*Income Level*				
	<5000	*5000-7500*	*7500-10000*	*>10000*	*Total*
Electrician	85 (82.5)	7 (6.8)	2 (1.9)	9 (8.7)	103 (100)
Cutting and Tailoring	28 (77.8)	5 (13.9)	3 (8.4)	-	36 (100)
Electronic Mechanic	13 (50.0)	9 (34.6)	-	4 (15.4)	26 (100)
Fitter	9 (50.0)	6 (33.3)	-	3 (16.7)	18 (100)
Turner	4 (40.0)	6 (60.0)	-	-	10 (100)
Machinist	5 (55.5)	4 (44.5)	-	-	9 (100)
Motor Mechanic	11 (52.4)	5 (23.8)	5 (23.8)	-	21 (100)
Tractor Mechanic	- ()	-	5 (100)	-	5 (100)
Welder	10 (41.7)	10 (41.7)	4 (16.7)	-	24 (100)
Carpenter	5 (31.2)	8 (50.0)	3 (18.8)	-	16 (100)
Plumber	19 (57.6)	9 (27.3)	5 (15.1)	-	33 (100)
Stenography	23 (48.9)	10 (21.3)	5 (10.6)	9 (19.1)	47 (100)
Computer Operator	26 (66.7)	7 (17.9)	-	6 (15.4)	39 (100)
Radio and TV Mechanic	9 (52.9)	5 (29.4)	3 (17.4)	-	17 (100)
Information Technology	-	3 (100)	-	-	3 (100)
Total	247 (60.7)	94 (23.1)	35 (8.6)	31 (7.6)	407 (100)

Table 35
Income Level of Employed ITI Pass Outs by Sector of Employment (Rs.)

Sector of Employment	*Income Group*				
	<5000	*5000-7500*	*7500-10000*	*>10000*	*Total*
Government	44	12	14	22	92
	(47.8)	(13.0)	(15.2)	(23.9)	(100)
Private	164	34	3	-	201
	(81.6)	(16.9)	(1.5)		(100)
NGO	12	10	-	-	22
	(54.5)	(45.5)			(100)
Self-employed	27	38	18	9	92
	(29.3)	(41.3)	(19.6)	(9.8)	(100)
Total	247	94	35	31	407
	(60.7)	(23.1)	(8.6)	(7.6)	(100)

PLACEMENT ASSISTANCE TO ITI PASS OUTS

In this section, data has been presented on placement assistance provided to ITI pass outs in finding employment, means of finding employment after training, factors helping find first job after training, employment and unemployment rates by type of course and obstacles faced by them in finding suitable employment. Iss

(a) **Specific Assistance Provided by ITI and Means of Finding Employment:** Less than one-third of the ITI pass outs have reported that ITIs have advertised/ display posts available. Similarly, more than one-third of them have reported that ITIs have provided counselling in finding a job. Likewise, more than one-fifth of them have reported that ITIs have provided them information on specific careers, which facilitated in finding a job. None of the ITIs have provided a recruitment service, sent curriculum vitae to companies, arranged visits to workplace, and linked to an employment agency to help the trainees finding out employment (see table 36), thus, there is need to provide these facilities by the ITIs to help the trainees in finding suitable employment.

Table 36
Types of Specific Assistance Provided by ITI in Finding Employment

Specific Assistance	*Very Important*	*Important*	*Somewhat Important*	*Least Important*	*Not Important*	*Total*
Advertised/display posts available	24 (7.6)	67 (21.3)	23 (7.3)	76 (24.1)	125 (39.7)	315 (100)
Distributed job application forms	-	-	15 (4.7)	43 (13.7)	257 (81.6)	315 (100)
Provided company details	-	-	17 (5.4)	33 (10.5)	265 (84.1)	315 (100)
Provided a recruitment service	-	-	-	55 (17.5)	260 (82.5)	315 (100)
Linked to a specific company	-	-	-	84 (26.7)	231 (73.3)	315 (100)
Provided counselling	17 (5.4)	93 (29.5)	55 (17.5)	50 (15.8)	100 (31.7)	315 (100)
Gave practical training	97 (30.8)	78 (24.8)	40 (12.7)	- (31.7)	100	315
Sent CVs to companies	-	-	-	92 (29.2)	223 (70.8)	315 (100)
Arranged visits to workplaces	-	-	-	67 (21.2)	248 (78.8)	315 (100)
Linked to an employment agency	-	-	-	84 (26.7)	231 (73.3)	315 (100)
Provided information on specific careers	23 (7.3)	34 (10.8)	41 (13.0)	97 (30.8)	120 (38.1)	315 (100)

Less than one-third of them found employment through personal contacts and one-fourth through relatives and one-fifth through an advertisement in the newspaper, and one-tenth through an employment agency. About 10.5 percent of them have reported help by the ITI staff in finding an employment (see table 37). The ITIs should facilitate the trainees with arranging placement services and inviting the recruiting agencies on the campus, so that the duration of job search may be minimized and they could be placed in suitable employment after training, which could reduce the incidence of unemployment and underemployment among the ITI pass outs.

Table 37
Means of Finding Employment After ITI Training

Means of Finding Employment	*Very Important*	*Important*	*Somewhat Important*	*Least Important*	*Not Important*	*Total*
Through personal contacts	36 (11.4)	59 (18.7)	60 (19.0)	43 (13.7)	117 (37.1)	315 (100)
Through relatives	33 (10.5)	46 (14.6)	52 (16.5)	64 (20.3)	120 (38.1)	315 (100)
Through a newspaper advertisement	37 (11.7)	28 (8.9)	67 (21.3)	48 (15.2)	135 (42.8)	315 (100)
Through an employment agency	11 (3.5)	23 (7.3)	87 (27.6)	53 (16.8)	141 (44.7)	315 (100)
Through my employer coming to the ITI to find employees	-	-	-	84 (26.7)	231 (73.3)	315 (100)
With the help of ITI	-	-	-	76 (24.1)	239 (75.9)	315 (100)
Through ITI teaching staff	-	-	33 (10.5)	-	282 (89.5)	315 (100)

(b) **Factors Helping ITI Pass Outs Securing First Job after Training:** The data presented in Table 38 reveals that ITI diploma/certificate and the course studied were rated important factors helping them find the first job after training followed by factors such as motivations by the instructors, strong work ethic, post-ITI education, computer training, references of the known persons and practical work experience during training have played a significant role in find the first job. The factors such as possession of bachelor degree and leadership qualities developed during the training have not contributed much in finding a job. The post-ITI education/training is very important factor influencing getting first job by them. Thus, there is need to introduce advance diploma courses in ITIs to enable the trainees to specialize and equip better to face the challenges of the labour market. Besides theoretical knowledge, the apprenticeship and development of work ethic should also be given due importance during the training.

Table 38

Factors Helping ITI Pass Outs Securing irst Job after Training

Means of Finding Employment	*Very Impor-tant*	*Impor-tant*	*Some-what Impor-tant*	*Least Impor-tant*	*Not Impor-tant*	*Total*
Having an ITI Diploma/ certificate	74 (23.49)	83 (26.35)	74 (23.49)	66 (20.95)	18 (5.71)	315 (100)
The programme/course I studied at the ITI	87 (27.62)	67 (21.27)	77 (24.44)	66 (20.95)	18 (5.71)	315 (100)
Having bachelor degree	-	-	32 (10.16)	179 (56.82)	104 (33.02)	315 (100)
Having leadership qualities that were developed at the ITI	-	-	131 (41.59)	93 (29.52)	91 (28.89)	315 (100)
Having been motivated by tutors at the ITI	65 (20.63)	34 (10.79)	76 (24.13)	80 (25.39)	60 (19.05)	315 (100)
Having a strong work ethic	83 (26.35)	28 (8.89)	67 (21.27)	73 (23.17)	64 (20.31)	315 (100)
Having gone through an apprenticeship	-	27 (8.57)	13 (4.13)	141 (44.76)	134 (42.54)	315 (100)
Having strong communication skills	-	44 (13.97)	25 (7.94)	122 (38.73)	124 (39.36)	315 (100)
Having previous job experience	-	85 (26.98)	48 (15.24)	102 (32.38)	80 (25.39)	315 (100)
Having a post-ITI education	33 (10.47)	54 (17.14)	23 (7.30)	128 (40.63)	77 (24.44)	315 (100)
Having received computer training	54 (17.14)	23 (7.30)	31 (9.84)	136 (43.17)	71 (22.54)	315 (100)
References from people who knew me	76 (24.12)	43 (13.65)	-	104 (33.01)	92 (29.21)	315 (100)
Practical/work experience acquired during course	67 (21.27)	42 (13.33)	28 (8.89)	83 (26.35)	95 (30.16)	315 (100)
Help, which the ITI gave me for the job interview	-	-	-	168 (53.33)	147 (46.67)	315 (100)
Being self-confident	-	-	94 (29.84)	137 (43.49)	84 (26.67)	315 (100)
Parental support	-	-	37 (11.75)	144 (45.71)	134 (42.54)	315 (100)

(c) **Employment and Unemployment Rates among ITI Pass Outs by Type of Course:** The data related to employment and unemployment rates among ITI pass outs by type of course is given in Table 39. It is significant to note that full employment was reported in trades like tractor mechanic and information technology, which may be due to the fact that their proportion was very low in the selected sample and these courses are offered to very small number of trainees in few ITIs. Besides above, the highest employment rate was recorded in the trades of plumber (82.5 percent), motor mechanic, welder and carpenter (80.0 percent each), followed by trades of fitter and machinist (75.0 percent each), and electrician (62.04 percent), computer operator (60.93 percent), and radio and T.V mechanic (60.71 percent). The highest unemployment rate was reported in the trade of cutting and tailoring, which is female dominated followed by stenography (61.8 percent), electronic mechanic (45.84 percent), electrician (37.95 percent), and computer operator (39.07 percent). The high unemployment rates among the ITI pass outs in trades such as stenography, electronic mechanic, electrician, and computer operator is due to the fact that a comparatively large sample of these trades was included in the study and besides, there is intense competition for the jobs in these trades in the labour market.

(d) **Obstacles Faced by ITI Pass Outs in Finding Suitable Employment:** Table 40 provides data on obstacles faced by ITI pass outs that were looking for a job and/or intending to change the current job. Out of 363 sample ITI pass outs, 28.37 percent, 21.46 percent, 17.35 percent and 10.74 percent have reported absence of required work experience, absence of opportunities in the field of specialization and lack of knowledge in information technology respectively as the main obstacles in finding suitable employment. Other important obstacles reported by them include lack of knowledge of English (9.9 percent) and lack of knowledge of management (8.81 percent). Thus, there is need to diversify the course structures to make them more competitive and employment oriented and emphasis should be paid on equipping them with knowledge of English language and information technology by arranging special classes during the training programmes.

Table 39
Employment and Unemployment Rates of ITI Pass Outs by Type of Course

Type of Trade	*Sector of Employment*				
	Employed	*Employment Rate*	*Unemployed*	*Unemployment rate*	*Total*
Electrician	103 (25.30)	62.04	63 (16.19)	37.95	166 (20.85)
Cutting and Tailoring	36 (8.84)	18.27	161 (41.39)	81.73	197 (24.75)
Electronic Mechanic	26 (6.38)	54.16	22 (5.65)	45.84	48 (6.03)
Fitter	18 (4.42)	75.00	6 (1.54)	25.00	24 (3.01)
Turner	10 (2.46)	100	0	0	10 (1.26)
Machinist	9 (2.21)	75.00	3 (0.77)	25.00	12 (1.51)
Motor Mechanic	21 (5.16)	80.76	5 (1.28)	19.23	26 (3.27)
Tractor Mechanic	5 (1.23)	100	0	0	5 (0.63)
Welder	24 (5.89)	80.00	6 (1.54)	20.00	30 (3.77)
Carpenter	16 (3.93)	80.00	4 (1.03)	20.00	20 (2.51)
Plumber	33 (8.11)	82.5	7 (1.80)	17.5	40 (5.02)

Contd....

Type of Trade	Sector of Employment				
	Employed	Employment Rate	Unemployed	Unemployment rate	Total
Stenography	47 (11.55)	38.21	76 (19.53)	61.8	123 (15.45)
Computer Operator	39	60.93	25 (6.42)	39.07	64 (8.04)
Radio and TV Mechanic	17 (4.18)	60.71	11 (2.83)	39.28	28 (3.52)
Information Technology	3 (0.74)	100	0	0	3 (0.37)
Total	407 (100)	51.13	389 (100)	48.87	796 (100)

Table 40
Obstacles Faced by ITI Pass Outs in Finding Suitable Employment

Obstacles Faced	No.	Percentage
Absence of required work experience	103	28.37
Absence of opportunities in the field of specialization	78	21.48
Absence of opportunities in the area of interest	63	17.35
Lack of knowledge in English	36	9.9
Lack of knowledge in Information Technology	39	10.74
Lack of knowledge in Management	32	8.81
Other	12	3.30
Currently looking for a job/intending to change job	363	100

LEVEL OF WORK SATISFACTION BY ITI PASS OUTS

In the last section of the chapter, the level of work satisfaction by the currently employed ITI pass outs has been examined, which includes the level of satisfaction with aspects of work situation, overall assessment of relationship between key aspects of job characteristics, extent of relevance of ITI training to current job and workplace, extent of usefulness of ITI training to current job and workplace, contribution of knowledge and skill acquired at ITI to present organization, overall benefits of ITI training to current job and workplace, opinion regarding work in ones own business/being self-employed, and changes needed to improve competitive edge of IIT pass outs.

(a) **Levels of Satisfaction with Aspects of Work Situation:** The data on levels of satisfaction with aspects of work situation by the currently employed ITI pass outs is given in Table 41, which reveals that 30.04 percent, 37.14 percent, 23.81 percent of them respectively perceived the content of work, the working conditions and opportunity to learn while working as very useful. About 30.0 percent of them have used the knowledge and skill acquired very significantly and 20.31 percent, 18.14 percent, 15.24 percent and 13.96 percent of them were very satisfied with job security, income, promotion opportunities and other fringe benefits respectively. At the same time, 30.47 percent, 35.23 percent and 41.58 percent of them have reported that the content of the work, working conditions and opportunities to learn while working was of little/not at all useful respectively. More than half of them have reported lack of job security, promotion opportunities and fringe benefits in current employment.

Table 41
Levels of Satisfaction with Aspects of Work Situation

Levels of satisfaction	*Very Useful*	*Somewhat Useful*	Little/not *at all Usefull*	Total
Content of work	123 (39.04)	96 (30.47)	96 (30.47)	315 (100)
Working conditions	117 (37.14)	87 (27.62)	111 (35.23)	315 (100)
Opportunity to learn while working	75 (23.81)	109 (34.60)	131 (41.58)	315 (100)
Use knowledge and skills acquired	95 (30.16)	98 (31.11)	122 (38.73)	315 (100)
Job security	64 (20.31)	92 (29.21)	159 (50.48)	315 (100)
Income	58 (18.41)	113 (35.87)	143 (45.39)	315 (100)
Promotion opportunities	48 (15.24)	105 (33.33)	162 (51.43)	315 (100)
Benefits (medical aid, housing allowance, pension, and so on)	44 (13.96)	89 (28.25)	182 (57.78)	315 (100)

More than one-fifth of them realized the career expected and used the knowledge acquired during training highly and one-third of them reported their current employment position appropriate with their level of education. About one-fourth of them were modestly satisfied with career expectation, use of acquired knowledge and appropriateness of position with the level of education. At the same time, it is significant to note that more than 39.0 percent of them were marginally satisfied with these key aspects of job characteristics Table 42.

Table 42
Overall Assessment of Relationships between Key Aspects of Job Characteristics

Assessment of Relationships	*Highly Satisfied*	*Monthly Satisfied*	*Marginally Satisfied*	*Total*
To what extent have you realized career expected during training	73 (23.17)	85 (26.98)	157 (49.84)	315 (100)
To what extent do you use knowledge acquired during study	89 (28.25)	76 (24.12)	150 (47.62)	315 (100)
To what extent is your position appropriate to your education	106 (33.66)	84 (26.67)	125 (39.68)	315 (100)

(b) **Relevance and Usefulness of ITI Training to Current Job and Workplace:** The data on relevance and usefulness of training to current job and workplace is presented in Tables 43 and 44 respectively. More than one-fourth of them have reported that the subject studied during training was relevant very often and sometimes in current job and workplace and 42.85 percent of them have reported that the subject studied was relevant seldom and never in current job and workplace. One-third of them have reported that relevance of the knowledge and skills acquired very often, sometimes and seldom and never. A more or less the similar is the case with relevance of the experience and exposure gained during training. From the above, it is clear that a significant proportion of them consider the courses, and knowledge and skill acquired during training as irrelevant in their current job and workplace, which call for restructuring of the courses in tune with changing labour market flexibility to make the ITI pass outs more efficient and productive.

Table 43

Extent of Relevance of ITI Training to Current Job and Workplace

Extent of Relevance	*Very Often and Often*	*Sometimes*	*Seldom and Never*	*Total*
The subjects studied under the programme	84 (26.67)	96 (30.47)	135 (42.85)	315 (100)
Used the knowledge/skills acquired through the course	107 (33.97)	104 (33.01)	104 (33.01)	315 (100)
Used experience and exposure gained at ITI	122 (38.73)	99 (31.43)	94 (29.84)	315 (100)
Passed on knowledge to colleagues and juniors informally	101 (32.06)	108 (34.28)	106 (33.65)	315 (100)

More than one-fourth of them have reported that ITI training is very useful for fulfilling the task and responsibilities and development of own personality/identity in current job and for the development of the workplace. Similarly, more than one-third of them have reported that ITI training is very useful for future professional development/career and development of the state economy. However, more or less similar proportion of them have reported that ITI training is little/not at all useful in various job aspects mentioned in Table 44, which needs to be taken cautiously by the relevant authorities so that the overall training programmes be modified to make them more relevant and highly useful to the trainees, their employers and the society and economy at large.

About one-fifth of the currently employed ITI pass outs have reported that the knowledge and skill acquired at ITI with regard to analytical skills for deeper understanding of problems and readymade technical skills to fit solutions to problems are very useful and more than one-third of them reported such knowledge and skills as somewhat useful to their present organization. It is significant to note that 43.81 percent of them have reported that such knowledge and skills are little not at all useful to their present organization (See table 45), and this needs to be taken with caution so that the overall knowledge and skills gained during training should be made more relevant and highly useful to their workplaces, failing which the retention capacity of the employers and/or their income and promotional avenues may be jeopardized and results in wastage of time and efforts made by the trainees as well as the trainers.

Table 44
Extent of Usefulness of ITI Training to Current Job and Workplace

Extent of Usefulness	*Very Useful*	*Somewhat Useful*	Little/not *at all Usefull*	Total
For fulfilling my present organizational tasks/ responsibilities	92 (29.21)	109 (34.60)	114 (36.19)	315 (100)
For future professional development/career	106 (33.65)	113 (35.87)	96 (30.47)	315 (100)
For the development of my personality/identity	91 (28.89)	103 (32.69)	121 (38.41)	315 (100)
For development of present organization	95 (30.16)	99 (31.43)	121 (38.41)	315 (100)
For the development of my state	119 (37.78)	97 (30.79)	99 (31.43)	315 (100)

Table 45
Contribution of Knowledge and Skill Acquired at ITI to Present Organization

Contribution of Knowledge and Skill Acquired	*Very Useful*	*Somewhat Useful*	Little/not *at all Usefull*	Total
Analytical skills for deeper understanding of problems	64 (20.31)	113 (35.87)	138 (43.81)	315 (100)
Readymade technical skills to fit solutions to problems	69 (21.90)	108 (34.28)	138 (43.81)	315 (100)

More than one-third of the currently employed ITI pass outs have reported that the knowledge and ideas gained, and the contacts and academic partnerships made during the training is very useful in current job and workplace. Similarly more than one-fourth of them reported that strength of professional partnership is highly useful in current job and workplace. Likewise, more than one-half of them reported that ITI training is little/not at all useful in improving the confidence in work performance, higher progression in the same job and recognition of enhanced skills at the workplace. More than 40.0 percent of them reported that ITI training is little/not at all useful in professional development, higher mobility across jobs and enhancing the income prospects Table 46. All these needs to be taken carefully, while restructuring the programme and making the courses offered at ITI as more relevant and highly useful to the trainees as well as the employers.

Table 46

Overall Benefits of ITI Training to Current Job and Workplace

Overall Benefits of ITI Training	*Very Useful*	*Somewhat Useful*	Little/not *at all Usefull*	Total
Gained ideas/knowledge that is useful in job	106 (33.65)	89 (28.25)	120 (38.09)	315 (100)
Useful contacts during the study period	118 (37.46)	113 (35.87)	84 (26.67)	315 (100)
Strength of academic partnerships	121 (38.41)	96 (30.47)	98 (31.11)	315 (100)
Strength of professional partnerships	84 (26.67)	89 (28.25)	142 (45.08)	315 (100)
Improved confidence about performing work	74 (23.49)	82 (26.03)	159 (50.47)	315 (100)
Higher progression in the same job	63 (20.00)	92 (29.20)	160 (50.80)	315 (100)
Higher mobility across jobs	53 (16.82)	114 (36.19)	148 (46.98)	315 (100)
Higher income	62 (19.68)	106 (33.65)	147 (46.67)	315 (100)
Recognition for enhanced skills in organization	54 (17.14)	96 (30.47)	165 (52.38)	315 (100)
Relevance of enhanced skills to country's needs	78 (24.76)	107 (33.96)	130 (41.27)	315 (100)

(c) **Opinion Regarding Work in Ones Own Business/ Being Self-Employed:** The opinions of the self-employed ITI pass-outs were sought regarding work in own business/being self-employed. More than one-fourth of them opined that being self-employed achieve a relatively high status is completely applicable and more than one-fifth opined that it is applicable and somewhat applicable and rest of them opined that it is least applicable and not applicable. More than one-fifth and one-third of them respectively opined that being self-employed means working very long hours is completely applicable and applicable (see table 47). More than 45.0 percent of

Table 47
Opinions Regarding Work in Ones Own Business/Being Self-Employed

Opinions Regarding Work	*Completely applicable*	*Applicable*	*Somewhat applicable*	*Least applicable*	*Not applicable*	*Total*
Being self-employed achieve a relatively high	26 (28.26)	21 (22.83)	22 (23.91)	15 (16.30)	8 (8.69)	92 (100)
Being self-employed have very long working hours	21 (22.83)	36 (39.13)	19 (20.65)	9 (9.78)	7 (7.61)	92 (100)
Trainees establish their own business	-	-	47 (51.08)	25 (27.17)	20 (21.74)	92 (100)
Technical education doesn't prepare ITI pass outs sufficiently	15 (16.30)	28 (30.43)	21 (22.82)	18 (19.56)	10 (10.87)	92 (100)
Favourable long term job prospect exist	11 (11.95)	15 (16.30)	33 (35.87)	16 (17.39)	17 (18.48)	92 (100)

them opined that technical education alone does not prepare them sufficiently to take up self-employment and therefore long term job prospects does not exist in majority of the cases, which implies that a higher proportion of them should be ready to take up self-employment as a source of livelihood, instead of depending on regular labour market.

Thus, the prospective trainees should be motivated to venture in to self-employment in high proportion to ease the job opportunities.

(d) **Opinion Regarding Changes Needed to Improve Competitive Edge of IIT Pass Outs:** The opinion regarding the changes needed to improve the competitive edge of ITI pass outs were also ascertained from the respondents. A perusal of the data presented in Table 48 makes it evident that they have advocated the need to review and update the curriculum and syllabi, add more major subjects, upgrade facilities, limit the class size, impart the theory of technology, propagate the use of computers, tools, machines, drawings and written instruction to improve their competitive edge. They have also advocated the need to impart the theory and practice of equipment maintenance, skills in communication and teamwork, knowledge of labour laws and industrial relations, safer working practices, discipline and accuracy, employ competent faculty, provide faculty development programmes, and provide job placement. The responses were so varied that the data analysis poses a big challenge. However, the use of computers and engagement of competent faculty and faculty development programmes were emphasized across the districts significantly. More than three-fourth of the respondents across the districts have advocated the job placement to be provided by the respective ITIs, for which the faculty members should be trained to take the challenge effectively. There is need to forge suitable linkages with different line departments in the government sector and business firms/ organizations in private sector, who should provide placements to the ITI pass outs in their respective firms/organizations.

At present, the ITIs are not adhering the practice of job placement and the faculty and staff members are not trained in

Table 48
Opinion Regarding Changes Needed to Improve Competitive Edge of IIT Pass Outs

Changes Needed	*I*	*II*	*III*	*IV*	*V*	*VI*	*VII*	*VIII*	*IX*	*X*	*XI*	*XII*	*XIII*	*XIV*
Review and update the curriculum and syllabi	6 (42.8)	21 (56.7)	67 (63.8)	22 (61.1)	24 (61.5)	43 (53.7)	22 (40.7)	19 (48.7)	17 (40.5)	32 (57.1)	12 (54.5)	35 (56.4)	43 (40.1)	47 (45.6)
Add more major subjects	5 (35.7)	13 (35.1)	56 (53.3)	18 (50.0)	21 (53.8)	37 (46.3)	18 (33.3)	17 (43.6)	21 (50.0)	34 (60.7)	15 (68.2)	32 (51.6)	54 (50.5)	55 (53.4)
Upgrade facilities	7 (50.0)	15 (40.5)	43 (40.9)	16 (44.4)	16 (41.0)	29 (36.2)	14 (25.9)	14 (35.9)	16 (38.1)	29 (51.8)	9 (40.9)	28 (45.1)	36 (33.6)	65 (63.1)
Limit the class size	4 (28.6)	20 (54.0)	33 (31.4)	19 (52.8)	19 (48.7)	33 (41.3)	26 (48.1)	12 (30.8)	18 (42.8)	26 (46.2)	11 (50.0)	22 (35.5)	43 (40.2)	39 (37.8)
Theory of technology	5 (35.7)	19 (51.3)	52 (49.5)	21 (58.3)	25 (64:1)	39 (48.7)	24 (44.4)	16 (41.0)	15 (35.7)	21 (37.5)	13 (59.1)	18 (29.0)	39 (36.4)	44 (42.7)
Use of computers	7 (50.0)	23 (62.1)	43 (40.9)	24 (66.7)	17 (43.6)	43 (53.7)	19 (35.2)	21 (53.8)	19 (45.3)	32 (57.1)	10 (45.4)	21 (33.8)	39 (36.4)	38 (36.9)
Use of tools	8 (57.1)	18 (48.6)	38 (36.2)	14 (38.9)	28 (71.8)	33 (41.2)	22 (40.7)	26 (66.7)	21 (50.0)	26 (46.2)	81 (36.4)	4 (22.6)	37 (34.6)	38 (36.9)
Use of machines	6 (42.8)	15 (40.5)	37 (35.2)	13 (36.1)	21 (53.8)	37 (46.2)	13 (24.1)	14 (35.9)	16 (38.1)	23 (41.1)	8 (36.4)	16 (25.8)	33 (30.8)	33 (32.0)
Use of drawings	4 (28.6)	13 (35.1)	40 (38.1)	15 (41.7)	13 (33.3)	21 (26.2)	11 (20.4)	18 (46.1)	15 (35.7)	17 (30.3)	9 (40.9)	15 (24.2)	29 (27.1)	39 (37.8)
Use of written instructions	6 (42.8)	19 (513)	58 (55.2)	20 (55.5)	19 (23.1)	38 (47.5)	26 (48.1)	23 (58.9)	21 (50.0)	21 (37.5)	11 (50.0)	19 (30.6)	39 (36.4)	51 (49.5)

Contd....

Changes Needed	*I*	*II*	*III*	*IV*	*V*	*VI*	*VII*	*VIII*	*IX*	*X*	*XI*	*XII*	*XIII*	*XIV*
Theory and practice of equipment maintenance	8 (57.1)	22 (59.4)	62 (59.0)	14 (38.9)	22 (56.4)	41 (51.2)	29 (53.7)	20 (51.3)	23 (54.8)	28 (50.0)	13 (59.1)	22 (35.5)	46 (43.0)	37 (35.9)
Communication and teamwork	9 (64.3)	17 (45.9)	77 (73.3)	11 (30.5)	26 (66.7)	46 (57.5)	31 (57.4)	26 (66.7)	22 (52.4)	24 (42.8)	14 (63.6)	26 (41.9)	43 (40.1)	38 (36.8)
Knowledge of labour laws and industrial relations	7 (50.0)	24 (64.8)	52 (49.5)	16 (44.4)	17 (43.6)	40 (50.0)	22 (40.7)	20 (52.3)	14 (33.3)	33 (58.9)	12 (54.5)	30 (48.4)	51 (47.6)	44 (42.7)
Safer working practices	9 (64.3)	26 (70.3)	57 (54.3)	24 (66.7)	19 (23.1)	44 (55.0)	29 (53.7)	31 (79.5)	19 (45.2)	27 (48.2)	10 (45.4)	32 (51.6)	33 (30.4)	54 (52.4)
Discipline and accuracy	12 (85.7)	29 (78.4)	78 (74.3)	22 (61.1)	26 (66.7)	34 (42.5)	32 (59.2)	27 (69.2)	23 (54.8)	32 (57.1)	13 (59.1)	35 (56.4)	49 (45.8)	56 (54.4)
Employ competent faculty	10 (71.4)	22 (59.4)	59 (56.2)	10 (27.8)	14 (35.9)	22 (27.5)	30 (55.5)	18 (46.1)	19 (45.2)	22 (39.3)	8 (36.4)	22 (35.5)	35 (32.7)	23 (22.3)
Provide faculty development programmes	11 (78.6)	13 (35.1)	33 (31.4)	11 (30.5)	16 (41.0)	26 (32.5)	21 (38.9)	15 (38.5)	18 (42.8)	27 (48.2)	6 (27.3)	17 (27.4)	38 (35.5)	19 (18.4)
Provide job placement	11 (78.6)	33 (89.1)	92 (87.6)	31 (86.1)	35 (89.7)	72 (90.0)	49 (90.7)	34 (87.2)	36 (85.7)	50 (89.3)	19 (86.4)	53 (85.5)	94 (87.8)	96 (93.2)
Total	14 (100)	37 (100)	105 (100)	36 (100)	39 (100)	80 (100)	54 (100)	39 (100)	42 (100)	56 (100)	22 (100)	62 (100)	107 (100)	103 (100)

Note: Same as Table 1

performing the task of job placement. Therefore, there is need to forge suitable linkages with local institutions of higher learning for providing job placement training to the faculty and staff. One of the options could be that the Management Faculty in the local Universities may be contacted to impart a short-term course to the selected staff of the ITIs in job placement. In all the ITIs, there is need to create a job placement cell, which should devise the mechanism of job placement. In order to evaluate the performance of respective ITIs, there is need to add one more criterion of the number of placement made by them. The better performing ITIs should be given additional infrastructure development grants, which could act as a bait to perform well in job placement.

4

DEMAND ASSESSMENT OF INDUSTRIES

The training institutions provide skills that improve productivity at work. It is important to remember that training is not an instrument to create jobs or reduce unemployment. A supply of skilled labour does not automatically create its own demand. Skills' training is unlikely to lead to employment and productivity growth if job opportunities are not expanding. When macroeconomic policies allow the labour market to expand, then the returns on training will be high, whereas in the context of low demand by industrial units and enterprises, training and active labour market policies will have little effect on reducing unemployment. Training programmes should therefore be guided by the needs and demand of industrial units and enterprises and the labour market. Macroeconomic policies that ensure economic and job growth provide the best environment for relevant and effective training programmes. However, in Jammu and Kashmir, training programmes are still often determined by supply considerations, *i.e.* the existing, often inadequate, qualifications profile of trainers, out-of-date training equipment and materials and erroneous assumptions about where trainees will manage to find jobs upon completing their training. This often means irrelevant and ineffective training.

Making industrial training a demand driven exercise is a challenging task, as it requires a fundamental reorientation of training policies, *i.e.* changes in the objectives and governance structures of industrial training, putting up mechanisms of identifying industrial training needs and priorities, and creating a new ethos and introducing new management practises in individual industrial training institutions. It will also call for a sharing of the costs of industrial training based on the principle that those who benefit from industrial training should also contribute to covering its costs. A quick examination of the employment structure in industrial units in Jammu and Kashmir suggests that the public sector is at best a small and possibly declining source of jobs for labour force. The industrial and service sectors of the economy and in particular activities in the urban and rural informal sectors are absorbing more and more workers. The single most important challenge for the industrial training system and institutions is therefore to equip students with the skills and motivation to engage in industrial work and self-employment and viable informal types of economic activity.

TRAINING PRIORITIES AND NEEDS

In market economies, movements in wages and employment signal changes in the demand for and supply of particular industrial skills and trades. By capturing these signals, planners can identify shortages or gluts of particular industrial skills and plan training programmes accordingly. This requires some structures and skills for collecting, analysing and disseminating information on employment and labour market trends and signals. At present, these are missing or underdeveloped in Jammu and Kashmir.

(a) **In-Service Training Opportunities for Industrial Workers:** Being for the most part a school-based system with a strong academic bias, industrial training in Jammu and Kashmir is also pre-employment training, *i.e.* training young people who will subsequently look for their first job in the labour market. There is very little in-service industrial training for the already employed workforce. Many workers have had little formal education and industrial training, a situation that has been reinforced by the long-standing relative easy access to employment in the informal sector of the economy. The impact on enterprise productivity of targeted industrial training interventions among employed workers is likely to be significant. Another major challenge for the industrial training system is therefore to expand the range of in-service industrial training opportunities in institutions, industrial units and enterprises.

(b) **Financing Industrial Training:** Jammu and Kashmir under invests in training for work and most of it is being provided by public and private training institutions and paid directly, or through subsidies, by the state. Industrial units, enterprises and individuals, the main beneficiaries of industrial training, contribute very little. Under investment in training has much to do with traditional neglect of vocational education and industrial training in Jammu and Kashmir, individuals' preference for white-collar credentials and employers' underestimation of the value of skills and industrial training for improving company performance. In order to increase the supply of industrial training, new partners, especially the private and voluntary sector have to be solicited to contribute to its financing and provision. This calls for a system of incentives that would encourage other stakeholders than government, in particular industrial units and enterprises, to invest more in industrial training and so share the burden of supplying industrial skills needed in the economy of Jammu and Kashmir.

(c) **Governance Structure of Industrial Training:** If stakeholders other than the state are to increase their share in financing industrial training, than they must have a say in governing the industrial training system on an equal footing with government. Governance reform would also have to address this issue, for example by decentralising decision making regarding course content, management and resource mobilisation to individual industrial training institutions and so make industrial training more responsive to local labour market needs.

DEMAND FOR INDUSTRIAL TRAINING

A fundamental principle underlying any industrial training provision is that it should be linked to identifiable job opportunities in industrial units and enterprises or to appropriate small-scale activities that have the prospect of generating sustainable income. Hence, there is need to assess industrial training demand in both formal and informal sector activities. However, as comprehensive and reliable labour market information in Jammu and Kashmir is lacking at present, this section will give a quantitative picture of industrial training needs in industrial units and enterprises.

Demand analysis implies studying the labour market: analysing the size and composition of the labour force, the current employment situation and prospects, the nature and extent of labour market regulations and possible future trends. Demand analysis can be done by applying various instruments, including economic and social statistics, labour market information and signalling. As an example of the latter, by monitoring movements or changes in wages and vacancies, the relative demand and supply of people in various occupations and skill categories can be identified and used as guidance for expanding or contracting training programmes. Special surveys of the industrial units have been used to access industrial skill and training demand in companies and among occupations.

An important element of a training needs assessment is to determine whose needs should be assessed. Is the focus to be on the local or regional level, at the enterprise or individual level? Or are they best determined at the level of occupations and skills? Which sectors should receive priority in assessing training needs: the informal or the formal sector, the agricultural or the industrial sectors? The answers to these questions largely depend on the economic and social priorities and needs and ultimately on political decisions regarding where the industrial training effort should be focussed. Increasingly, there is much to commend assessments to be undertaken at the local, sectoral and enterprise levels and involving the relevant stakeholders in the process. The centralised manpower planning is today increasingly in disuse.

SMALL SCALE INDUSTRIAL SECTOR IN JAMMU AND KASHMIR

Industrialisation is one of the important segments of the Jammu and Kashmir economy. The small-scale sector plays an important role in accelerating industrial growth and economic growth. It has emerged as a dynamic and vibrant sector, which comprises of modern and traditional industrial units and covers a wide spectrum of industries broadly categorized as small, ancillary and tiny industrial units. It has contributed significantly to the overall growth of state gross domestic product as well as in terms of employment and export earnings. Despite numerous difficulties, the state of Jammu and Kashmir witnessed an industrial boom during 1977-1997. The number of registered small industrial units has increased from 6387 at the end of the 5th Plan to 39538 by the end of 1998 and increased further since then. The level of investment in small industrial units has also increased from Rs. 30 crores in 1985 to Rs. 330 crores in the beginning of the 1990s. However, the state of Jammu and Kashmir is facing insurgency for the last couple of years, which has affected the industrial investment and hampers the process of industrial development and generation of employment opportunities in industrial units. Besides, the industries in the state are confronted with problems of inadequate availability of capital, raw material, and poor infrastructure, which are contributing towards industrial sickness.

A perusal of the data given in Table 1 reveals that during ten-year period (1987-88 to 1997-98), the number of registered SSI units has increased by 170.23 per cent in the state of Jammu and Kashmir. Against this, the increase in employment is much slow and stands at 58.11 per cent and production has recorded a growth of 212.28 per cent. The increase in average wage is comparatively higher in rural areas (81.45 per cent) than urban areas (51.62 per cent) of the state. The number of industrial units engaged in job working has recorded a tremendous increase of 509.07 per cent, followed by manufacturing units. However, SSI units engaged in possessing, and repairing and servicing has declined by 65.26 per cent and 1.33 per cent respectively.

Table 1
Industrial Development in the State

Items	*1987-88**	*1997-98***	*% Change*
Registered SSI units (No.)	14631	39538	170.23
Employment (No.)	40655	64281	58.11
Production (Rs. in lakhs)	30309	94650	212.28
Average wage (Rural)	4400	8049	81.45
Average wage (Urban)	4680	7096	51.62
Units engaged in			
a. Manufacturing	4733 (52.12)	7510 (49.58)	58.67
b. Processing	927 (10.21)	606 (4.00)	-65.26
c. Job working	716 (7.88)	4361 (28.79)	509.07
d. Repairing & servicing	2704 (29.77)	2668 (17.61)	-1.33
e. Total	9080 (100.00)	15145 (100.00)	66.79

Note: *as per All India Census, and **as per State Census

The functional small-scale industries have generated an average employment of 4.24 persons per industrial units. Out of total employment generated, 44798 persons were employed on regular basis and 19483 were employed on contract basis. They have employed 3855 technically trained persons (6 per cent) and 33232 skilled persons (51.7 per cent) in 1997-98. The high level of employment has been provided by non-metallic product units followed by wooden products group, and hosiery Most of the SSI units were engaged in garments (20 per cent), wood products (13.82 per cent), repair and services (11.87 per cent), food products (11.60 per cent), metal products (10.77 per cent), textiles (5.20 per cent) and beverages (0.24 per cent) in 1997-98.

Out of 15145 functional units under different industrial groups in the state of Jammu and Kashmir, 7096 were located in urban areas, 8079 in rural areas and 743 were located in different Industrial Estates, which clearly reflects that a high proportion of the SSI units are concentrated in rural areas with greater scope of rural livelihood diversification. Ownership pattern determines the strength of the industrial units. The proprietary and limited companies firms are dominating the ownership of SSI units in the state. The schemes of employment generation have been instrumental in increasing the number of proprietary firms.

The total number of SSI units in the state of Jammu and Kashmir has increased from 43689 in 2001-02 to 46919 in 2004-05 recording an increase of 7.16 per cent, and the employment generated has increased from 193285 persons in 2001-02 to 209322 persons in 2004-05 recording an increase of 8.30 per cent. Seven districts viz. Anantnag, Jammu, Srinagar, Pulwama, Kupwara, Kargil and Badgam have shown the higher rate of increase in SSI units and six districts viz. Jammu, Leh, Pulwama, Kupwara, Kargil and Badgam have shown the higher rate of increase in employment than the state between 2001-02 and 2004-05. Five districts viz. Badgam, Kargil, Kupwara, Pulwama and Jammu show double-digit growth in SSI units and two districts viz. Kargil and Leh show double-digit growth in employment during 2001-02 to 2004-05 (see table 2).

The data presented in Table 3 makes it clear that the number of the producing SSI units in Industrial Estates of Jammu and Kashmir have declined from 351 in 1990-91 to 452 in 1999-2000 and further to 432 in 2001-02 and remained constant during 2002-03 and 2003-04 and then increased to 467 in 2004-05. The per centage decline was 28.77 during 1990-91 to 1999-2000, which clearly reflects the impact of on-going insurgency on the SSI units. A decline of 4.42 per cent has been recorded in SSI units functioning in Industrial Estates during 1999-2000 and 2001-02. However, with the introduction of more incentives and improvement in investment, the SSI units has increased by 8.10 per cent during 2003-04 and 2004-05, after remaining unchanged during 2001-02 to 2003-04. The data related to annual production

Table 2
Registered SSI Units and Employment (No./Persons)

District	2001-02		2002-03		2003-04		2004-05		2001-02 to 2004-05 (% Increase)	
	Units	Employment	Units	Employment	Units	Employment	Units	Employment	Units	Employment
Anantnag	3377	15166	3479	15540	3587	15954	3707	16374	9.77	7.96
Baramulla	3661	14326	3522	14522	3582	14764	3674	15112	0.36	5.48
Doda	1571	3665	1589	3712	1611	3783	1635	3854	4.07	5.16
Jammu	8950	53835	9123	55506	9291	57285	9468	58818	10.22	9.26
Kathua	4381	15304	4418	15540	4452	15856	4542	16390	3.67	7.10
Leh	876	2285	906	2404	916	2453	923	2539	5.36	11.12
Poonch	1429	3114	1468	3198	1495	3256	1529	3355	7.00	7.74
Rajouri	1245	3094	1259	3139	1272	3161	1292	3205	3.77	3.59
Srinagar	7871	38697	8105	39716	8355	40799	8606	41903	9.33	8.28
Udhampur	3531	9089	3605	9267	3668	9472	3698	9667	4.73	6.36
Pulwama	2066	9578	2117	9850	2175	10113	2276	10492	10.16	9.54
Kupwara	1390	4862	1460	5104	1499	5231	1534	5346	10.36	9.95
Kargil	527	1292	553	1369	572	1426	591	1494	12.14	15.63
Budgam	3014	18978	3097	19471	3197	19875	3343	20773	10.92	9.56
Total	43689	193285	44701	198338	45672	203428	46818	209322	7.16	8.30

Source: Directorate of Industries and Commerce

Table 3

SSI Units in Industrial Estates, Production and Employment (No.)

Particulars	*1980-81*	*1990-91*	*1999-00*	*2001-02*	*2002-03*	*2003-04*	*2004-05*
Functioning Units	224	351	452	432	432	432	467
Producing Units	204	351	452	432	432	432	467
Production (Annual/Rs. in Lakhs)	85.86	923	1462.50	32465.00	10674.71	10674.71	15922.00
Average Daily Employment	2513	2125	2136	4241	2636	2636	3102

Source: Directorate of Industries and Commerce

and average daily employment raises eyebrows, as it remained the same during two years (2002-03 and 2003-04) and declined by 67.12 per cent and 50.95 per cent and 37.61 per cent and 26.86 per cent respectively during 2001-02 to 2002-03 and 2001-02 to 2004-05.

PROFILE OF INDUSTRIAL UNITS

In the following paragraphs, district-wise analysis of the data collected on the various aspects of demand of industrial training from the organised industrial units has been presented, which includes ownership, activities, category, employment, product and services, and level of technology of the sample industrial units.

Table 4
Ownership of the Sample Industrial Units

District	*Proprietary*	*Partnership*	*Total*
Anantnag	18 (75.00)	6 (25.00)	24 (100)
Baramulla	12 (80.00)	3 (20.00)	15 (100)
Doda	8 (100.00)	-	8 (100)
Jammu	24 (77.42))	7 (22.58)	31 (100)
Kathua	13 (81.25)	3 (18.75)	16 (100)
Leh	7 (100.00)	-	7 (100)
Poonch	11 (100.00)	-	11 (100)
Rajouri	12 (100.00)	-	12 (100)
Srinagar	16 (84.21)	3 (15.79)	19 (100)
Udhampur	9 (81.81)	2 (18.19)	11 (100)
Pulwama	8 (72.72)	3 (27.28)	11 (100)
Kupwara	6 (100)	-	6 (100)
Kargil	6 (100)	-	6 (100)
Budgam	12 (75.00)	4 (25.00)	16 (100)
Total	162 (83.93)	31 (16.07))	193 (100)

(a) **Ownership of Industrial Units:** Out of 193 sample industrial units, 83.93 per cent and 16.07 per cent respectively were proprietary and partnership firms. A cursory glance at data given in Table 4 makes it evident that majority of the industrial units were proprietary firms and they were cent per cent in districts of Doda, Leh, Poonch, Rajouri, Kupwara and Kargil. Thus, partnership firms were non-existing the sample industrial units.

(b) **Activity of Industrial Units:** The sample industrial units were engaged in various activities such as manufacturing (21.24 percent), assembling (9.84 percent), processing (19.17), job working (27.46 percent), repairing (17.09 percent) and services (5.18 percent). Thus, higher proportions of industrial units were engaged in activities like job working followed by manufacturing, processing and repairing. The manufacturing units were found in all districts except Leh, Kargil and Badgam. Similarly assembling units were found in all districts except Doda, Leh, Poonch, Rajouri, Kupwara, Kargil and Badgam, and processing units were found in all districts except Kathua, Leh, Kupwara and Kargil. In the districts of Doda, Udhampur, Pulwama and Kupwara none of the sample industrial units was engaged in repairing activities and service units were concentrated in districts of Anantnag, Jammu, Kathua and Badgam. Thus, the sample industrial units were distributed across the districts but with wide variations in their location and concentration.

(c) **Category of Industrial Units:** Out of the sample industrial units, 68.91 per cent, 20.21 per cent, and 10.88 per cent were found in the category of SSI, ancillary and tiny units. Thus, SSI units were dominant. None of the tiny units were reported in Doda, Leh, Poonch, Udhampur, Kupwara, Kargil and Badgam, and the ancillary units were found in all the districts except Leh, Kupwara and Kargil. From the above it is not wrong to infer that in the districts of Leh, Kupwara and Kargil, all the industrial units were reportedly SSI units and their share across other districts stood at more than half.

Table 5
Activity of the Sample Industrial Units

District	*Manufacturing*	*Assembling*	*Processing*	*Job Working*	*Repairing*	*Service*	*Total*
Anantnag	6 (25.00)	3 (12.50)	4 (16.67)	6 (25.00)	4 (16.67)	1 (4.16)	24 (100)
Baramulla	3 (20.00)	2 (13.33)	4 (26.67)	4 (26.67)	2 (13.33)	-	15 (100)
Doda	4 (50.00)	-	2 (25.00)	2 (25.00)	-	-	8 (100)
Jammu	7 (22.58)	2 (6.45)	6 (19.35)	7 (22.58)	6 (19.35)	3 (9.67)	31 (100)
Kathua	3 (18.75)	2 (12.50)	-	3 (18.75)	5 (31.25)	3 (18.75)	16 (100)
Leh	-	-	-	4 (57.14)	3 (42.86)	-	7 (100)
Poonch	2 (18.18)	-	4 (36.36)	3 (27.28)	2 (18.18)	-	11 (100)
Rajouri	3 (25.00)	-	3 (25.00)	4 (33.33)	2 (16.67)	-	12 (100)
Srinagar	6 (31.57)	3 (15.78)	3 (15.78)	4 (21.05)	3 (15.78)	-	19 (100)
Udhampur	2 (18.18)	3 (27.28)	4 (36.36)	2 (18.18)	-	-	11 (100)
Pulwama	3 (27.28)	4 (36.36)	2 (18.18)	2 (18.18)	-	-	11 (100)
Kupwara	2 (33.33)	-	-	4 (66.67)	-	-	6 (100)
Kargil	-	-	-	4 (66.67)	2 (33.33)	-	6 (100)
Budgam	-	-	5 (31.25)	4 (25.00)	4 (25.00)	3 (18.75)	16 (100)
Total	41 (21.24)	19 (9.84)	37 (19.17)	53 (27.46)	33 (17.09)	10 (5.18)	193 (100)

Table 6
Category of Industrial Units

District	*SSI*	*Ancillary*	*Tiny*	*Total*
Anantnag	16 (66.67)	3 (12.50)	5 (20.83)	24 (100)
Baramulla	8 (53.33)	4 (26.67)	3 (20.00)	15 (100)
Doda	4 (50.00)	4 (50.00)	-	8 (100)
Jammu	19 (61.29)	6 (19.35)	6 (19.35)	31 (100)
Kathua	11 (68.75)	3 (18.75)	2 (12.50)	16 (100)
Leh	7 (100.00)	-	-	7 (100)
Poonch	8 (72.72)	3 (27.28)	-	11 (100)
Rajouri	7 (58.33)	4 (33.33)	1 (8.34)	12 (100)
Srinagar	13 (68.42)	4 (21.05)	2 (10.53)	19 (100)
Udhampur	9 (81.81)	2 (18.19)	-	11 (100)
Pulwama	7 (63.63)	2 (18.19)	2 (18.19)	11 (100)
Kupwara	6 (100.00)	-	-	6 (100)
Kargil	6 (100.00)	-	-	6 (100)
Budgam	12 (75.00)	4 (25.00)	-	16 (100)
Total	133 (68.91)	39 (20.21)	21 (10.88)	193 (100)

(d) **Employment of Skilled and Unskilled Workers:** The sample 193 industrial units employs 1461 workers, out of which 35.18 per cent, 37.57 per cent, 17.45 per cent and 9.79 per cent were technical, skilled, unskilled and other category workers respectively. In the districts of Jammu and Kashmir too, more or less the same pattern is noticed. For example, in district Anantnag, out of 168 workers, majority of them were skilled workers (40.47 percent) followed by technical workers (32.14 percent), whereas in district Baramulla, majority of them were technical workers (48.97 percent) followed by skilled workers (32.65 percent). Thus, the employability of the technically trained and skilled personnel is very high in the industrial units as compared to unskilled and other workers, and the potential for further absorption of such workers is high, if there is improvement in political scenario and consequent investment in industrial infrastructure by the government and private sector.

Table 7
Employment of Skilled and Unskilled Workers

District	*Technical*	*Skilled*	*Unskilled*	*Others*	*Total*
Anantnag	54 (32.14)	68 (40.47)	33 (19.64)	13 (7.73)	168 (100)
Baramulla	48 (48.97)	32 (32.65)	8 (8.16)	10 (10.20)	98 (100)
Doda	32 (43.24)	26 (35.13)	9 (12.16)	7 (9.46)	74 (100)
Jammu	73 (33.95)	106 (49.30)	26 (12.09)	10 (4.65)	215 (100)
Kathua	34 (36.95)	28 (30.43)	17 (18.48)	13 (14.13)	92 (100)
Leh	19 (28.35)	26 (38.81)	14 (20.89)	8 (11.94)	67 (100)
Poonch	24 (32.43)	29 (39.19)	11 (14.84)	10 (13.51)	74 (100)
Rajouri	34 (36.17)	34 (36.17)	15 (15.95)	11 (11.70)	94 (100)
Srinagar	38 (33.33)	39 (34.21)	23 (20.17)	14 (12.28)	114 (100)
Udhampur	36 (34.61)	32 (30.77)	28 (26.92)	8 (7.69)	104 (100)
Pulwama	31 (30.39)	37 (36.27)	24 (23.53)	10 (9.8)	102 (100)
Kupwara	23 (35.38)	22 (33.84)	11 (16.92)	9 (13.84)	65 (100)
Kargil	14 (24.13)	27 (46.55)	9 (15.52)	8 (13.79)	58 (100)
Budgam	54 (39.70)	43 (31.61)	27 (19.85)	12 (8.82)	136 (100)
Total	514 (35.18)	549 (37.57)	255 (17.45)	143 (9.79)	1461 (100)

(e) **Product and Services of the Industrial Units:** The data on product and services provided by the sample industrial units is presented in Table 8, which clearly

Table 8
Product and Services of the Industrial Units

Description	*Proprietary*	*Partnership*	*Total*
Food Products	32 (88.89)	4 (11.11)	36 (100)
Beverages	17 (77.27)	5 (22.73)	22 (100)
Wool and Silk	11 (100.00)	-	11 (100)
Hosiery and Garments	23 (79.31)	6 (20.69)	29 (100)
Paper Products & Printing	12 (100.00)	-	12 (100)
Plastic Products	14 (66.67)	7 (33.33)	21 (100)
Chemical Products	6 (66.67)	3 (33.33)	9 (100)
Metal Products	9 (100.00)	-	9 (100)
Machinery Parts	4 (100.00)	-	4 (100)
Other Manufacturing	34 (85.00)	6 (15.00)	40 (100)
Total	162 (83.93)	31 (16.06)	193 (100)

reveals that manufacturing is dominant activities followed by food products, hosiery and garments, beverages, plastic products and wool and silk products in the proprietary firms and manufacturing of plastic products and hosiery and garments products are dominant activities in partnership firms.

(f) **Technology Level of the Industrial Units:** The technology levei of the industrial units was reportedly mix one and there was use of simple hand tools, machine-driven tools, powered hand tools, besides the use of automatic machineries. The machine-driven tools were used by all the industrial engaged in manufacturing food products, beverages, paper products and printing, plastic products and machinery parts. All industrial units engaged in beverages, plastic products, chemical products, and machinery parts were using automatic machinery (See Table 9). Besides, they also used simple hand tools and powered hand tools.

Table 9
Technology Level of the Industrial Units

Description	*Simple Hand Tools*	*Machine-Driven Equipment*	*Powered Hand Tools*	*Automatic Machinery*	*Total Units in Operation*
Food Products	27 (75.00)	36 (100.00)	21 (58.33)	24 (66.67)	36 (100)
Beverages	18 (81.82)	22 (100.00)	11 (50.00)	22 (100.00)	22 (100)
Wool and Silk	11 (100.00)	4 (36.36)	-	-	11(100)
Hosiery and Garments	27 (93.10)	23 (79.31)	6 (20.68)	23 (79.31)	29(100)
Paper Products & Printing	12 (100.00)	12 (100.00)	4 (33.33)	9 (75.00)	12(100)
Plastic Products	18 (85.71)	21 (100.00)	6 (28.57)	21 (100.00)	21(100)
Chemical Products	-	9 (100.00)	-	9 (100.00)	9 (100)
Metal Products	9 (100.00)	3 (33.33)	5 (55.55)	-	9 (100)
Machinery Parts	4 (100.00)	4 (100.00)	4 (100.00)	4 (100.00)	4 (100)
Other Manufacturing	36 (90.00)	27 (67.50)	23 (57.50)	13 (32.50)	40 (100)

CONSIDERATION OF TECHNICAL QUALIFICATIONS IN RECRUITMENT

In the following paragraphs, an attempt has been made to analyze the data on the type of technical qualifications considered in recruiting new employees, rating of the courses/ trades offered by ITIs, other qualifications required in recruiting new employees, recruitment of technically trained workers in the past, sources of new technically trained workers' recruitment, opinion regarding new technically trained worker's recruitment, provision of additional training after new worker's recruitment, reasons for additional training after worker's recruitment, rating of skill levels of workers recruited from ITIs, type of technical trained workers with better job prospects, and perceptions regarding lack of knowledge and skill by ITI pass outs.

(a) **Technology Level of the Industrial Units:** The industrial training in the course/trades of electronic mechanic, turner, and welder was considered very significantly in recruiting new employees followed

Table 10
Type of Technical Qualifications Considered in Recruiting New Employees

Technical Qualification	*Proprietary*	*Partnership*	*Total*
Electrician	13 (86.67)	2 (13.33)	15 (100)
Instrument Mechanic	23 (85.18)	4 (14.81)	27 (100)
Electronic Mechanic	16 (100.00)	-	16 (100)
Fitter	13 (76.47)	4 (23.53)	17 (100)
Turner	16 (100.00)	-	16 (100)
Welder	9 (100.00)	-	9 (100)
Machinist	19 (82.61)	4 (17.39)	23 (100)
Motor Mechanic	11 (73.33)	4 (26.67)	15 (100)
Stenography	7 (70.00)	3 (30.00)	10 (100)
Diesel Mechanic	14 (87.50)	2 (12.50)	16 (100)
Computer Operator	13 (72.22)	5 (27.78)	18 (100)
Information Technology	8 (72.72)	3 (27.28)	11 (100)
Total Units in Operation	162 (83.94)	31 (16.06)	193 (100)

by diesel mechanic, electrician, instrument mechanic and machinist by the proprietary firms. Other courses/trades such as fitter, motor mechanic, computer operator, information technology, and stenography were also considered significantly high in recruiting new employees. The courses/trades of computer operator, information technology, stenography, motor mechanic and fitter were considered by about one-fourth of partnership firms in recruiting new employees (See Table 10).

(b) **Rating of Technical Qualifications in Recruiting New Employees:** The course/trade of electrician was rated very high and high by one-third and one-fifth of the industrial units respectively in recruiting new employees and 40.0 per cent and 6.67 per cent of the industrial units respectively in recruiting new employees. One-fourth and one-fifth of them rated the course/trade of instrument mechanic as very high, high and low in recruiting new employees (See Table 11). The course/trade of electronic mechanic was rated high and middle by one-fourth of them and 31.25 per cent and 18.75 per cent of them rated it middle high and low respectively in recruiting new employees. Besides, the courses/trades like machinist and motor mechanic were also rated very high in recruiting new employees and computer operator and information technology were also rated high and middle high by 33.33 per cent and 44.44 per cent, and 36.36 per cent and 54.54 per cent respectively in recruiting new employees. It is significant to note that none of them rated the courses/trades of electrician, fitter, welder, machinist, motor mechanic, computer operator and information technology as low, which implies that these courses/trades needs to be propagated more and their course curriculum and programmes should be restructured to cater to the demand of the industrial units and make them more competitive.

Table 11
Rating of Type of Technical Qualifications in Recruiting New Employees

Technical Qualification	*Very high*	*High*	*Middle high*	*Middle*	*Low*	*Total*
Electrician	5 (33.33)	3 (20.00)	6 (40.00)	1 (6.67)	-	15 (100)
Instrument Mechanic	7 (25.92)	6 (22.22)	5 (18.51)	3 (11.11)	6 (22.22)	27 (100)
Electronic Mechanic	-	4 (25.00)	5 (31.25)	4 (25.00)	3 (18.75)	16 (100)
Fitter	-	6 (35.29)	7 (41.17)	4 (23.53)	-	17 (100)
Turner	-	5 (31.25)	3 (18.75)	4 (25.00)	4 (25.00)	16 (100)
Welder	-	-	4 (44.44)	5 (55.56)	-	9 (100)
Machinist	6 (26.08)	5 (21.74)	7 (30.43)	5 (21.74)	-	23 (100)
Motor Mechanic	3 (20.00)	-	8 (53.33)	4 (26.67)	-	15 (100)
Stenography	-	-	4 (40.00)	3 (30.00)	3 (30.00)	10 (100)
Diesel Mechanic	-	-	-	9 (56.25)	7 (43.75)	16 (100)
Computer Operator	-	6 (33.33)	8 (44.44)	4 (22.22)	-	18 (100)
Information Technology	-	4 (36.36)	6 (54.54)	1 (9.10)	-	11 (100)
Total Units in Operation	21 (10.88)	39 (20.21)	63 (32.64)	47 (24.35)	23 (11.91)	193 (100)

(c) **Main Consideration of Qualifications in Recruiting New Employees:** From the 193 sample industrial units, the main considerations of qualifications in recruiting new employees such as professionals/ managers, technicians, clerks and related workers, sales & service workers, craft & related workers, machine operators and low skilled workers were ascertained and they had reported educational certificates, vocational training certificates, experience, recommendations from employees/ employers, and recommendations from referees as the basis for new recruitment with varying degree of importance. 43.0 per cent of the industrial units have reported that educational certificates as the main considerations and 29.01 per cent of them reported experience as the main consideration in recruiting in professionals/managers, while recruiting new technicians, 39.38 per cent and 36.27

Table 12

Main Consideration of Qualifications in Recruiting New Employees

Type of Jobs *Qualifications*	*A*	*B*	*C*	*D*	*E*
Professionals/Managers	83	22	56	14	18
	(43.00)	(11.40)	(29.01)	(7.25)	(9.32)
Technicians	25	76	70	10	12
	(12.95)	(39.38)	(36.27)	(5.18)	(6.22)
Clerks and related workers	95	16	54	18	10
	(49.22)	(8.29)	(27.97)	(9.32)	(5.18)
Sales & Service Workers	29	80	48	24	12
	(15.02)	(41.45)	(24.87)	(12.43)	(6.21)
Craft & Related Workers	13	44	100	16	20
	(6.73)	(22.79)	(51.81)	(8.29)	(10.36)
Machine Operators	24	104	39	10	16
	(12.43)	(53.88)	(20.20)	(5.18)	(6.29)
Low Skilled Workers	12	17	113	26	25
	(6.21)	(8.80)	(58.54)	(13.47)	(12.95)

Note: A - Educational certificates,
B - Vocational training certificates,
C - Experience,
D - Recommendations from employees/employers,
E - Recommendations from referes
The responses given are out of the total sample units in operation *i.e.* 193.

per cent of them gave main importance to vocational training certificates and experience respectively. Similarly, 49.22 per cent and 27.97 per cent of them respectively gave main importance to educational certificates and experience and 41.45 per cent and 24.87 per cent, 22.79 per cent and 51.81 per cent, and 53.88 per cent and 20.20 per cent of the industrial units respectively gave main importance to vocational training certificates and experience in recruiting new sales & service workers, craft & related workers, and machine operators, whereas in recruiting new low skilled workers the main consideration was experience, recommendations from the employees/employers and referees. Thus, one can infer that technical qualifications and experience was the main considerations in recruiting new technicians and technically trained workers, whereas in recruiting the low skilled workers, the main consideration was experience and recommendations from employers/employees and referees.

(d) **Recruitment of Technically Trained Workers in Past:** The data on recruitment of technically trained workers in the past, their sources of recruitment, and opinions regarding them and provision for additional training and reasons there of is presented in Tables 13, 14, 15, 16 and 17. About 75 industrial units have recruited technically trained workers in recent past, out of which majority of them were recruited by SSI units (42.10 percent), followed by ancillary units (33.33 percent) and tiny units (28.57 percent). Thus, SSI units have recruited significantly the technically trained workers in the past.

It is significant to note that out of 56 SSI units, which have recruited technically trained workers, 76.36 per cent of them were ITI pass outs, whereas the pass outs of the vocational training institutes have also been recruited by SSI units (57.14 percent), ancillary units (28.57 percent) and tiny units (14.28 percent). Out of the 75 industrial units, which have recruited new technically trained workers, 72.0 per cent have reported their performance as satisfactory and the highest level of satisfaction has been reported for technical level and craft and related workers. 34 industrial units have the provision of additional training after new worker's recruitment to expose them to the work atmosphere. The data shown in table 16 makes it clear that about half of the tiny and ancillary units and 42.86 per cent of the SSI units gave gone for additional training to newly recruit technical workers.

They have given varied reasons for additional training after worker's recruitment, which includes lack of relevant theoretical knowledge, lack of adequate practical/application skills, lack of proper attitudes, values, work ethics, and to provide firm-specific training. It is significant to note that a majority of them reported lack of adequate practical/application skills followed by lack of proper attitudes, values and work ethics on the part of newly recruits, which needs to be taken care of at the ITIs itself during their trainings by making appropriate provision for practical training and application skills and imbibing in them the proper attitudes, values and work ethics, so that their employability and competitiveness can be enhanced in labour market.

Table 13

Recruitment of Technically Trained Workers in Past

Type of Unit	*Yes*	*No*	*Total*
SSI	56 (42.10)	77 (57.59)	133 (100)
Ancillary	13 (33.33)	26 (66.67)	39 (100)
Tiny	6 (28.57)	15 (71.43)	21 (100)
Total	75 (38.86)	118 (61.13)	193 (100)

Table 14

Sources of New Technically Trained Workers' Recruitment

Sources	*SSI*	*Ancillary*	*Tiny*	*Total*
Industrial Training Institute	42 (76.36)	9 (16.36)	4 (7.27)	55 (100)
Polytechnic	3 (100.00)	-	-	3 (100)
Engineering Colleges	3 (100.00)	-	-	3 (100)
Vocational Training Institute	8 (57.14)	4 (28.57)	2 (14.28)	14 (100)
Total	56 (74.67)	13 (17.77)	6 (8.00)	75 (100)

Table 15
Opinion Regarding New Technically Trained Worker's Recruitment

Level of Recruitment	*Satisfactory*	*Unsatisfactory*	*Total*
Technical level	28 (75.67)	9 (24.32)	37 (100)
Clerks and related workers	7 (63.63)	4 (36.36)	11 (100)
Sales & Service Workers	9 (69.23)	4 (30.77)	13 (100)
Craft & Related Workers	6 (75.00)	2 (25.00)	8 (100)
Low Skilled workers	4 (66.67)	2 (33.33)	6 (100)
Total	54 (72.00)	21 (28.00)	75 (100)

Table 16
Provision of Additional Training After New Worker's Recruitment

Type of Unit	*Yes*	*No*	*Total*
SSI	24 (42.86)	32 (57.14)	56 (100)
Ancillary	7 (53.84)	6 (46.15)	13 (100)
Tiny	3 (50.00)	3 (50.00)	6 (100)
Total	34 (45.33)	41 (54.67)	75 (100)

Table 17
Reasons for Additional Training After Worker's Recruitment

Reasons	*SSI*	*Ancillary*	*Tiny*	*Total*
Lack of relevant theoretical knowledge	6 (100.00)	-	-	6 (100)
Lack of adequate practical/application skills	9 (64.28)	5 (35.72)	-	14 (100)
Lack of proper attitudes, values, work ethics	6 (75.00)	2 (25.00)	-	8 (100)
To provide firm-specific training	3 (100.00)	-	3 (100.00)	6 (100)
Total	24 (70.58)	7 (20.58)	3 (8.82)	34 (100)

(e) **Rating and Perceptions of Skill Levels of Workers Recruited from ITIs:** The data regarding rating of skill levels of workers recruited from ITIs are presented in Table 18. It evident that out of 55 industrial units, who have recently employed ITI pass outs, 61.82 per cent rated the ITI pass outs better than those school leavers who have acquired skills on-the-job in the firm, 23.64 per cent and 14.55 per cent respectively rated ITI pass outs as good as good as those school leavers who have acquired skills on-the-job in the firm, and not as good as the school leavers who have acquired skills on-the-job in the firm. At the same time, majority of the SSI units have also rated the recently ITI pass outs better than those school leavers who have acquired skills on-the-job in the firm.

Table 18
Rating of Skill Levels of Workers Recruited from ITIs

Rating of Workers	*SSI*	*Ancillary*	*Tiny*	*Total*
Better than those school leavers who have acquired skills on-the-job in the firm	26 (76.47)	6 (17.64)	2 (5.88)	34 (61.82)
As good as those school leavers who have acquired skills on-the-job in the firm	8 (61.54)	3 (23.07)	2 (15.38)	13 (23.64)
Not as good as the school leavers who have acquired skills on-the-job in the firm	8 (100.00)	-	-	8 (14.55)
Total	42 (76.36)	9 (16.36)	4 (7.28)	55 (100)

The data on the perceptions regarding lack of knowledge and skill of ITI pass outs is given in Table 19. A perusal of the Table 19 makes it evident that more than one-third of the SSI units perceived lack of knowledge and skill in the use of computers and drawings, communication and teamwork practices and knowledge of labour laws and industrial relations, more than one-fifth perceived lack of knowledge and skill in discipline and accuracy, theory and practice of equipment maintenance and safer working practices and less than one-fifth perceived lack of knowledge and skill in theory of technology and use of tools, machines and written instructions. The data related to perception of ancillary and tiny units also reveals more or less the same picture with variations across responses and level of perceptions. Thus, it is not wrong to infer that there is need to put more attention on the perceived lack of knowledge and skill in aforementioned areas to improve their competitive edge and performance in job market.

Table 19
Perceptions Regarding Lack of Knowledge and Skill of ITI Pass Outs

Knowledge and Skill	*SSI*	*Ancillary*	*Tiny*
Theory of technology	23 (17.29)	9 (23.07)	7 (33.33)
Discipline and accuracy	28 (21.05)	11 (28.20)	6 (28.57)
Use of computers	58 (43.60)	13 (33.33)	9 (42.85)
Use of tools	23 (17.29)	3 (7.69)	4 (19.04)
Use of machines	18 (13.53)	5 (12.82)	6 (28.57)
Use of drawings	34 (25.56)	9 (23.07)	8 (38.09)
Use of written instructions	22 (16.54)	14 (35.89)	11 (52.38)
Theory and practice of equipment maintenance	29 (21.80)	16 (41.02)	8 (38.09)
Communication and teamwork practices	43 (32.33)	14 (35.89)	9 (42.85)
Knowledge of labour laws and industrial relations	48 (36.09)	13 (33.33)	14 (66.67)
Safer working practices	33 (24.81)	8 (20.51)	7 (33.33)
Total Sample Units in Operation	133 (100.00)	39 (100.00)	21 (100.00)

Table 20
Type of Technically Trained Workers with Better Job Prospects

Criteria	*Type of Technically Trained Workers* 1	2	3	4	5
Monthly income/earnings	42 (21.76)	36 (18.65)	18 (9.33)	17 (8.81)	80 (41.45)
Promotions	72 (37.30)	74 (38.34)	13 (6.7)	10 (5.18)	24 (12.43)
Permanent long-term employment	36 (18.65)	34 (17.61)	10 (5.18)	18 (9.32)	95 (49.22)
Career progression	60 (31.00)	48 (24.87)	12 (6.21)	24 (12.43)	49 (25.38)

Note: 1. Workers with sound secondary educational qualifications and institutional / technical/ vocational training qualifications,
2. Workers with incomplete secondary education and vocational training qualifications,

3. Workers with incomplete secondary education but with long years of experience,
4. Workers with sound secondary educational qualifications and on-the-job training in the firm, 5 - Workers who have followed apprenticeship training.

The responses given are out of the total sample units in operation *i.e* 193.

Lastly, the data on the perceptions of the industrial units were ascertained to know the types of technically trained workers with better job prospects and the same is presented in Table 20. The technically trained workers who have followed apprenticeship training and sound secondary educational qualifications and institutional/vocational training, and incomplete secondary education but with vocational training has better income prospects than the workers with incomplete secondary education but with long years of experience, and the workers with sound secondary educational qualifications and on-the-job training in the firm. Similarly, the technically trained workers with sound and incomplete secondary but with vocational and technical training have better promotion prospects than other types of workers mentioned in table 20. However, the workers with apprenticeship training, and sound secondary qualifications respectively have better prospects for long-term permanent employment and smooth career progression. One thing which is quite clear that secondary qualifications may or may not significant in industrial jobs and not a potent qualification in better job prospects than better technical and apprenticeship training and this should be given due weight-age, while admitting the prospective trainees in ITIs.

To conclude, it is not wrong to say that the ITIs have played a considerable role in producing a skilled workforce for the organized economy. Our surveys of sample industrial units revealed that a significant proportion of all employees and skilled workers have been trained in the ITIs. The economic situation has been changing rapidly in the state of Jammu and Kashmir and the state is recovering from the insurgency and political turmoil. It is expected that both government sector and private sector industrial enterprises will have better employment opportunities with improved investment climate. At the same time, the self-employed and unorganized sector has more employment potential, which needs to be propagated by the relevant agencies. The potential of unorganized sector needs to be tapped in a significant manner by introducing new guidelines and policies. The SSI units and proprietary firms therein have recruited more workers in recent past than the ancillary and tiny units and the partnership firms.

The employment scenario of ITI pass outs raises the issue of relevance of training courses to the current situation in the local labour markets. Most of the ITIs continue to focus on producing basic industrial skills, such as fitters, welders, etc., that are long-term and orientated towards formal employment. Given the current employment environment, the course structures and programmes should be reviewed to improve the job success of the ITI pass outs. The current courses/trades offered by ITIs provided very little job opportunity, if any. The new courses/trades that could be relevant to the local labour markets needs to be introduced, which may includes auto mechanic, AC and refrigerator mechanic, handicraft and handloom weaving, multi-skilled fabricator, etc. Besides, courses/trades in travel, tourism and hospitability, sales and service, hotel and catering, etc. needs to be introduced. At the same time, the duration of the training programmes remains a major problem as a majority of young people look for shorter courses that more flexibly reflect job possibilities, which needs to be given due consideration of the relevant authorities.

The industrial units do not consider the ITI pass outs as suitable for immediate employment. They gave more preference to the ITI pass out with apprenticeship training or prefer to apprentices and train them for few months after which they may be considered fit for regular employment. Therefore the total period of skills training involving the ITI-based as well as on-the-job may amount to three-four years, which is quite long period of time, ending up with small salaries. Therefore, self - employment could be a much shorter way to enter the labour market. The combined duration of ITI-based training and of apprenticeship also suggests that the courses/trades offered by the ITIs are extremely long and generate very few incentives for young people to invest in training. Thus, there is need to rationalise the duration of training and apprenticeship and their content enabling integration of ITI courses/trades with apprenticeships and the total duration of ITI-based training plus apprenticeship should be within two to three years, which should lead to the skilled worker qualification. Further, it seems that the programming of ITI courses is done at the state level, which is not based on the assessed potential demand for skills and results in mismatch between local demand and supply of the skills. The concerned authorities have not conducted assessment of the labour market to monitor training demand and ITI pass outs potentiality and employability in labour market success has not been made due to which the ITI courses continue to have only far-fetched links with local labour markets. For example, the courses such as electronic mechanics suitable for advanced industries located in urban areas are conducted in ITIs located in semi-rural areas.

On the whole, the mismatch between demand and supply of ITI pass outs may only be corrected through conduct of regular surveys and studies of both organized and unorganized sectors as well as of the ITI pass outs' labour market destinations and making judgments on the best mix of training courses/ trades. The more accurate planning of training would require knowledge of the occupational structures of the unorganized economy and of the role of training institutes in supplying the workforce to it. The observed mismatch is aggravated by factors such as shortage of funds for replacing/introducing training programmes and low staffing flexibility because ITI teaching staff are civil servants who cannot be easily moved or replaced by other instructors needed for implementing new training courses. Besides above, the major role in identifying demand for skills and implementing planning of training should be assigned to the ITIs themselves and they should be given greater autonomy and offered considerable incentives for achieving better results.

5

DEMAND ASSESSMENT OF PROSPECTIVE TRAINEES

The issues of youth unemployment and underemployment have come to the forefront in recent years. The unemployment and underemployment figures for young people are staggering. Education and training are important means of addressing youth employability. This chapter seeks to address the demand assessment of prospective trainees and issue of skills development for youth-at-risk, including the economically vulnerable and the socially excluded. A micro-level approach is used to identify training programmes and skills demanded by prospective vulnerable young women and men. Almost everywhere, not only in developing states like Jammu and Kashmir, but also in other states, there is a tendency toward the informalisation of the economy. The informal economy has been able to absorb large numbers of unemployed and underemployed persons and it has been a primary generator of jobs.

Youth unemployment and underemployment impose a heavy cost upon individuals, employers, government and societies. Unemployment in early life may permanently impair employability and the patterns of behaviour and attitudes established at an early stage persist later in life. For employers, youth unemployment means that young people have less to spend on their products and services, and their personal savings that would be invested in product consumption are reduced, resulting in loss of production for enterprises. For the government, youth unemployment means they have a reduced taxation base and higher social welfare costs, that investments in education and training are wasted, and that their voter support among young people is weak. Moreover, rising unemployment levels among youth may be a source of social instability, increased drug abuse and crime.

YOUTH UNEMPLOYMENT AND UNDEREMPLOYMENT

In the following paragraphs, an attempt has been made to explain some of the reasons why youth, generally, are at greater risk of unemployment and underemployment. It covers such things as work experience, economic considerations, lack of understanding and/or appreciation of the value of young people and perceptions of youth. An examination of the factors that affect the employability of disadvantaged youth helps us to understand the sources of social exclusion of many young women and men. The mainstream education and training is an important component of a strategy to promote employability. Developing young people's employability is central to ensuring their successful transition to the labour market and their access to career-oriented employment. Youth need to acquire the skills, knowledge, competencies and attitudes that will allow them to find work and to cope with an unpredictable labour market.

Majority of young people live in rural areas where many are especially vulnerable to extreme poverty and working long hours for low pay, struggling to survive in the informal economy. A significant proportion of young people between 15 and 17 years of age are engaged in hazardous forms of work. Young people actively seeking to participate in work are more than older generations seeking employment. Decent and productive work is an unfulfilled aspiration of many young people.

There is need for a commitment to develop and implement strategies for decent and productive work for youth, recognising that it is a significant problem, with implications for persistent poverty, job instability, and social exclusion. Youth poverty and exclusion are widespread and increasing. Inadequate, insufficient and/or inappropriate education, training and employment, lack of assets, property rights and access to credit and lack of decision-making opportunities exacerbate the social and economic vulnerability of youth, generally. The vulnerability of disadvantaged youth is even greater. Investing in youth is an urgent matter; appropriate policies and programmes must be established and adequate resources allocated in order to address this issue.

Unemployment at the onset of one's working life can lead to serious problems. Lack of employment lowers household income and blocks the crucial development of skills, which come from work experience and on-the-job training. Early workplace skill development is crucial to future earnings growth and unemployment early in working life increases the probability of future joblessness. Evidence has shown that early unemployment can permanently affect future employability. Gaining employment is particularly difficult for already poor and socially excluded youth. For those employed, much of that work is in the informal economy under precarious conditions and low pay. The vast majority of the youth work in the informal economy. The decline of the formal economy, accompanied by decreased public or family income support means jobless young people are increasingly forced to find work in the informal economy.

It is important to note that almost everywhere, not only in state of Jammu and Kashmir, but also in other states, there is a tendency to the informalization of the economy. The informal economy has been able to absorb large numbers of unemployed and underemployed persons and it has been a primary generator of jobs. As such, it has often contributed to a minimum of social cohesion; social safety nets have been either nonexistent or not functioning properly. In Jammu region, displaced workers and migrants compose the bulk of informal labour. Most youth working in the informal economy lack adequate incomes, social protection, security and representation. In a vicious cycle, poorly productive enterprises, low incomes and inadequate working conditions interact to undermine enterprise competitiveness, which in turn undermines the capability to provide decent employment conditions. If current trends continue, it is likely that most of the jobs available to young people in the future will be low paid and of poor quality.

Recognising the concentration of women in the informal economy, many government schemes and NGOs have focused on income-generation activities. Characterized by more emphasis on credit provision and group formation than on skill training provision, such interventions are generally based on the assumption that women are supplementing the family income. The interventions in this area are usually aimed at providing them with skills not for profit but for survival. This disregards the fact that women are often the sole or major earners, increasingly so with the growing number of female-headed households. Run by small organizations with limited staff and resources, the training courses provided tend to be of poor quality. Additionally, such courses are often in gender-stereotyped skills, such as sewing or cooking, which do not lead into profitable areas of work. Functional adult literacy courses have also been accompanied by small-scale vocational training, usually for women, and often attract similar criticisms.

Underemployment is typically categorised into visible and invisible underemployment, where the former consists of work of inadequate duration, *i.e.*, both involuntary part-time employment and temporary short-term work, while the latter encompasses work of inadequate productivity. Attention tends to focus on visible underemployment rather than "inadequate" productivity. The large numbers of youth are underemployed, working fewer hours than they would like. Young people may be able to obtain only part-time work, as is often the case particularly among young women and underemployment is also high among many young men who work in the household production unit in the rural and urban informal economy.

There is a serious lack of data and information on unemployment and underemployment rates for disadvantaged youth. This partially reflects the range of vulnerabilities some youth face, resulting from discrimination, economic hardship or geographic location, for example. It also reflects societal norms about assessing which youth can work. Often people with disabilities, for example, are classified as "unable to work" and are placed in a category of those in need of social protection. The number of "disadvantaged young people with employment problems" greatly exceeds the number of "young unemployed". Yet, in most cases, policies are not aimed at those most disadvantaged because they constitute a minority and, therefore, are not cost-effective. The most socially disadvantaged youth generally experience more problems obtaining employment. They are less likely to obtain good basic education, and are often discriminated against on the basis of social class, ethnic origin, gender, disability, etc. Poor young people are even more prone to unemployment, and particularly to inactivity. In several villages, youth joblessness is more and more concentrated in households in which no member is employed.

Thus, youth face greater barriers in accessing the labour market; the magnitude of the youth unemployment and underemployment problem is very clear. There is concrete evidence of the impact of double discrimination in case of young female. Being young and being female means facing multiple hurdles in making the transition from school to work. Poor youth are also ignored in mainstream development thinking and action. In addition to the problems faced by youth in mainstream development strategies, they have a second burden of poverty, which gives them fewer choices. Poor young women have a triple burden. Rural youth constitute approximately more than half of the young people. With increasing industrialisation, rural areas have experienced a decline in employment opportunities. Young people face difficulties in sustaining jobs in traditional agricultural sectors and in gaining access to education and training. Many groups of young people are more likely to suffer higher unemployment and underemployment rates due to the nature of their circumstances. These disadvantaged youth must be given more choices, more opportunities for education, skills training, micro credit and more effort must be made to address these issues.

II. PROFILE OF PROSPECTIVE TRAINEES

In the following paragraphs, the profile of the sample prospective trainees has been given, which includes the age, sex ratio, marital status, educational status and educational status of their fathers and mothers. This information is useful in examining their training and skill needs assessment.

(a) **Age, Sex and Marital Status:** The data presented in Tables 1, 2 and 3 respectively gives the age, sex and marital status of the sample prospective trainees. A perusal of the data in table 1 reveals that 43.1 percent, 26.57 percent, 22.0 percent and 8.3 percent of the prospective trainees were found in the age group of below 20 years, between 20-25 years, between 25-30 years and above 30 years of age. It is significant to note that a significant proportion of the respondents in the age group more than 25 years have already undergone through some informal apprenticeship training and shown their desire to upgrade the skills they possess. The district level analysis of the data presented in table 1 also makes it evident that a majority of the respondents were below the age of 25 years. In district Doda, 48.0 percent of them were found in the age group of 25-30 years, which reveals that youth population in the upper ages are also in need of getting technical training and/or desire to upgrade the skill possessed by them.

More than two-third and less than one-third of the sample prospective trainees respectively were males and females. However, in the districts of Badgam, Doda, Poonch, Rajouri, and Jammu, more than one-third of them were females, whereas in districts of Kupwara, Baramulla, Anantnag, Kargil, and Leh, their proportion was less than one-third. It is significant to note that in the districts of Baramulla, Anantnag, and Leh, more the three-fourth of them were males (See table 2). Thus, the training

Table 1

District-wise Distribution of Prospective ITI Trainees by Age

Age Years	*I*	*II*	*III*	*IV*	*V*	*VI*	*VII*	*VIII*	*IX*	*X*	*XI*	*XII*	*XIII*	*XIV*	*Total*
< 20	16	13	11	9	8	10	12	8	7	13	11	14	10	9	151
	(64.0)	(52.0)	(44.0)	(36.0)	(32.0)	(40.0)	(48.0)	(32.0)	(28.0)	(52.0)	(44.0)	(56.0)	(40.0)	(36.0)	(43.1)
20-25	7	5	6	11	10	7	4	7	6	4	6	7	6	7	93
	(28.0)	(20.0)	(24.0)	(44.0)	(40.0)	(28.0)	(16.0)	(28.0)	(24.0)	(16.0)	(24.0)	(28.0)	(24.0)	(28.0)	(26.57)
25-30	2	7	4	3	4	8	5	6	12	3	8	4	5	6	77
	(8.0)	(28.0)	(16.0)	(12.0)	(16.0)	(32.0)	(20.0)	(24.0)	(48.0)	(12.0)	(32.0)	(16.0)	(20.0)	(24.0)	(22.0)
> 30	-	-	4	2	3	-	4	4	-	5	-	-	4	3	29
			(16.0)	(8.0)	(12.0)		(16.0)	(16.0)		(20.0)			(16.0)	(12.0)	(8.3)
Total	25	25	25	25	25	25	25	25	25	25	25	25	25	25	350
	(100)	(100)	(100)	(100)	(100)	(100)	(100)	(100)	(100)	(100)	(100)	(100)	(100)	(100)	(100)

Note: I. Kupwara; II. Baramulla; III. Srinagar;
IV. Badgam; V. Pulwama; VI. Anantnag;
VII. Leh; VIII. Kargil; IX. Doda;
X. Udhampur; XI. Poonch; XII. Rajouri;
XIII. Jammu; and XIV. Kathua

Table 2

District-wise Distribution of Prospective ITI Trainees by Sex

Sex	*I*	*II*	*III*	*IV*	*V*	*VI*	*VII*	*VIII*	*IX*	*X*	*XI*	*XII*	*XIII*	*XIV*	*Total*
Male	18	21	17	15	17	20	19	18	16	17	16	15	16	17	242
	(56.0)	(84.0)	(68.0)	(60.0)	(68.0)	(80.0)	(76.0)	(72.0)	(64.0)	(68.0)	(64.0)	(60.0)	(64.0)	(69.0)	(69.1)
Female	7	4	8	10	8	5	6	7	9	8	9	10	9	8	108
	(28.0)	(16.0)	(32.0)	(40.0)	(32.0)	(20.0)	(24.0)	(28.0)	(36.0)	(32.0)	(36.0)	(40.0)	(36.0)	(32.0)	(30.9)
Total	25	25	25	25	25	25	25	25	25	25	25	25	25	25	350
	(100)	(100)	(100)	(100)	(100)	(100)	(100)	(100)	(100)	(100)	(100)	(100)	(100)	(100)	(100)

Note: Same as Table 1

Table 3

District-wise Distribution of Prospective ITI Trainees by Marital Status

Marital Status	*I*	*II*	*III*	*IV*	*V*	*VI*	*VII*	*VIII*	*IX*	*X*	*XI*	*XII*	*XIII*	*XIV*	*Total*
Married	6	8	4	8	4	8	5	6	10	6	7	6	7	9	94
	(24.0)	(32.0)	(16.0)	(32.0)	(16.0)	(32.0)	(20.0)	(24.0)	(40.0)	(24.0)	(28.0)	(24.0)	(28.0)	(36.0)	(26.9)
Unmarried	19	17	21	17	21	17	20	19	15	19	18	19	18	16	256
	(76.0)	(68.0)	(84.0)	(68.0)	(84.0)	(68.0)	(80.0)	(76.0)	(60.0)	(76.0)	(56.0)	(76.0)	(56.0)	(64.00)	(73.1)
Total	25	25	25	25	25	25	25	25	25	25	25	25	25	25	350
	(100)	(100)	(100)	(100)	(100)	(100)	(100)	(100)	(100)	(100)	(100)	(100)	(100)	(100)	(100)

Note: Same as Table 1

needs of the young male population are high as compared to the females in the same age groups. About three-fourth of the sample prospective trainees were unmarried and the proportion of the married respondents was significantly low Table 3. Demographically, it reflects a significant trend that people postpone the process of family formation and enter the marriage market at later age. However, among the majority of the sample respondents, it is not due to the sheer desire for higher social status, but the high incidence of unemployment and underemployment compel them not to enter the marriage ties. However, some of them are reportedly married males with employment in informal sector or without any job, depending on their parents with the hope that sooner or later they may be able to get one and sustain their livelihood.

(b) **Educational Status of Respondents and Parents:** The data on educational status of the respondents and their fathers and mothers is presented in Tables 4, 5 and 6 respectively. A cursory glance at the data given in Table 4 makes it evident that more than one-fifth of them were educated up to middle and high school levels and less than one-fifth of them were educated up to primary standard and a small proportion of them were without any formal education, but were having some informal technical training and shown their desire to upgrade the skills they possess by pursuing a course/trade of their if the same is available or offered. More than one-fourth of the respondents were educated up to higher secondary level. It is significant to note that none of the respondents in the districts of Srinagar, Badgam, Anantnag, Kargil, Udhampur, Poonch and Jammu was without any formal education. Almost in all the districts, about one-fifth of the prospective trainees were educated up to high school level, except two districts of Anantnag and Udhampur. Thus, the prospective trainees who were educated above the high school standard consisting more than half of the prospective trainees are already covered

Table 4

District-wise Distribution of Prospective ITI Trainees by Educational Status

Educational Status	*I*	*II*	*III*	*IV*	*V*	*VI*	*VII*	*VIII*	*IX*	*X*	*XI*	*XII*	*XIII*	*XIV*	*Total*
No formal education	3 (12.0)	4 (16.0)	-	-	2 (8.0)	-	3 (12.0)	-	3 (12.0)	-	-	3 (12.0)	-	5 (20.0)	23 (6.57)
Primary	6 (24.0)	6 (24.0)	-	5 (20.0)	5 (20.0)	7 (28.0)	4 (16.0)	6 (24.0)	6 (24.0)	5 (20.0)	3 (12.0)	5 (20.0)	7 (28.0)	4 (16.0)	69 (19.7)
Middle	8 (32.0)	4 (16.0)	8 (32.0)	3 (12.0)	7 (28.0)	3 (12.0)	6 (24.0)	8 (32.0)	4 (16.0)	9 (36.0)	7 (28.0)	4 (16.0)	9 (36.0)	3 (12.0)	83 (23.7)
High School	6 (24.0)	5 (20.0)	7 (28.0)	8 (32.0)	6 (24.0)	4 (16.0)	5 (20.0)	5 (20.0)	5 (20.0)	4 (16.0)	6 (24.0)	7 (28.0)	5 (20.0)	8 (32.0)	81 (23.1)
Higher Secondary	2 (8.0)	6 (24.0)	10 (40.0)	9 (36.0)	5 (20.0)	11 (44.0)	7 (28.0)	6 (24.0)	7 (28.0)	7 (28.0)	9 (36.0)	6 (24.0)	4 (16.0)	5 (20.0)	94 (26.9)
Total	25 (100)	25 (100)	25 (100)	25 (100)	25 (100)	25 (100)	25 (100)	25 (100)	25 (100)	25 (100)	25 (100)	25 (100)	25 (100)	25 (100)	350 (100)

Note: Same as Table 1

Table 5
Highest Educational Level of Father of Prospective ITI Trainees

Educational Status	*I*	*II*	*III*	*IV*	*V*	*VI*	*VII*	*VIII*	*IX*	*X*	*XI*	*XII*	*XIII*	*XIV*	*Total*
No formal Education	6 (24.0)	7 (28.0)	-	-	5 (20.0)	-	5 (20.0)	-	7 (28.0)	-	6 (24.0)	7 (28.0)	-	7 (28.0)	50 (14.3)
Primary	4 (16.0)	5 (20.0)	-	6 (24.0)	4 (16.0)	8 (32.0)	3 (12.0)	4 (16.0)	8 (32.0)	7 (28.0)	5 (20.0)	7 (28.0)	4 (16.0)	6 (24.0)	71 (20.3)
Middle	3 (12.0)	4 (16.0)	6 (24.0)	3 (12.0)	3 (12.0)	5 (20.0)	4 (16.0)	6 (24.0)	4 (16.0)	7 (28.0)	7 (28.0)	4 (16.0)	6 (24.0)	5 (20.0)	67 (19.1)
High School	6 (24.0)	5 (20.0)	9 (36.0)	3 (12.0)	4 (16.0)	4 (16.0)	5 (20.0)	5 (20.0)	6 (24.0)	6 (24.0)	7 (28.0)	7 (28.0)	5 (20.0)	6 (24.0)	78 (22.3)
Higher Secondary	2 (8.0)	4 (16.0)	5 (20.0)	6 (24.0)	3 (12.0)	4 (16.0)	3 (12.0)	6 (24.0)	-	5 (20.0)	-	-	4 (16.0)	1 (4.0)	43 (12.3)
Bachelor's degree	4 (16.0)	-	2 (8.0)	4 (16.0)	6 (24.0)	4 (16.0)	5 (20.0)	4 (16.0)	-	-	-	-	3 (12.0)	-	32 (9.1)
Master's degree	-	-	3 (12.0)	3 (12.0)	-	-	-	-	-	-	-	-	3 (12.0)	-	9 (2.6)
Total	25 (100)	25 (100)	25 (100)	25 (100)	25 (100)	25 (100)	25 (100)	25 (100)	25 (100)	25 (100)	25 (100)	25 (100)	25 (100)	25 (100)	350 (100)

Note: Same as Table 1

Table 6
Highest Educational Level of Mother of Prospective ITI Trainees

Educational Status	*I*	*II*	*III*	*IV*	*V*	*VI*	*VII*	*VIII*	*IX*	*X*	*XI*	*XII*	*XIII*	*XIV*	*Total*
No formal Education	10 (40.0)	11 (44.0)	-	3 (12.0)	8 (32.0)	4 (16.0)	8 (32.0)	-	9 (36.0)	8 (32.0)	9 (36.0)	9 (36.0)	-	6 (24.0)	85 (24.3)
Primary	7 (28.0)	6 (24.0)	-	6 (24.0)	7 (28.0)	6 (24.0)	4 (16.0)	10 (40.0)	6 (24.0)	4 (16.0)	4 (16.0)	5 (20.0)	6 (24.0)	8 (32.0)	79 (22.6)
Middle	8 (32.0)	4 (16.0)	8 (32.0)	6 (24.0)	6 (24.0)	8 (32.0)	6 (24.0)	8 (32.0)	5 (20.0)	6 (24.0)	7 (28.0)	4 (16.0)	5 (20.0)	5 (20.0)	86 (24.6)
High School	-	4 (16.0)	4 (16.0)	5 (20.0)	4 (16.0)	3 (12.0)	5 (20.0)	5 (20.0)	5 (20.0)	4 (16.0)	5 (20.0)	7 (28.0)	3 (12.0)	6 (24.0)	60 (17.1)
Higher Secondary	-	-	6 (24.0)	5 (20.0)	-	4 (16.0)	2 (8.0)	2 (8.0)	-	3 (12.0)	-	-	4 (16.0)	-	26 (7.4)
Bachelor's degree	-	-	3 (12.0)	-	-	-	-	-	-	-	-	-	4 (16.0)	-	7 (2.0)
Master's degree	-	-	4 (16.0)	-	-	-	-	-	-	-	-	-	3 (12.0)	-	7 (2.0)
Total	25 (100)	25 (100)	25 (100)	25 (100)	25 (100)	25 (100)	25 (100)	25 (100)	25 (100)	25 (100)	25 (100)	25 (100)	25 (100)	25 (100)	350 (100)

Note: Same as Table 1

in the mainstream industrial training system prevalent in the state of Jammu and Kashmir; however, the rest of them need careful attention and planning by the relevant authorities.

The data on the educational status of the fathers and mothers of the prospective trainees was collected to understand their attitudes towards the vocational and technical training. It is presumed that the better-educated parents may understand the labour market better and appreciate the need to provide vocational and technical training to their sons and daughters, so that their prospects of better employment and earnings may be enhanced. A perusal of the data in Tables 5 and 6 reveals that 14.3 percent and 24.3 percent of the fathers and mothers of the prospective trainees respectively were without any formal education and about one-fifth of them were educated up to primary, middle and high school levels. The proportion of the parents educated above high school level was reportedly low. The district-wise analysis of the data pertained to the educational levels of the parents also reveals more or less the same with minor variations across the districts. On the whole, the educational level of the parents of the prospective trainees presents a comfortable picture and one can infer that there may exists positive attitudes of the parents towards the desire and need for undergoing vocational and technical training of their sons and daughters, if the training skills are provided to them based on the educational level and the skill possession by them.

(c) **Traditional/Technical Skill Possession in Vocational Activities:** The data presented in Table 7 clearly reveals the traditional/technical skills possessed by the sample prospective trainees. It is significant to note that 40.3 percent of them were without any traditional/technical skills and rest of them have multiple traditional/technical skills, which needs to be upgraded to enhance their employability and level of earnings. More than one-tenth of them have traditional/technical skills in rope making, handling machinery, bee-keeping, pottering, and tailoring. Besides, a smaller

Table 7
Traditional/Technical Skill Possession in Vocational Activities by Prospective ITI Trainees

Traditional Skill	*I*	*II*	*III*	*IV*	*V*	*VI*	*VII*	*VIII*	*IX*	*X*	*XI*	*XII*	*XIII*	*XIV*	*Total*
Rope Making	5 (20.0)	8 (32.0)	-	-	7 (28.0)	-	4 (16.0)	-	6 (24.0)	-	5 (20.0)	4 (16.0)	-	6 (24.0)	45 (12.9)
Handling Machinery	-	-	8 (32.0)	3 (12.0)	3 (12.0)	5 (20.0)	-	6 (24.0)	4 (16.0)	7 (28.0)	-	4 (16.0)	6 (24.0)	5 (20.0)	51 (14.6)
Bee-keeping	6 (24.0)	5 (20.0)	-	3 (12.0)	4 (16.0)	-	5 (20.0)	5 (20.0)	-	6 (24.0)	-	7 (28.0)	-	6 (24.0)	47 (13.4)
Dairy Technology	2 (8.0)	4 (16.0)	-	-	3 (12.0)	4 (16.0)	-	6 (24.0)	-	5 (20.0)	-	-	4 (16.0)	-	28 (8.0)
Barber	4 (16.0)	-	2 (8.0)	-	-	4 (16.0)	-	4 (16.0)	-	-	-	-	3 (12.0)	-	17 (4.9)
Typist/ Stenographer	-	-	3 (12.0)	3 (12.0)	-	-	-	-	-	-	-	-	3 (12.0)	-	9 (2.6)
Black Smith	6 (24.0)	-	-	-	5 (20.0)	-	-	-	-	-	-	4 (16.0)	-	3	18 (5.1)
Pottering	3 (12.0)	4 (16.0)	-	3 (12.0)	3 (12.0)	-	4 (16.0)	-	4 (16.0)	7 (28.0)	-	4 (16.0)	-	5 (20.0)	37 (10.6)
Tailoring	6 (24.0)	-	-	3 (12.0)	4 (16.0)	-	5 (20.0)	5 (20.0)	6 (24.0)	-	-	-	5 (20.0)	6 (24.0)	40 (11.4)
Shoe Making	2 (8.0)	-	5 (20.0)	6 (24.0)	-	4 (16.0)	3 (12.0)	-	-	5 (20.0)	-	-	4 (16.0)	-	29 (8.3)

Contd....

Traditional Skill	*I*	*II*	*III*	*IV*	*V*	*VI*	*VII*	*VIII*	*IX*	*X*	*XI*	*XII*	*XIII*	*XIV*	*Total*
Spinning &	-	6	4	-	5	-	5	-	-	-	-	7	-	7	34
Weaving		(24.0)	(16.0)		(20.0)		(20.0)					(28.0)		(28.0)	(9.7)
Basket	-	-	-	3	-	-	4	-	4	-	-	4	-	5	20
Making				(12.0)			(16.0)		(16.0)			(16.0)		(20.0)	(5.7)
Book	2	4	5	-	3	4	-	6	-	5	-	-	4	1	34
Binding	(8.0)	(16.0)	(20.0)		(12.0)	(16.0)		(24.0)		(20.0)			(16.0)	(4.0)	(9.7)
Toy	4	-	2	4	-	4	-	4	-	-	-	-	3	-	21
Making	(16.0)		(8.0)	(16.0)		(16.0)		(16.0)					(12.0)		(6.0)
No Skill	12	11	9	13	10	11	8	12	9	11	13	7	9	6	141
	(48.0)	(44.0)	(36.0)	(52.0)	(40.0)	(44.0)	(32.0)	(48.0)	(36.0)	(48.0)	(52.0)	(28.0)	(36.0)	(24.0)	(40.3)
Total	25	25	25	25	25	25	25	25	25	25	25	25	25	25	350
	(100)	(100)	(100)	(100)	(100)	(100)	(100)	(100)	(100)	(100)	(100)	(100)	(100)	(100)	(100)

Note: Same as Table 1

proportion go them possess the traditional/technical skills in book binding, spinning and weaving, shoe making, dairy technology, toy making, basket making, black smith, barber, and typing and stenography in decreasing order. The district-wise analysis of the data also reveals more or less the same picture with minor variations across the districts. For example, none of the sample respondents in districts of Kupwara, Baramulla, Leh, and Pooch have reported possession of skill in handling machinery, which is one of the prime requirements in industrial sector employment. Similarly, none of the prospective trainees have reported the skills of typing/stenography in all the districts except Srinagar, Badgam, and Jammu, whereas in the districts of Baramulla, Srinagar, Anantnag, Udhampur, Poonch, and Rajouri, none of the prospective trainees possess the skills in tailoring. A part of the sample respondents have got informal apprenticeship training and currently engaged in informal sector on wage employment or as self-employed and earning meager income to eke out a livelihood. Thus, there is no denying the fact that the upgradation of their skills through formal training will result in improved employability and income prospects.

(d) **Vocational Courses Preferred by Prospective ITI Trainees:** The data on the preferences of vocational courses by the prospective trainees is presented in Table 8. A perusal of the data given in Table 8 makes it evident that the prospective trainees have shown their preference for multiple courses. The most highly preferred courses were in the field of travel and tourism (46.3 percent) followed by hospitality (41.1 percent) and secretarial practice (38.0 percent), which clearly reveals that a significant proportion of the sample prospective trainees prefer those of the courses, which are highly demanded in the

Table 8
Vocational Courses Preferred by Prospective ITI Trainees

Traditional Skill	*I*	*II*	*III*	*IV*	*V*	*VI*	*VII*	*VIII*	*IX*	*X*	*XI*	*XII*	*XIII*	*XIV*	*Total*
Furniture	7	9	7	7	8	9	6	5	7	11	5	4	7	6	98
Making	(28.0)	(36.0)	(28.0)	(28.0)	(32.0)	(36.0)	(24.0)	(20.0)	(28.0)	(25.0)	(20.0)	(16.0)	(24.0)	(24.0)	(28.0)
Handloom	9	8	9	6	7	8	5	6	9	8	10	11	3	7	106
and Weaving	(36.0)	(32.0)	(36.0)	(24.0)	(28.0)	(32.0)	(20.0)	(24.0)	(36.0)	(32.0)	(40.0)	(44.0)	(12.0)	(28.0)	(30.3)
AC and	8	5	9	13	4	11	5	5	7	6	9	7	9	6	104
Refrigerators	(32.0)	(20.0)	(36.0)	(52.0)	(16.0)	(44.0)	(20.0)	(20.0)	(28.0)	(24.0)	(36.0)	(28.0)	(36.0)	(24.0)	(29.7)
Auto	7	5	7	3	4	8	5	5	7	6	8	7	7	6	85
Mechanic	(28.0)	(20.0)	(28.0)	(12.0)	(16.0)	(32.0)	(20.0)	(20.0)	(28.0)	(24.0)	(32.0)	(28.0)	(28.0)	(24.0)	(24.3)
Secretarial	9	8	12	7	12	6	10	7	9	11	9	11	13	9	133
Practice	(36.0)	(32.0)	(48.0)	(28.0)	(48.00)	(24.0)	(40.0)	(28.0)	(36.0)	(44.0)	(36.0)	(44.0)	(52.0)	(36.0)	(38.0)
Candle	5	6	8	5	8	9	7	9	6	8	7	7	9	7	101
Making	(20.0)	(24.0)	(32.0)	(20.0)	(32.0)	(36.0)	(28.0)	(36.0)	(24.0)	(32.0)	(28.0)	(28.0)	(36.0)	(28.0)	(28.8)
Handicrafts	4	5	4	7	10	5	6	8	4	6	5	4	7	5	80
	(16.0)	(20.0)	(16.0)	(28.0)	(40.0)	(20.0)	(24.0)	(32.0)	(16.0)	(24.0)	(20.0)	(16.0)	(28.0)	(20.0)	(22.8)
Hospitality	9	9	14	13	8	11	14	9	9	13	8	7	16	5	145
	(36.0)	(36.0)	(56.0)	(56.0)	(32.0)	(44.0)	(56.0)	(36.0)	(36.0)	(52.0)	(32.0)	(28.0)	(64.0)	(20.0)	(41.4)
Travel and	13	11	16	16	11	9	15	14	9	11	9	7	15	6	162
Tourism	(52.0)	(44.0)	(64.0)	(64.0)	(44.0)	(36.0)	(60.0)	(56.0)	(36.0)	(44.0)	(36.0)	(28.0)	(60.0)	(24.0)	(46.3)
Hair and	6	7	9	4	3	5	5	4	6	6	7	8	8	6	84
skin care	(24.0)	(28.0)	(36.0)	(16.0)	(12.0)	(20.0)	(20.0)	(16.0)	(24.0)	(24.0)	(28.0)	(32.0)	(32.0)	(24.0)	(24.0)
Driver-cum	8	3	6	5	4	6	8	6	5	4	8	3	8	7	81
-mechanic	(32.0)	(12.0)	(24.0)	(20.0)	(16.0)	(24.0)	(32.0)	(24.0)	(20.0)	(16.0)	(32.0)	(12.0)	(32.0)	(28.0)	(23.1)
Total	25	25	25	25	25	25	25	25	25	25	25	25	25	25	350
	(100)	(100)	(100)	(100)	(100)	(100)	(100)	(100)	(100)	(100)	(100)	(100)	(100)	(100)	(100)

Note: Same as Table 1

> growing service and self-employed sector. With improved political scenario and investment in infrastructure and the revival of tourism economy of the state, the scope of the expansion is widely perceived and expected. Therefore, the preference for courses on travel and tourism, and hospitality is rightly justified with better chances of adoption by the unskilled and semi-skilled youth. The course of secretarial practice is also in high demand in the labour market. With the growth in the service sector especially the telecom, banking and insurance, the demand for skilled workers in secretarial practice is keeping up and likely to increase in near future with better chances of sustainability.

The other courses preferred by them includes handloom and weaving (30.3 percent), followed by repairs and maintenance of A.C and refrigerators, (29.7 percent), candle making (28.8 percent), furniture making (28.0 percent), auto-mechanic (24.3 percent), hair and skin care (24.0 percent), driver-cum-mechanic of light vehicle (23.1 percent) and handicrafts (22.8 percent) and their distribution across the districts is noticed more or less in similar fashion with minor variations. From the above, it is clear that the prospective trainees are well versed with the situation in local labour market and employment scenario prevailing in the state of Jammu and Kashmir due to which they have shown preferences towards only those of the courses/trades which have high potential in self-employed as well as private sector most particularly the growing informal sector of the economy, which is currently the largest employment generating sector.

To conclude, it is not wrong to say that a significant part of the labour force is engaged in the informal sector and this phenomenon is here to stay and that government policies for economic and social development, including education and training policies, should target those who work or expected to enter in this sector. The training, skill formation and education for workers in informal sector have received much less attention than it deserves. Building knowledge and skills for the masses in this sector is one of the ways of promoting poverty alleviation. In recent years, government and non-governmental education and training providers have taken steps to develop and deliver training for decent work in the informal economy. There is limited information about the current quality of training for or in the informal sector. For effective policy formulation, there is a need to identify the factors of training and skill transfer, which lead to an improvement of living and working conditions of the beneficiaries.

Generally, the issues of diversification and "vocationalisation" of secondary education are dealt with purely in economic terms (earning opportunities, better jobs and higher technical fields). Public technical and vocational training do not have a good track record, particularly in terms of efficiency and flexibility and such training is sometimes also far away from local, cultural, social and market realities. Many trainees pursuing technical/vocational training are unlikely to obtain the full-time wage employment they sought. At the same time, the technically educated, as well as the 'general line' graduates are out of touch with working and technical conditions as well as possibilities in micro and small enterprises. There is little or no attempt to cater to the needs of those who wish to continue living and working in rural areas and this compels them to join the urban informal sector because of their shortage of skills. In most rural areas, facilities for elementary education are absent, let alone vocational facilities. Some efforts at developing such facilities are being made, but are unfortunately not meeting with any success, apart from a few isolated examples.

The informal sector generally comprises small entrepreneurs, paid and unpaid establishment workers, independent workers and casual workers. For the small entrepreneurs the need is for managerial and marketing skills besides the technical skills, as well as regular upgrading of skills and access to knowledge and information. The majority of informal workers learn their skills on the job, something that is common to both the formal and informal sectors. However, the apprenticeship might provide basic skills but does not familiarise the workers with new technologies or managerial skills. Constraints of both time and money often prevent workers in the formal and informal sectors from acquiring further training, even when such facilities exist.

In the manufacturing sector, indigenous forms of training may be sufficient for adapting technology to simple production and labour-intensive activity, but that does not necessarily mean more efficient production or market competitivity. Modern technical training probably needs to complement, rather than replace indigenous work techniques. Outside the manufacturing sector, the issue remains as to how independent workers, auto-drivers and hawkers and the like can be trained. They are often highly unorganized and may not be operating from fixed locations. Besides, these workers have irregular working hours. Coupled with all this, they have limited resources and little time to undergo training. Many are so poor that they may not be able to afford even minimal extra expenses. Finding the time to attend training programmes or courses is a major constraint, as their time needs to be spent earning a livelihood. Rampant illiteracy too restricts the potential of retraining and upgrading their skills.

Casual workers, a most disadvantaged category, rely heavily on manual labour. These jobs need little training and earnings are usually low, although some may earn more than their counterparts in the formal sector. Work skills are usually learnt on the job. Due to the high level of horizontal mobility amongst sectors and employment status, many individuals end up with multiple skills, having moved through different jobs in the course of their working life. Such occupational mobility complicates the formulation of approaches to training. But if vocational training and education are to cater to both formal and informal sectors, it is essential to take into account the traditions and values of the system of vocational learning in working life. Such training needs to cater to the requirements of local development and be based on an understanding of the kinds of competencies people in the informal sector want, need and utilize; the socio-economic and cultural contexts within which they work and how they cope; and the skills, capabilities, attitudes and values that are required to sustain their livelihood strategies. Indeed, the understanding of the livelihood strategies in specific social and cultural settings, disaggregated along caste, ethnic, class and gender lines, as well as the labour market conditions, is of paramount importance if a meaningful re-orientation of the approaches to training and skill-building has to be made.

6

CONCLUSIONS AND RECOMMENDATIONS

CONCLUSIONS

The regular assessments of the demand and supply of technically trained manpower and its impact are vital issues to identify the gaps between the demand and supply and to take suitable policy initiatives to avoid the overproduction or shortage and facilitate the policy changes to improve the quality of technically trained manpower by changing the existing curriculum to meet the requirements of the labour market. The present study is one such attempt to assess the impact of training courses in the ITIs, including the track record of the placement of the trainees and demand assessment of the ITI pass outs in industries and by prospective trainees. The main conclusions drawn in the study are presented in the following paragraphs.

- The total enrolment of the trainees in various courses/trades offered during the reference period of five years was 10985 in the 29 ITIs (for which data was available) of the state of Jammu and Kashmir, out of which 66.91 per cent and 33.09 per cent were males and females respectively. Out of 7351 males and 3634 females enrolled, 66.29 per cent and 75.75 per cent respectively appeared in the final test and of those who appeared in the final test, 62.57 per cent and 71.70 per cent of males and females respectively were declared pass. Thus, the drop out rate was one-third and one-fourth respectively for males and females. The course-wise enrolment, retention and pass outs reveals that all male ITI trainees appeared in the final test of instrument mechanic and more than 80 per cent in Urdu calligraphy and diesel mechanic were declared pass. Similarly, more than 70 per cent of the male ITI trainees appeared in the final test of the courses of computer operator, A.C & refrigerator, electrician, motor and mechanic and more than 60 per cent in the courses of electronic mechanic, plumber, fitter, and machinist were declared pass. The proportion of the pass outs was comparatively higher in case of female trainees in courses of Urdu calligraphy followed by computer operator, cutting and tailoring, and electronic mechanic. The pass outs in radio & T.V mechanic, turner, and tractor mechanic were less than one-half, which needs attention of the authorities so that the proportion of the ITI pass outs in these specific courses could be increased further.

- In some of the courses, the enrolment was comparatively lower than the number of sanctioned trainees per course and the female trainees were confined to 33.0 per cent of the courses offered by the ITIs. The enrolment of the female trainees was virtually non-existent in the courses catering to the supply of technically trained manpower for the industrial sector and they were mostly enrolled in courses like cutting and tailoring, stenography and computer operator. Thus, there is gender bias in enrolment in the ITI courses and therefore, there is urgent need to remove such biases by motivating more and more young women to enroll in the courses catering to the employment in industrial sector. There are wide variations and gaps between enrolment and retention and the proportion of the trainees declared pass across by course/trade in the ITIs of the state.

- The proportion of the male trainees enrolled in ITIs was comparatively more than the female trainees except the ITIs of Udhampur, Leh, and Tral. The retention rate for male trainees was comparatively low (less than 60 percent) in ITIs of Jammu, Samba, Udhampur, Rajouri, Leh, Bandipore, Baramulla, Tral, Handwara, Kulgam, and Chararisharief, whereas the retention rate for female trainees was comparatively low (less than 50 percent) in ITIs of Leh, Handwara, and Pattan. The lower retention rate implies high drop out and wastage, which needs immediate attention of the relevant authorities so that the rate of retention should be enhanced from the present lower levels. Similarly, the cent percent retention of enrolled female trainees in ITIs of Kathua, Bhaddu/Billawar, Mendhar, Kargil, and Tral; above 80.0 per cent in ITIs of Reasi, Doda, Srinagar, Ganwderbal, Bandipore, Baramulla, Anantnag, and Shopian deserve appreciation and incentives. In ITIs of Reasi, Ramban, Handwara, Kulgam, and Pattan, the proportion of the male ITI pass outs stood at less than one-half and in the ITIs of Reasi, Bhaddu/Billawar, Mendhar, Leh, Bandipore, Tral, and Handwara, the proportion of the female ITI pass outs were recorded at less than one-half, which implies the need for improvement in teaching methodology, library and laboratory infrastructure, etc. In some of the ITIs, the availability of the teaching and non-teaching staff is also reportedly inadequate to cater to the need of effective training, which also need attention of the relevant authorities.
- A majority of the ITI pass outs have rated the academic during their training as good and a small proportion of them have rated their academic rating

as bad. The district-wise academic rating by the training also reveals more or less the same picture with exceptions of the districts of Kupwara, Baramulla, Badgam, Pulwama, Doda, Udhampur and Poonch, where none of the ITI pass outs has rated their academic as bad and very bad during training. About one-third of the ITI pass outs had opted for courses/trades like electrician, cutting and tailoring, and stenography. Two of the courses/trades viz. electrician, and cutting and tailoring were opted by the ITI pass outs in all the districts and were more common among males (electrician) and females (cutting and tailoring), followed by courses/trades of stenography, computer operator, electronic mechanic and plumber. The courses/trades of tractor mechanic and information technology were opted by a meager proportion of the ITI pass outs, which is due to the fact that only two ITIs viz. ITI Baramulla and ITI Jammu are providing training in trade of tractor mechanic and ITI Jammu is providing training in the field of information technology. This needs immediate attention of the authorities so that emerging and highly employment oriented courses like information technology may be introduced in all the ITIs.

- All the courses/trades were not provided and opted in each of the ITI. For example, the sample ITI pass outs of ITI Handwara had opted three courses/trades (electrician, cutting and tailoring, and electronic mechanic), four courses/trades (electrician, cutting and tailoring, stenography and Radio and T.V mechanic) in ITI Leh and ITI Kargil, and in ITI Mendhar (electrician, cutting and tailoring, plumber, and Radio and T.V mechanic). Thus, there is urgent need to add more vocational courses in those of the ITIs, where fewer courses/trades is currently being operationalized, which would provide more options to the prospective trainees. A majority of the ITI pass outs have rated the courses/ trades offered by ITIs as middle high to very high. For example, 14.45 per cent, 25.90 per cent and 19.87 per cent of the ITI pass outs have rated the course/ trade of electrician as very high, high and middle high respectively. A more or less similar rating of the courses/trades of cutting and tailoring, plumber, stenography and computer operator has been made by them. The courses/trades such as fitter, turner, machinist, motor mechanic, tractor mechanic, welder and carpenter have also been rated as high and very high. This is due to the fact that most of the ITI pass outs in these courses/trades are currently employed or self-employed and earning sustainable livelihoods. Keeping in view the high level of incidence of unemployment and underemployment in the state of Jammu and Kashmir, the prospective trainees should also be trained in management aspects to enable them to venture in self-employment after completing their courses/trades at ITIs. The prospective trainees should also be educated about various self-employment programmes being run by government agencies, for which regular visits of the functionaries of the line departments, banking and industries be arranged to expose the trainees to the need and importance of self-employment and means and ways to be engaged as self-employed.

- The respondents were asked to give the reasons for their decisions to enroll in ITIs. More than half of them wanted to focus on a field that they were interested in ITI as very important and important reason and 43.28 per cent of them also reported that they do not know what they really wanted to do as very important and important reason, which clearly reveals the lack of awareness and motivation and non-seriousness on the part of the ITI trainees in pursuing a course/trade. Thus, there is urgent need to provide proper counselling and awareness to the prospective trainees before getting them admitted in various courses/trades, which would help them in taking up only those of the courses/trades in which they are really interested. A majority of them enrolled in the courses/trades in ITIs because they were interested in them and to get a job as very important and important factors influencing their decisions. However, more than two-third of them enrolled in courses/trades at ITIs because of the easy programme structure. A similar proportion of them reported that the courses they wanted to study at ITI were full, so they were compelled to enoll in other courses/trades of least interest, which is really cause of concern and calls for immediate attention of the appropriate authorities so that a proportional balance is maintained in demand and supply of the courses/trades being offered at ITIs.

- A significant proportion of the respondents respectively were satisfied with quality of teaching, study methods, language of instruction and provisioning of library materials. At the same time, one-third and one-fifth of them were unsatisfied and very unsatisfied respectively in terms of availability of the staff to help them when needed and one-fourth of them were very unsatisfied with the conditions of buildings. The level of satisfaction was also very low in case of provisioning of lecture handouts to the trainees. Thus, there is need to improve the conditions of the existing building and availability of staff to help the trainees in need and the staff may be motivated to provide the lecture handouts to the trainees so that they could use them and supplement with other reading materials.
- About two-third of the ITI pass outs were satisfied with the assistance/advice offered by the instructors, opportunity of out for examinations, academic advice offered, teaching quality of lectures, structure of the programmes, provision of practical works,

contacts with fellow trainees, availability of teaching equipments, quality of laboratories, and equipment and stocking of libraries. More than one-third of them were satisfied with supply of teaching materials, catering facilities and quality of buildings. Thus, there is urgent need to improve the provisioning of supply of teaching materials and conditions of catering facilities and buildings so that the overall quality of study provisions and conditions at ITI could be improved, which would go a long way in improving the performance and quality of ITI pass outs. More than one-third of the sample respondents were satisfied with interpersonal skills, written communication skills, oral communication skills and problem-solving skills, self-confidence development and teamwork and leadership skills acquired during training in their respective courses/trades at ITIs. The skill gained in creative thinking and independent learning was rated low and more than two-third of the respondents were unsatisfied or very unsatisfied in creative thinking aspect and about one-half of ITI pass outs were unsatisfied or very unsatisfied in aspect of independent learning. Thus, the aspects of creative thinking and independent learning needs to improved, which could improve their employability, productivity and levels of earnings and help facilitate innovations and modifications in work processes.

- Out of sampled 796 ITI pass outs, 48.8 per cent and 51.2 per cent were unemployed and employed respectively. Out of 389 unemployed ITI pass outs, 89.2 per cent were never employed before and 10.8 per cent have resigned/laid off/ separated from the previous employment. Those of the respondents who were gainfully employed, 48.3 per cent, 22.4 per cent and 22.4 per cent respectively were employed locally, within the respective districts, and outside their respective districts and 22.6 per cent were self-employed. About half of the ITI pass outs were gainfully employed in all the districts of the state of Jammu and Kashmir except the districts of Pulwama and Leh, where the proportion of gainfully employed ITI pass outs stood at 43.6 per cent and 42.6 per cent respectively. About one-fourth of the employed ITI pass outs were self-employed in districts of Srinagar, Badgam, Leh, Kargil, Doda, Poonch and Rajouri, whereas in other districts the proportion of self-employed were about one-fifth except Kupwara, where self-employed were reportedly 37.5 per cent. Thus, self-employment is one of the lucrative options for ITI pass outs to eke out a livelihood and there is need to promote awareness regarding self-employment programmes and schemes among the prospective trainees during the tenure of their stay at ITIs.

- Out of 407 employed ITI pass outs, 78.4 per cent and 21.6 per cent were males and females respectively. In district Kupwara, all the employed ITI pass outs were males. In all other districts, the proportion of male employed ITI pass outs was higher than females except the district Kargil, where they were reportedly in equal proportion. In districts of Leh and Udhampur, the gender imbalance in employment was not so sharp as in other districts and 43.5 per cent and 41.1 per cent of the employed ITI pass outs were females. The main reason for lower proportion of the employed female ITI pass outs is their enrollment pattern, as a higher proportion of them were enrolled in the course/ trade of cutting and tailoring, which provides them meager job opportunities in organized as well unorganized sectors. However, they could be motivated to take up self-employment as the market for their services is very large and returns are also very lucrative, for which there is need to make them aware regarding various schemes being run by governmental and non-governmental agencies for assisting them to start their own small enterprises on individual as well as group basis.

- The private sector is the dominant employment-providing sector to the ITI pass outs, where about half of them were employed and 22.6 per cent each were employed in government and self-employed sector. Non-governmental organizations (NGOs) are providing employment opportunities to a very small proportion (5.4 per cent) of the ITI pass outs. NGO sector jobs for ITI pass outs are virtually non-existing in most of the districts. Thus, the programmes and schemes of self-employment needs to propagated among the ITI pass outs so that they could productively engaged in building and advancing the economy of the state of Jammu and Kashmir. The electricity/gas and water supply is the dominant economic activity followed by manufacturing, wholesale/retail/repairs/hotels, construction, transport and storage, real estate and business services. The manufacturing, and electricity/gas/ water supply are the main economic activities of employment of ITI pass outs in districts of Kupwara and Baramulla. In districts of Jammu, Kathua and Srinagar, the ITI pass outs were engaged almost all types of economic activities with minor modifications of agriculture and forestry in Srinagar.
- One-fourth of them were engaged as technician followed by supervisory position, sales and service personnel, and operator, and skilled workers. A smaller proportion of them were engaged in managerial position, clerks, craft workers and elementary workers. All of the employed ITI pass outs in district Kupwara were engaged as technician and operators. Similarly, technician is dominant cadre in district Baramulla also. The districts of Anantnag, Jammu and Kathua represents all the

positions occupied by ITI pass outs. Similar is the situation in district Srinagar except the elementary occupation. The districts of Leh and Udhampur are dominant in terms of managerial position occupied by employed ITI pass outs. This is mainly due to the fact that these respondents have also educated up to graduation and post-graduation level, which have paved their ways up to managerial position. Thus, technical training supplemented by higher education has helped the employed ITI pass outs to attain better employment.

- Out of 103 employed ITI pass outs in electrician course/trade, majority of them were reportedly engaged in private sector followed by government sector and self-employment sector. Those of the ITI pass outs that have opted for trade of cutting and tailoring, majority of them were working as self-employed followed by private sector. Almost all the ITI pass outs who have pursued the course of cutting and tailoring were reportedly females and in order to provide them with better income, it is required to motivate them to avail the benefits of the on-going programmes and schemes of self-employment run by the government and NGOs. None of the ITI pass outs in trades of fitter, turner, machinist, stenography and information technology was engaged as self-employed. On the whole, the private sector is the dominant sector in absorbing higher proportion of the ITI pass outs in almost all courses/trades except tractor mechanic and information technology. However, in case of the trade like information technology, this appears false in real practice, because the private sector is the highest absorber of the informational technology professionals elsewhere. The current situation is due to the fact that only three ITI pass outs have been included in the sample and all of them were engaged in government sector.

- Out of 389 unemployed ITI pass outs, 82.0 per cent are currently looking for a job. The duration of job search by the unemployed ITI pass outs varies from less than 6 months in case of 12.6 per cent to less than 2 years in case of 22.9 per cent. The main reasons reported by unemployed ITI pass outs for not finding a job were economic recession/no jobs available, very few job opening and there is strong competition, lack of work experience, poor preparation/training, lack of professional requirements, and no personal connections/no strong referrals. The job search interval is not very long in majority of the currently employed ITI pass outs, which also includes those who are currently engaged in self-employment. The lack of initial capital to start own business, lack of confidence to venture into self-employment, and generally parents expectation to be supported after they have done their part in educating their children may be compelling reasons for the ITI pass outs to seek employment as opposed to self employment, which may have increased the duration of job search. Over the period, more than half of the employed ITI pass outs have changed their jobs. Thus, there is low level of job satisfaction among the currently employed. However, more than one-third of the currently employed ITI pass outs were working with their current employer for more than three years.
- Out of 315 currently employed ITI pass outs, 37.8 per cent, 30.5 per cent, 16.5 per cent and 15.2 per cent respectively were engaged on contractual, temporary, probationary and permanent basis. Due to liberalization measures, the employers in government sector as well as private sector prefer to employ the labour on non-permanent basis, so that they could be retrenched as and when required, which is causing a lot of hardships to the ITI pass outs. This needs careful examination by the

manpower planners and decision-makers. Out of 267 non-permanent employed ITI pass outs, one-third of them cited low standard of English as the main reason for the failure to get a permanent employment. The poor performance at tests and interviews conducted by recruiting agencies were cited by more than one-fifth as a reason followed by discrimination by race, caste, religion and politics, and poor performance at ITI (more than one-tenth) of the ITI pass outs for their failure to obtain a permanent job. About 79.0 per cent of the employed ITI pass outs were engaged in jobs related to the field of training and those who were landed in jobs not related to the field of training, more than half of them could not get a satisfactory job in their field of training because either the pay was low or they do not like the job available A similar proportion of them have reported that their training was inadequate and they could not compete with other pass outs in the same field, and there was an opening in currently employed field, for which they immediately applied. Two-third of them intend to change their jobs in future, which clearly reflects strong level of dissatisfaction with the current jobs.

- The majority of the employed ITI pass outs (69.8 percent) were getting gross monthly income of less than Rs. 5000. In districts of Badgam, Pulwama, and Poonch, all of the employed ITI pass outs were getting lower gross monthly income, whereas in the districts of Kupwara, Kargil, Leh, and Doda, all of them belong to the income group of below Rs. 7500 per month. In the districts of Rajouri, Jammu and Srinagar, 14.8 per cent, 12.7 per cent and 10.5 per cent of them were found in monthly income group of above Rs. 10000. Out of 92 self-employed ITI pass outs, 41.3 per cent were earning between Rs. 5000-7500 on monthly basis. About a tenth of them were found in higher income group and they were concentrated in districts of Srinagar and Jammu. Thus, the gross monthly income of the self-employed ITI pass outs is comparatively more than those of employed ITI pass outs. Thus, self-employment is comparatively more lucrative avenues for the prospective trainees and needs to be strongly propagated during the training periods at respective ITIs so that a greater proportion of them should venture into self-employment as their career. Out of 319 male and female-employed ITI pass outs, about two-third were earning less than Rs. 5000 per month. None of the female ITI pass out was earning above Rs. 7500, which clearly reflects gender disparity in levels of earnings, as can be noticed elsewhere.

- The income level of the employed ITI pass outs by the type of course/trade pursued by them reveals that 82.5 per cent, 77.8 per cent and 66.7 per cent of the ITI pass outs in courses/trades like electrician, cutting and tailoring and computer operator respectively were earning monthly income to the tune of less than Rs. 5000. Half of the ITI pass outs in courses/trades such as electronic mechanic, motor mechanic, machinist, plumber and radio and T.V mechanic were earning less than Rs. 5000 per month. At the same time, electrician (8.7 per cent), electronic mechanic (14.5 percent), fitter (16.7 percent), stenography (19.1 percent) and computer operator (15.4 percent) were earning more than Rs. 10000. Thus, it is not wrong to infer that even in the same trade the level of earning differ largely on account of longer duration of employment, better employment opportunities, higher educational attainments, etc. Similarly, a significantly high proportion (81.6 percent) of the ITI pass outs working in private sector were earning less than Rs. 5000 and 47.8 per cent, 54.5 per cent and 29.3 per cent of ITI pass outs respectively working in government, NGO and self-employed sector were earning less than Rs. 5000. At the same time, 23.9 per cent and 9.8 per cent of the ITI pass out respectively working government sector and self-employed sector were earning above Rs. 10000. Thus, high variations are noticed in income levels of the workers in government, private and self-employed sector. The private sector is comparatively low-paid sector to the ITI pass outs as compared to government and self-employed sector. Keeping in view the limitations of the government sector to expand, the opportunities lies in expanding more and more the rapidly growing self-employed sector.

- Less than one-third of the ITI pass outs have reported that ITIs have advertised/display posts available. Similarly, more than one-third of them have reported that ITIs have provided counselling in finding a job. Likewise, more than one-fifth of them have reported that ITIs have provided them information on specific careers, which facilitated in finding a job. None of the ITIs have provided a recruitment service, sent curriculum vitae to companies, arranged visits to workplace, and linked to an employment agency to help the trainees finding out employment, thus, there is need to provide these facilities by the ITIs to help the trainees in finding suitable employment. Less than one-third of them found employment through personal contacts and one-fourth through relatives and one-fifth through an advertisement in the newspaper, and one-tenth through an employment agency. About 10.5 per cent of them have reported help by the ITI staff in finding an employment. The ITIs should facilitate the trainees with arranging placement services and inviting the recruiting agencies on the campus, so that the duration of job search may be minimized and they could be placed in suitable employment after training, which could reduce the incidence of unemployment and underemployment among the ITI pass outs.

- The ITI diploma/certificate and the course studied were rated important factors helping them find the first job after training followed by factors such as motivations by the instructors, strong work ethic, post-ITI education, computer training, references of the known persons and practical work experience during training have played a significant role in find the first job. The factors such as possession of bachelor degree and leadership qualities developed during the training have not contributed much in finding a job. The post-ITI education/training is very important factor influencing getting first job by them. Thus, there is need to introduce advance diploma courses in ITIs to enable the trainees to specialize and equip better to face the challenges of the labour market. Besides theoretical knowledge, the apprenticeship and development of work ethic should also be given due importance during the training.
- The full employment was reported in trades like tractor mechanic and information technology, which may be due to the fact that their proportion was very low in the sample and these courses are offered to very small number of trainees in few ITIs. Besides above, the highest employment rate was recorded in the trades of plumber, motor mechanic, welder and carpenter, followed by trades of fitter and machinist, and electrician, computer operator, and radio and T.V mechanic. The highest unemployment rate was reported in the trade of cutting and tailoring, which is female dominated followed by stenography, electronic mechanic, electrician, and computer operator. The high unemployment rates among the ITI pass outs in trades such as stenography, electronic mechanic, electrician, and computer operator is due to the fact that a comparatively large sample of these trades was included in the study and besides, there is intense

competition for the jobs in these trades in the labour market.

- Out of 363 sample ITI pass outs, 28.37 per cent, 21.46 per cent, 17.35 per cent and 10.74 per cent have reported absence of required work experience, absence of opportunities in the field of specialization and lack of knowledge in information technology respectively as the main obstacles in finding suitable employment. Other important obstacles reported by them include lack of knowledge of English and lack of knowledge of management. Thus, there is need to diversify the course structures to make them more competitive and employment oriented and emphasis should be paid on equipping them with knowledge of English language and information technology by arranging special classes during the training programmes.
- About 30.04 per cent, 37.14 per cent, 23.81 per cent of employed ITI pass outs respectively perceived the content of work, the working conditions and opportunity to learn while working as very useful. About one-third of them have used the knowledge and skill acquired very significantly and a smaller proportion of them were very satisfied with job security, income, promotion opportunities and other fringe benefits. About 43.81 per cent of them have reported that such knowledge and skills are little not at all useful to their present organization, and this needs to be taken with caution so that the overall knowledge and skills gained during training should be made more relevant and highly useful to their workplaces, failing which the retention capacity of the employers and/or their income and promotional avenues may be jeopardized and results in wastage of time and efforts made by the trainees as well as the trainers. More than one-third of the currently employed ITI pass outs have reported that the knowledge and ideas gained, and the contacts and

academic partnerships made during the training is very useful in current job and workplace. More than 40.0 per cent of them reported that ITI training is little/not at all useful in professional development, higher mobility across jobs and enhancing the income prospects. All these needs to be taken carefully., while restructuring the programme and making the courses offered at ITI as more relevant and highly useful to the trainees as well as the employers.

- The opinions of the self-employed ITI pass-outs were sought regarding work in own business/being self-employed. More than one-fourth of them opined that being self-employed achieve a relatively high status is completely applicable and more than one-fifth opined that it is applicable and somewhat applicable and rest of them opined that it is least applicable and not applicable. More than one-fifth and one-third of them respectively opined that being self-employed means working very long hours is completely applicable and applicable. More than 45.0 per cent of them opined that technical education alone does not prepare them sufficiently to take up self-employment and therefore long term job prospects does not exist in majority of the cases, which implies that a higher proportion of them should be ready to take up self-employment as a source of livelihood, instead of depending on regular labour market. Thus, the prospective trainees should be motivated to venture in to self-employment in high proportion to ease the job opportunities.
- The opinion regarding the changes needed to improve the competitive edge of ITI pass outs were also ascertained. They have advocated the need to review and update the curriculum and syllabi, add more major subjects, upgrade facilities, limit the class size, impart the theory of technology, propagate the use of computers, tools, machines, drawings and

written instruction to improve their competitive edge. They have also advocated the need to impart the theory and practice of equipment maintenance, skills in communication and teamwork, knowledge of labour laws and industrial relations, safer working practices, discipline and accuracy, employ competent faculty, provide faculty development programmes, and provide job placement. More than three-fourth of the respondents across the districts have advocated the job placement to be provided by the respective ITIs, for which the faculty members should be trained to take the challenge effectively. There is need to forge suitable linkages with different line departments in the government sector and business firms/organizations in private sector, who should provide placements to the ITI pass outs in their respective firms/organizations.

- At present, the ITIs are not adhering the practice of job placement and the faculty and staff members are not trained in performing the task of job placement. Therefore, there is need to forge suitable linkages with local institutions of higher learning for providing job placement training to the faculty and staff. One of the options could be that the Management Faculty in the local Universities may be contacted to impart a short-term course to the selected staff of the ITIs in job placement. In all the ITIs, there is need to create a job placement cell, which should devise the mechanism of job placement. In order to evaluate the performance of respective ITIs, there is need to add one more criterion of the number of placement made by them. The better performing ITIs should be given additional infrastructure development grants, which could act as a bait to perform well in job placement.
- Training programmes should be guided by the needs and demand of industrial units and enterprises and the labour market, however, in the state of Jammu

and Kashmir, training programmes are still often determined by supply considerations, which often means irrelevant and ineffective training. In order to make industrial training a demand driven exercise, there is need for a fundamental reorientation of training policies. One of the most important challenges for the industrial training system and institutions is to equip the trainees with the skills and motivation to engage in industrial work and self-employment and viable informal types of economic activity. The sample 193 industrial units employs 1461 workers, out of which 35.18 per cent, 37.57 per cent, 17.45 per cent and 9.79 per cent were technical, skilled, unskilled and other category workers respectively. In the districts of Jammu and Kashmir too, more or less the same pattern is noticed. Thus, the employability of the technically trained and skilled personnel is very high in the industrial sector as compared to unskilled and other workers, and the potential for further absorption of such workers is high, if there is improvement in political scenario and consequent investment in industrial infrastructure by the government and private sector.

- The industrial training in the course/trades of electronic mechanic, turner, and welder was considered very significantly in recruiting new employees followed by diesel mechanic, electrician, instrument mechanic and machinist by the proprietary firms. Other courses/trades such as fitter, motor mechanic, computer operator, information technology, and stenography were also considered significantly high in recruiting new employees. The courses/trades of computer operator, information technology, stenography, motor mechanic and fitter were considered by about one-fourth of partnership firms in recruiting new employees. None of them rated the courses/trades of electrician, fitter, welder, machinist, motor mechanic, computer operator and information technology as low, which implies that these courses/ trades needs to be propagated more and their course curriculum and programmes should be restructured to cater to the demand of the industrial units and make them more competitive.

- The technical qualifications and experience was the main considerations in recruiting new technicians and technically trained workers, whereas in recruiting the low skilled workers, the main consideration was experience and recommendations from employers/employees and referees. SSI units have recruited significantly the technically trained workers in the past. Out of 56 SSI units, which have recruited technically trained workers, 76.36 per cent of them were ITI pass outs. The industrial units, which have recruited new technically trained workers, about three-fourth of them have reported their performance as satisfactory and the highest level of satisfaction has been reported for technical level and craft and related workers. 34 industrial units have the provision of additional training after new worker's recruitment to expose them to the work atmosphere. A majority of them reported lack of adequate practical/application skills followed by lack of proper attitudes, values and work ethics on the part of newly recruits, which needs to be taken care of at the ITIs itself during their trainings by making appropriate provision for practical training and application skills and imbibing in them the proper attitudes, values and work ethics, so that their employability and competitiveness can be enhanced in labour market.
- Out of 55 industrial units, who have recently employed ITI pass outs, 61.82 per cent rated the ITI pass outs better than those school leavers who have acquired skills on-the-job in the firm, 23.64 per cent and 14.55 per cent respectively rated ITI pass outs

as good as good as those school leavers who have acquired skills on-the-job in the firm, and not as good as the school leavers who have acquired skills on-the-job in the firm. More than one-third of the SSI units perceived lack of knowledge and skill in the use of computers and drawings, communication and teamwork practices and knowledge of labour laws and industrial relations, more than one-fifth perceived lack of knowledge and skill in discipline and accuracy, theory and practice of equipment maintenance and safer working practices and less than one-fifth perceived lack of knowledge and skill in theory of technology and use of tools, machines and written instructions. Thus, there is need to put more attention on the perceived lack of knowledge and skill in aforementioned areas to improve their competitive edge and performance in job market.

- Thus, the ITIs have played a considerable role in producing a skilled workforce for the organized economy. Our surveys of sample industrial units revealed that a significant proportion of all employees and skilled workers have been trained in the ITIs. The economic situation has been changing rapidly in the state of Jammu and Kashmir and the state is recovering from the insurgency and political turmoil. It is expected that both government sector and private sector industrial enterprises will have better employment opportunities with improved investment climate. At the same time, the self-employed and unorganized sector has more employment potential, which needs to be propagated by the relevant agencies. The potential of unorganized sector needs to be tapped in a significant manner by introducing new guidelines and policies.
- The issues of youth unemployment and underemployment have come to the forefront in recent years. The unemployment and

underemployment figures for young people are staggering. Education and training are important means of addressing youth employability. About 43.1 per cent, 26.57 per cent, 22.0 per cent and 8.3 per cent of the prospective trainees were found in the age group of below 20 years, between 20-25 years, between 25-30 years and above 30 years of age. A significant proportion of them in the age group more than 25 years have already undergone through some informal apprenticeship training and shown their desire to upgrade the skills they possess. A majority of the prospective trainees were below the age of 25 years, however, in district Doda, 48.0 per cent of them were found in the age group of 25-30 years, which reveals that youth population in the upper ages are also in need of getting technical training and/or desire to upgrade the skill possessed by them. About 40.3 per cent of them were without any traditional/technical skills and rest of them have multiple traditional/technical skills, which needs to be upgraded to enhance their employability and level of earnings. More than one-tenth of them have traditional/technical skills in rope making, handling machinery, bee-keeping, pottering, and tailoring. Besides, a smaller proportion go them possess the traditional/technical skills in book binding, spinning and weaving, shoe making, dairy technology, toy making, basket making, black smith, barber, and typing and stenography in decreasing order.

- The district-wise analysis also reveals more or less the same picture with minor variations across the districts. For example, none of the sample respondents in districts of Kupwara, Baramulla, Leh, and Pooch have reported possession of skill in handling machinery, which is one of the prime requirements in industrial sector employment. Similarly, none of the prospective trainees have reported the skills of typing/stenography in all the districts except Srinagar, Badgam, and Jammu, whereas in the districts of Baramulla, Srinagar, Anantnag, Udhampur, Poonch, and Rajouri, none of the prospective trainees possess the skills in tailoring. A part of the sample respondents have got informal apprenticeship training and currently engaged in informal sector on wage employment or as self-employed and earning meager income to eke out a livelihood. Thus, there is no denying the fact that the upgradation of their skills through formal training will result in improved employability and income prospects.

- The prospective trainees have shown their preference for multiple courses. The most highly preferred courses were in the field of travel and tourism (46.3 percent) followed by hospitality (41.1 percent) and secretarial practice (38.0 percent), which clearly reveals that a significant proportion of the sample prospective trainees prefer those of the courses, which are highly demanded in the growing service and self-employed sector. With improved political scenario and investment in infrastructure and the revival of tourism economy of the state, the scope of the expansion is widely perceived and expected. Therefore, the preference for courses on travel and tourism, and hospitality is rightly justified with better chances of adoption by the unskilled and semi-skilled youth. The course of secretarial practice is also in high demand in the labour market. With the growth in the service sector especially the telecom, banking and insurance, the demand for skilled workers in secretarial practice is keeping up and likely to increase in near future with better chances of sustainability.
- The other courses preferred by them includes handloom and weaving (30.3 percent), followed by repairs and maintenance of A.C and refrigerators,

(29.7 percent), candle making (28.8 percent), furniture making (28.0 percent), auto-mechanic (24.3 percent), hair and skin care (24.0 percent), driver-cum-mechanic of light vehicle (23.1 percent) and handicrafts (22.8 percent) and their distribution across the districts is noticed more or less in similar fashion with minor variations. From the above, it is clear that the prospective trainees are well versed with the situation in local labour market and employment scenario prevailing in the state of Jammu and Kashmir due to which they have shown preferences towards only those of the courses/trades which have high potential in self-employed as well as private sector most particularly the growing informal sector of the economy, which is currently the largest employment generating sector.

- To conclude, a significant part of the labour force is engaged in the informal sector and this phenomenon is here to stay and that government policies for economic and social development, including education and training policies, should target those who work or expected to enter in this sector. The training, skill formation and education for workers in informal sector have received much less attention than it deserves. Building knowledge and skills for the masses in this sector is one of the ways of promoting poverty alleviation. In recent years, government and non-governmental education and training providers have taken steps to develop and deliver training for decent work in the informal economy. There is limited information about the current quality of training for or in the informal sector. For effective policy formulation, there is a need to identify the factors of training and skill transfer, which lead to an improvement of living and working conditions of the beneficiaries.

RECOMMENDATIONS

In the state of Jammu and Kashmir, the demand for skilled labour has risen significantly as a result of decline in the incidence of insurgency, improved political situation and better investment climate and the consequent changing organization of work. Inadequate skills and skills mismatch reduce employability and increase the risk that under-educated and under-trained youth face in the labour market. Thus, education and training are essential components in addressing the challenge. Education and training are essential requirements of a strategy to promote employability. They give youth the opportunity to take advantage of job opportunities and income earning possibilities. Developing young people's employability is central to ensuring their successful transition to the labour market and their access to career-oriented employment. Youth need to acquire the skills, knowledge, competencies and attitudes that will allow them to find work and to cope with an unpredictable labour market.

- Historically, apprenticeship has been the principal means of training semi-skilled and skilled workers. Systems of apprenticeship have evolved and adapted to meet industry needs. It continues to be the most common method of training for semi-skilled trades, crafts and occupations. It becomes much more complex and structured, when combines on-the-job apprenticeship with school-based education. In most developing countries, informal systems of apprenticeship remain the dominant form of learning skills; in many of these countries, apprenticeship systems are highly regulated by custom and tradition. Although it varies from society to society, it is typically characterized by an informal arrangement between a trainee and a "master" trainer, whereby the trainee learns through observation and assistance, through "serving" the "master". Through this process, the trainee learns about the operation of the enterprise, how to deal with suppliers, price and market products and how to keep records of accounts.

- Eventually, the trainees start his/her own business upon completion of training and development of their skills in the workshop. It is important to note that, under conditions of extreme poverty, informal apprenticeships can result in the exploitation of cheap labour and/or can end up passing on existing skills, without teaching new ones. Is informal apprenticeship better for disadvantaged youth? The informal apprenticeship training presents both opportunities and barriers for disadvantaged youth. Informal apprenticeships often result in self-employment in the informal economy, while formal schemes usually lead to wage employment in the formal economy. Despite the potential success of apprenticeship training, there are many barriers to some groups of young women and men. Discrimination undoubtedly impacts on access to apprenticeship for many youth. The consequences of devaluation of certain skills, accreditation, and experience, based on discriminatory hiring practices, may lead to lower rates of apprenticeship training participation, or perhaps, render apprenticeship training less attractive for disadvantaged youth.
- Apprenticeships are potentially exploitative unless certain conditions are fulfilled. They should be well structured and supervised; the period of training should be fixed; apprentices should be taught a range of skills; and written contracts and certificates, demonstrating completion of training, should be provided. Apprenticeship systems should be subject to inspections with penalties for violations. Disadvantaged youth are more susceptible to exploitation under apprenticeship schemes because of the added barriers they face. But the dual training system appears to be the most flexible of mainstream education and training and flexibility is important

to meet the needs of many disadvantaged young people.

- The employers are increasingly demanding higher skills for many types of jobs. These jobs are potentially available to at-risk young women and men, but the skills of many of these young people are inadequate to meet employer demands. Relying entirely on mainstream education and training systems to address the situation is insufficient. Well-structured work-based learning is more likely to impact the life chances of at-risk young people. It is important to recognize that employers' demand for entry-level workers is variable. Employers are heterogeneous, operate in very different markets, and therefore, have a range of different needs. Yet mainstream education systems operate under a relatively homogeneous curriculum. The recruitment and hiring practices of employers also affect the ability of disadvantaged youth to embark on a career. The job requirements, screening devices, and recruitment strategies clearly place at-risk youth at a serious disadvantage in the job market. Disadvantaged youth need to acquire these skills through alternative training methods.
- When the supply of youth, generally, is greater than the demand for apprenticeships, vulnerable or marginalized youth are largely ignored. The current systems are insufficient or inappropriate with regard to needs of youth who are vulnerable to marginalization and exclusion. Where programmes targeting various marginalized and excluded groups do exist, they have functioned outside the mainstream – special programmes, specialized institutions, and specialist educators. Notwithstanding the best intentions, too often the result has been exclusion: "second-rate" educational opportunities that do not lead to employment, leaving many young women and men outside the

mainstream of education and training and later, as adults, outside community, social and cultural life in general.

- In any education system, the curriculum is one of the major obstacles or tools to facilitate the development of more inclusive system. In many contexts, the curriculum is extensive and demanding, or centrally designed and rigid, leaving little flexibility for local adaptations or for teachers to experiment with new approaches. The content might be irrelevant to the reality in which the students live, and therefore inaccessible and unmotivating. The curriculum might also be gender biased and degrading. Research on inclusive education in a number of centres of learning around the world suggests some key elements for curricula that seek to ensure more inclusive education. These include: defining broad common goals for all, including the knowledge, skills and values to be acquired; developing a flexible structure to facilitate the diversity and providing diverse opportunities for practice and performance in terms of content, methods and level of participation; conducting assessment based on individual progress; acknowledging cultural, religious and linguistic diversity of learners; and ensuring that content, knowledge and skills are relevant to learners' context.
- Enterprises have the ability to provide practical, on-the-job skills that meet the immediate demands of the market. But because enterprise training tends to be job-specific, it often focuses on better skilled workers, and does not necessarily enhance the individual's flexibility and labour market mobility. It tends to be uncertified and non-accredited. It may also ignore training needs that have long-term strategic importance to the economy as a whole or to the career objectives of individuals, focusing on

the needs of the enterprise. Enterprise training tends to exclude the unemployed; the self-employed; and informal sector workers; and, by association, disadvantaged youth. Employers' organizations can play an important role in influencing training policy and governance, drawing attention to the need for long-term investment in continuous training and encouraging learning within enterprises, promoting the inclusion of disadvantaged youth in these training schemes.

- Enterprises continue to play a critical role both in the pre-employment training of youth through informal and organized apprenticeship and on-the-job training, while voluntary non-profit agencies have focused efforts on training the most disadvantaged. The role of the private sector in the provision of skills has been largely overlooked in official policy making, as has the contribution of vocational education and training institutions operated by enterprises. Private sector institutions can respond quickly to changing requirements and can readily adapt their curricula, while public vocational education and training institutions tend to suffer from rigid regulatory frameworks, a lack of accountability, entrepreneurial know-how and capital to respond to demand quickly and adequately to the needs of the market. The large modern sector enterprises employ only a small fraction of the workforce; the bulk of the labour force is beyond the reach of enterprise-based training programmes. At the same tome, large enterprises employ fewer and fewer people, and growing numbers of vulnerable young men and women have little or no access to training opportunities. Targeted government sponsored training schemes are often the only opportunity available to these groups.
- The non-profit voluntary sector has the advantage of being able to reach the grassroots level effectively,

even in remote areas, and to provide access to training for the poorest and most disadvantaged population groups. These areas and groups tend to be of little interest to most enterprises and cannot be easily reached by mainstream public providers. NGOs, for example, have played a positive role in developing supported employment, including job coaching, which has impacted on opportunities for youth with disabilities. However, voluntary agencies often provide training with little or no impact. Public policy needs to support enhanced capacity building in the voluntary training sector.

- Broadly speaking, formal, informal and non-formal education and training are considered to be the most effective preventive interventions to improve the employability of all youth. It empowers individuals by opening up avenues for communication that would otherwise be closed, expands personal choice and enhances control over their environment and is a prerequisite for the acquisition of many other skills. It gives people access to information and equips them to cope better with work and family life. It strengthens their self-confidence to participate in community affairs and influence political issues. Education and training gives disadvantaged youth the tools they need to move from exclusion to full participation in their society.
- In order for all youth to take advantage of the opportunities that arise from education and training, several weaknesses must be addressed. The first is the inability of many parents to send their children to school because of local economic and social conditions. The second concerns the poor educational opportunities for the more disadvantaged subgroups of youth: girls and young women, migrants, refugees, displaced persons, street children, indigenous youth, minorities, young people in rural areas and young people with

disabilities. The third concerns the quality of education, its relevance to gainful employment and its usefulness for assisting young people in the transition to full adulthood and active citizenship, as well as to nurture their idealism and creative thinking so that they may become agents in creating their own future.

- Keeping the above in view, there is need to review, rethink and re-orient the education, vocational training and labour market policies to facilitate the school-to work transition and to give young women and men – particularly those who are disadvantaged because of disabilities or who face discrimination because of race, religion or ethnicity – a head start in working life. Young women and men also need a set of "core work skills" such as communication, problem solving and teamwork skills to develop their employability and prepare them for work in the knowledge and skills based society. Clearly this is the direction that policies should be headed. There are many groups or subgroups of youth who are currently prohibited by the system or, despite policy changes, will not be able to access mainstream programmes.
- A significant proportion of children drop out before the completion of primary school, leaving many adolescents and youth at the margin of the education and training system. The result is that young people are often not in the position to acquire marketable knowledge and skills in the formal system. There is need to give high priority to the development of non-formal education and training opportunities, in youth friendly venues and through decentralized mechanisms that can better capture the skills needs and work opportunities of local youth communities. There is need to emphasize the importance of non-formal education to support young people in: obtaining essential life skills; strengthening self-

awareness and self-confidence; developing a sense of identity; and learning to value cooperation and teamwork. Alternatives to formal education and training systems tend to tackle those who fail to make the transition from school to work, i.e. unemployed youth. There is need for launching "second chance" training programmes for youth who have lost their jobs to try to enhance employability. Most youth-related policies today involve training, subsidized employment and public work. There is also need to adopt a preventive strategy based on a greater integration of school and work and aimed at easing the entry into the labour force before youth encounter obstacles.

- There are several criteria for determining what makes a training practice good. These criteria reflect broad categories and guidelines to be followed in order to maximize the opportunities for success.
- In order to meet the criteria laid out above, key features have been identified to guide the development of good training practices. These include data collection and mapping of marginalized populations; the training component; needs-based assessment; coordination, cooperation and commitment; labour market and social support services (including vocational guidance and counselling); financial support mechanisms; information sharing and awareness-raising; and physical infrastructure. It is important to emphasize that all aspects of the skills development of disadvantaged youth must be gender sensitive and recognize the heterogeneity amongst and between young men and women.
- The range of innovative techniques in supplying skills training is varied. Clearly it must address the obstacles, but how it does this is dependent on numerous factors. These include resources (human and financial), capacity and commitment, among

Box 1

Criteria for Determining Good Training Practices

Criterion	*Explanation*
Innovative	It has unique characteristics, which address the weaknesses in other training practices in addressing the disadvantaged youth; appeals to the interest of all stakeholders.
Feasible	It can, realistically, be implemented; there is sufficient support, funding, and capacity.
Gender sensitive	Young women as well as young men are given a voice in all aspects of the development, implementation and follow-up of the practice to ensure that their interests are taken into account.
Responsive	The practice is consistent with the needs identified by young women and men; it has involved a consensus-building approach; it is responsive to the interests and desires of the participants and others.
Relevant	The practice contributes, directly or indirectly, to demands of the market and the needs of the participants.
Ethical	It is consistent with principles of social and professional conduct; it operates in accordance with international labour standards.
Effective	The practice actually makes a difference in addressing youth employability; the impact is measured either formally or otherwise.
Efficient:	Resources (human, financial, and material) are used in a way that maximizes impact.
Sustainable	The practice can continue after its initial piloting; its benefits, to the individual, the community, the economy and/or the society, are likely to continue to be effective over the medium to long term.
Replicable	The practice can be replicated in other situations or settings; it can be adapted to be useful in other situations or settings; some elements of a practice are useful for other programmes.
Upscaleable	The practice can be expanded to operate on a wider level.

other things. Programmes should focus on the wide range of skills youth need to be successful in the workplace, emphasizing both job readiness skills and job search skills. Job readiness skills cover such things as effective workplace communication skills, including conflict resolution, active listening, and negotiation and getting along with co-workers. Job search skills refer to writing a résumé and covering letters, interview skills and networking with employers. These skills help youth feel more confident to go out and find employment as well as more confident and comfortable in resolving issues that arise in the workplace and have a good attitude about work.

- Team-building activities that allow young people to bond and teach the importance of working, as a team should be included. An on-the-job training component in various work placements in the community is important for both community awareness and establishing future employment contacts. Programmes must be flexible and learner-centred, as they will be catering to youth of differing capabilities, interests and potential. Competent peers to encourage and model responsible autonomy are seen as means by which to motivate young women and men.
- The importance of conducting accurate focused, gender-sensitive needs assessment before engaging in the design, and production and/or implementation of a training programme cannot be understated. Too often programmes are put in place, which do not meet the needs, or do not even reach the intended beneficiaries. It is important to identify the important issues, obstacles, targets and strategies. In order to ensure that the programmes are responsive, relevant and ethical needs assessment must be conducted. Needs assessment takes on many forms and levels of complexity. The approach is

dictated by a number of factors such as availability of information, funding and capacity. It is paramount that conducting a needs assessment for disadvantaged youth includes extensive consultation with individual youth and/or their organizations. Throughout the process one must be aware of the different circumstances, needs and strategies of disadvantaged young women and men.

- Gender-sensitive social support networks, during and following training, facilitate the responsitivity, efficiency and effectiveness of training practices for youth at risk. Many young people and their families need support services to gain knowledge of the training resources available, how to access them, alternatives to mainstreaming and information on the job market, writing a résumé, amongst other things. The range of possible support services is endless but the most common tend to be: career counselling; guidance; job placement; mentoring/coaching; technical assistance; and provision of market information.
- Rural youth face different kinds of challenges, which need to be addressed in effective ways. There is need to address these challenges by empowering rural youth through developing their technological skills for jobs in the labour market, while including career guidance, skills upgrading, latent talent promotion and entrepreneurial skills development in their vocational training programme. The career guidance component created awareness among jobseekers about available career options, job vacancies and facing interviews; assistance with suitable placement was also offered.
- For many of disadvantaged youth, the main obstacle to education and training is financial. To overcome this, innovative financial support mechanisms such as micro credit, flexible loan schemes and grants must be made available to ease the burden. The

micro credit system has tremendous potential as an instrument for poverty reduction, if accompanied by literacy promotion and training to help those who lack the skills to make credit work for them. The micro credit programmes are effective in reducing poverty among those poor people who have the requisite skills to become self-employed. Micro credit is a prerequisite for accessing the skills training, yet training is often required in order to obtain the credit.

- Programmes, which combine the two, increase the chances of being able to take advantage of the benefits. Income-generating training is another alternative, which allows economically disadvantaged youth to be able to enter and complete education and training. The discrimination in access to credit (due to age and inexperience) is a significant barrier for young entrepreneurs. The availability of micro credit to young entrepreneurs is important. Young entrepreneurs often demonstrate initiative and innovative skills to earn their living. The creation of funds and support from financial and other institutions should be encouraged. As it is important for new and young business people to be aware of the problems associated with establishing a business, it would be sensible for some sort of workshop to be arranged to train the young entrepreneurs in the management of their operations.
- Access to information on alternative education and training programmes and financial and/or social support schemes for youth and their families is essential in facilitating the transition to work. The improved information sharing reaches numerous professionals that work with young women and men in difficult circumstances. Community awareness about the value of all youth serves to challenge social attitudes about disadvantaged youth who often suffer discrimination resulting from

misunderstanding about their potential.

- The major constraint is the serious shortage of resources - lack of training institutes or inadequate facilities, lack of teachers and/or shortage of qualified staff, lack of learning materials, poor transportation networks and absence of support. The divide between rural and urban is an important issue. The out migration of many young people from the rural regions due to the lack of opportunity is seen as an increasing social problem. Thus, there is need to invest in the physical infrastructure in the rural communities, which in turn will provide opportunities for the young.
- The movements in wages and employment signal changes in the demand for and supply of particular skills and trades. By capturing these signals, planners can identify shortages or gluts of particular skills and plan training programmes accordingly. This requires some structures and skills for collecting, analysing and disseminating information on employment and labour market trends and signals. At present, these are missing in Jammu and Kashmir. Being for the most part a school-based system with a strong academic bias, training in the state of Jammu and Kashmir is also pre-employment training, i.e. training young people who will subsequently look for their first job in the labour market. There is very little in-service training for the already employed workforce. Many workers have had little formal education and training, a situation that has been reinforced by the long-standing relative easy access to employment in informal sector. The impact on enterprise productivity of targeted training interventions among employed workers is likely to be significant. Another major challenge for the training system is therefore to expand the range of in-service training opportunities in institutions and enterprises.

- The state of Jammu and Kashmir under-invests in training for work and most of it is being provided by public and private training institutions and paid directly, or through subsidies, by the state or central government. Enterprises and individuals, the main beneficiaries of training, contribute very little. Under-investment in training has much to do with traditional neglect of vocational education and training, individuals' preference for white-collar credentials and employers' underestimation of the value of skills and training for improving company performance. In order to increase the supply of training, new partners have to be solicited to contribute to its financing and provision. This calls for a system of incentives that would encourage other stakeholders than government, in particular enterprises, to invest more in training and so share the burden of supplying skills needed in the economy.
- If stakeholders other than the state are to increase their share in financing training, than they must have a say in governing the training system on an equal footing with government. Governance reform would also have to address this issue, for example by decentralising decision making regarding course content, management and resource mobilisation to individual training institutions and so make training more responsive to local labour market needs.
- The state of Jammu and Kashmir currently lacks comprehensive information on training needs, as well as the structure to collect demand and supply information on a regular basis. So far no comprehensive needs survey has been undertaken, not to speak of surveys undertaken regularly, which should be the ultimate goal. In the absence of mechanisms to link training supply to actual demand, and without adequate information on training needs, training programmes tends to be

largely supply driven. This means that programmes are conditioned more by the available skill profiles of existing teachers (or lack of such skills) and rely on often obsolete training equipment and training materials. Such supply driven training may result in poor employment outcomes and mean a waste of scarce training resources.

- A fundamental principle underlying any training provision is that it should be linked to identifiable job opportunities or to appropriate small-scale activities that have the prospect of generating sustainable income. Hence, there is need to assess training demands in both formal and informal sector activities. However, as comprehensive and reliable labour market information in Jammu and Kashmir is lacking at present. The vast majority of people in the state of Jammu and Kashmir make a living in the informal sector and in subsistence agriculture, where productivity, incomes and working conditions are almost invariably poor. However, the present study indicated that more than one-fifth of the ITI pass outs ended up in self-employment, and it is the sector where most people in the future will have to find a living. Training policy development should therefore prioritise training to improve productivity and income generation in these parts of the economy. The relevance of the training could be increased with the introduction of 'self-employment training' (i.e. business, management and marketing skills training) in order to enlarge the scope of potential employment openings for the ITI pass outs.
- Training resources are scarce and therefore need careful targeting, and diagnosis of demand, are essential in order to determine precisely who should benefit and why. A critical element is to determine whether informal sector workers are facing problems for which training can bring a solution. Training can

assist in improving product quality or in reducing accidents at work; it may be a conduit for product diversification or for the adoption of more appropriate technologies. In many cases, training for the informal sector must be combined with other interventions in support of the sector, e.g. credit, technology or legal support. Without these necessary complementary inputs training interventions are bound to fail. Training interventions should be affordable and use existing mechanisms if these are efficient. Thus, conventional training institutions can be encouraged to provide short courses for informal sector operators.

- Formal vocational education and training institutions have in some cases been able to redirect their objectives and curricula so that they correspond to the skill needs in formal as well as in informal manufacturing and services. If their adaptability to meet new training objectives and cater for a new clientele is limited, other options will have to be explored, e.g. strengthening traditional apprenticeship to help them improve their coverage and the quality of their training services, and establishing micro-enterprise extension facilities or small business advisory services that can address training needs of informal sector enterprises in an integrated manner.
- Training provision is expensive and the question of who should pay for it should be addressed as a matter of priority. So far most training, and that means pre-employment the government has financed training, in Jammu and Kashmir. If a reorientation of the training system towards training for the already employed workforce in order to improve their skills and productivity is accepted, this would mean that a formula would have to be devised for sharing the costs of training between various stakeholders. This could mean that the

government would assume the task of financing pre-employment training, while the beneficiaries, primarily the enterprises but also the individuals themselves, would take up the costs of employment-based training and further and upgrading training. In order to have individuals increase their contributions, a system of fees and loans would have to be devised.

In nutshell, education and training are important means of addressing youth employability, but vulnerable youth are, to a great extent, ignored in mainstream systems. Formal education and training systems often do not reach marginalized youth. Alternative methods of delivering training need to be explored. Good training practices for disadvantaged youth are innovative approaches to skills acquisition employment and income generation. They include procedures for systematically identifying employment- and income-generating opportunities at the local level, designing and delivering appropriate training programmes, and providing necessary post-training support services, including credit, technical assistance and market information. They include such things as needs-based assessment; coordination, cooperation and commitment; labour market and social support services; financial support mechanisms; information sharing and awareness-raising; and physical infrastructure.

- All aspects of the skills development of disadvantaged youth must be gender sensitive and recognize the heterogeneity amongst and between young men and women. An integrated programme at community level generally requires the support of several agencies and consultations with the social partners. Similarly, local training committees, in the selected areas, are key to identifying opportunities and needs, and provide the best means of organizing delivery. In the implementation phase, flexibility is essential. Training should be delivered as close to the clients as possible, with particular attention to ensuring that young women, as well as men, benefit fully from programmes. Important aspects in this respect are training of trainers, selection of trainees and finding sources of credit to make up lost income during training and help start up small businesses based on the new skills.

BIBLIOGRAPHY

Anand, Harjit (2001), "Linkages between informal and formal sectors: Some findings from micro level studies", in Kundu and Sharma (Ed.) *Informal Sector in India-Perspectives and Policies*, Manohar Publishers, New Delhi.

Ashton, D.; Sung, J. (2002), Supporting workplace learning for high performance working, Geneva, ILO.

Bangasser, Paul E. (2000), "The ILO and the informal sector: An institutional history", Employment paper, ILO, Geneva.

Bednarzik, R.W. (1975), "Involuntary part-time work: A cyclical analysis", *Monthly Labour Review*, Vol. 98, pp. 12-18.

Benhabib, J.; Spiegel, M.M. (1994), "The role of human capital in economic development: Evidence from aggregate cross country data", *Journal of Monetary Economics*, Vol. 34, pp. 143-173.

Bhattacherjee, D. (2002), "Organised labour and economic liberalisation in India: Past, present and future", in Jose, A.V. (Ed) *Organised Labour in the Twenty First Century*, International Institute of Labour Studies, Geneva.

Booth, A.; Snower, D. (eds.) (1996), *Acquiring Skills: Market Failures, Their Symptoms and Policy Responses*, Cambridge, Cambridge University Press.

Boserup, E. (1989), *Women's Role in Economic Development*, Earthscan, London.

Bowers, N.; Sonnet, A.; Bardonne, L. (2000), Giving young people a good start: The experience of OECD countries, OECD, Background Report for the OECD Ministers Conference on Youth Employment, 8-9 February.

Byrne, B. (1996), "Gender, conflict and development: An overview", *IDS Bulletin*, Vol. 1, IDS Sussex, July.

Cáceres, J.M.M. (2002), "More training, less security? Training and the quality of life at work in Argentina, Brazil and Chile", *International Labour Review*, Vol. 141, No. 4.

Capt, J. (2001), "What skills are needed to ensure survival and growth of enterprises?", Paper presented at the International Conference on Linking Work, Skills and Knowledge: Learning for Survival and Growth, Interlaken, Switzerland, 10-12 September.

Chandra, Ashoka (1999), "Retraining for redeployment: NRF initiative and challenge in training," *The Indian Journal of Labour Economics*, Vol. 42, No 1.

Dantwala Committee (1970), Report of the committee of experts on unemployment estimates, Government of India, Planning Commission, New Delhi.

Dhakal, S. (2002), Youth unemployment: Indignity of idleness and insecurity, *Nepal News*, June 28.

Fawcett, C. (2002), Latin American youth in transition: A policy paper on youth unemployment in Latin America and the Caribbean, School of International Service, American University, Sustainable Development Department, Social Development Division, Labour Markets Policy Briefs Series, Inter-American Development Bank.

Gasskov V. and M. Burns (2001), "Training for employment promotion in Muktsar district, Punjab", ILO, New Delhi.

Gill, I.S.: Fluitman, F. (eds.) (1998), Skills and change: Constraints and innovation in the reform of vocational education and training, Geneva, ILO.

Godfrey, M. (2003), "Youth employment policy in developing and transition countries: Prevention as well as cure", presentation by the World Bank, Youth Employment Workshop, Washington, DC, 2 June.

Goodale, G. (1989), Training for women in the informal sector, ILO Discussion Paper No. 36, Geneva, ILO.

Government of India (2001), Approach paper to the tenth five year plan, Planning Commission, New Delhi.

Government of India (2001), Targeting ten million employment opportunities per year, Planning Commission, New Delhi.

Government of India (2002), Recommendations of the 2nd National Commission on Labour, Ministry of Labour, New Delhi.

Grubb, W.N. (1996), Working in the middle: Strengthening education and training for the mid-skilled labour force, San Francisco, Jossey-Bass.

Han, H.C. (2004), Synthesis study: Training for work in the informal economy, IFP/SKILLS Working Paper, Informal Economy Series.

Hart, K, (1973), Informal income opportunities and urban employment in Ghana, *Journal of Modern African Studies*, Vol. 2.

Higgins, N. O. (2001), Youth unemployment and employment policy: A global perspective, ILO, Geneva.

Heidemann, W. (2000), Combating youth unemployment – The German approach, Training, Labour Education and Training Research Network.

Holger, G.; Strobl, E. (2001), The incidence of visible underemployment: Evidence for Trinidad and Tobago, Centre for Research in Economic Development and International Trade, University of Nottingham.

ILO (1998), "Employability in the global economy: How training matters", *World Employment Report*, Geneva, 1998.

ILO (2000), Training for employment: Social inclusion, productivity and youth employment, International Labour Conference, 88th Session, 2000.

ILO (2001), Meeting the youth employment challenge: A guide for employers, InFocus Programme on Skills Knowledge and Employability (IFP/SKILLS) and the Bureau for Employers' Activities (ACTRAV), Geneva.

ILO (2002), Youth and work: Global trends, Report prepared jointly by the ILO Employment Sector (InFocus Programme on Skills, Knowledge and Employability, and the Key Indicators of the Labour Market) and the ILO Bureau of Labour Statistics.

ILO (2003), Global Employment Trends 2003, Geneva.

ILO (2004), "Global labour market trends for women", Annex to the Global Employment Trends, Geneva.

Jhavbala, R. and Subrahmanya, R. K. A. (2000), *The Unorganised Sector: Work Security and Social Protection*, Sage Publications, New Delhi.

Kanyenze, G. et al (2000), Strategies to combat youth unemployment and marginalization in anglophone Africa, ILO/SAMAT Discussion Paper No. 14, Harare.

Knowles, J.C. and J.R. Behrman (2003), The economic returns to investing in youth in developing countries: A review of the literature, University of Pennsylvania mimeo for World Bank Human Development Network.

Kundu, A. and Sharma, A.N, (ed) (2001), "Informal sector in India: Perspectives and policies", Manohar Publishers, New Delhi.

Leach, F. (1998), "Gender, education and training: An international perspective", in Sweetman, C.(ed.), *Gender, Education and Training*, Oxfam Focus on Gender.

Leach, F. (1999), "Women in the informal sector: The contribution of education and training", in Eade, D. (ed.), *Development with Women*, Oxfam, Oxford.

Leach, F. (2000), "Gender implications of development agency policies on education and training", *International Journal of Educational Development*, Vol. 20, Issue 4, 2000, pp. 333-347.

Leppel, K. and S. Heller Clain (1988), "The growth of involuntary part-time employment of men and women", *Applied Economics*, Vol. 20, pp. 1155-1166.

Liimatainen, Marjo-Riitta (2002), Training and skills acquisition in the informal sector: A literature review, IFP/SKills - Informal Economy Series, ILO, Geneva.

McGrath, Simon and Kenneth King (1995), Education and training for the informal sector, Vol.2, Education Research Occasional Papers, ODA, London, UK, March.

McKernan, Signe-Mary (2002), "The impact of microcredit programmes on self-employment profits: Do non-credit programme aspects matter?", *The Review of Economics and Statistics*, February, Vol. 84, No. 1, pp. 93-115.

Middleton, J., A. Ziderman and A. Van Adams (1993), Skills for productivity: Vocational education and training in developing countries, Oxford, Oxford University Press, and Washington, DC, World Bank.

Mitra, Amit (2002), Training and skill formation for decent work in the informal sector: Case studies from South India, InFocus Programme on Skills, Knowledge and Employability; Informal Economy, Working Paper No. 8, ILO, Geneva, 2002.

Mroz, T.A. and T.H. Savage (2001), The long-term effects of youth unemployment, Employment Policy Institute, October.

Pant, K.C. (2003), Speech at Asian summit on youth entrepreneurship and employment on 29 October.

Ryan, P. (2001), "The school-to-work transition: A cross-national perspective", *Journal of Economics Literature,* Vol XXXIX (March), pp. 34-92.

Rees, A. (1986), "An essay on youth joblessness", *Journal of Economic Literature,* Vol. XXIV (June), pp. 613-628.

Samorodov, Alexander (1999), Aging and labour markets for older workers, ILO.

Singh, M. (2001), "Reflections on colonial legacy and dependency in Indian vocational education and training (VET): A societal and cultural perspective", *Journal of Work.*

Singh, S. (1992), "Training for employment: Some lessons from experience", *Journal of Educational Planning and Administration,* Vol. 6, No. 2.

Stratton, L.S. (1996), "Are 'involuntary' part-time workers indeed involuntary?", *Industrial and Labour Relations Review,* Vol. 49, pp. 522-536.

Sundaram, K. and Suresh D. Tendulkar (2002), "Working poor in India: Employment poverty linkages and employment policy options", Discussion paper 4, Issues in employment and poverty, ILO, Geneva.

Wignaraja, P. (2002), Employment: Double Burden of Poor Youth in Search of Work and Dignity, An Issues Paper on Innovative Thinking and Practice in Mobilising Resources for Youth, Education Development Center, Inc.

World Bank (2002), Modova: Youth inclusion, learning and innovation credit, Updated Project Information Document, Report No. AB205, Bank approval date: December 29.

Zagha, R. (1999), " Labour and India's economic reform", in Sachs, J.D., A.Varshney and N. Bajpai (Eds), *India in the Era of Economic Reforms,* Oxford University Press, Oxford.

